Internal Conflicts in Myanmar

Transnational Consequences

Internal Conflicts in Myanmar

Transnational Consequences

Editor

V.R. Raghavan

Published for
Centre for Security Analysis
Chennai, India

Vij Books India Pvt Ltd
New Delhi, India

Published   by

Vij Books India Pvt Ltd

2/19, Ansari Road, Darya Ganj
New Delhi - 110002
Phones: 91-11-65449971, 91-11- 43596460
Fax: 91-11-47340674
e-mail : vijbooks@rediffmail.com
web : www.vijbooks.com

Centre for Security Analysis
"9-B" Ninth Floor,
Chesney Nilgiri, 71, Ethiraj Salai,
Egmore, Chennai-600008
Tamil Nadu, India
+91-44-65291889
office@csa-chennai.org
www.csa-chennai.org

First Published : 2011

ISBN 13 : 978-93-80177-63-2

Acknowledgement

The Centre for Security Analysis (CSA) has undertaken a three year research project **Internal Conflicts and Transnational Consequences** supported by the John D and Catherine T MacArthur Foundation. This volume is part of the ongoing project and its publication has been possible by the project grant.

TABLE OF CONTENTS

FOREWORD

Internal conflicts have overtaken inter-state wars as the primary conflict paradigm in the decades spanning the 20th and 21st Centuries. The scale and intensities of internal conflicts- conflicts within states – have widened. The consequences of such internal conflicts are no longer internal to the state but extend beyond the borders of such states. This is a new dimension of internal conflicts which has led to substantial trans-border consequences affecting other states. Since such internal conflicts have overwhelmingly been of long duration, even extending to decades, there are strategic, economic, social and political outcomes which need to be understood.

In most of the states affected by internal conflicts and their trans-border effects, the original causes of conflicts have been subsumed by their lasting consequences. In many cases the consequences have become the cause of continuing conflicts. These developments have made the resolution of internal conflict complex and beyond the capacities of the states in which the conflicts continue.

The Centre for Security Studies, Chennai, has conceptualized a new approach to understanding longstanding internal conflicts, by examining their trans-border consequences. It is felt that this approach will throw new light on the relationship between internal conflicts and their external outcomes. This may in turn help show up new policy choices, towards finding a way forward to resolve the conflicts.

The three year project on Internal Conflicts and Transnational Consequences looks at India, Nepal, Myanmar and Sri Lanka. These states have had internal conflicts which are of long duration. These four states have faced largely similar conflict scenarios with different governing systems of democracy, monarchy and military governments. The manner in which these governments have dealt with conflicts, and the manner in which parties to the conflict responded to them, makes a valuable study. The consequences of such conflicts in neighbouring states offer a new perspective on managing and resolving them.

This volume focuses on the internal conflicts in Myanmar and their consequences on its neighbours. Every state around Myanmar has had to bear range of consequences, lasting over decades, from the conflict. The seminar conducted in Singapore, with the valuable assistance of Institute of South East Asian Studies, and the support of MacArthur Foundation, provided useful insights into the reality of internal conflicts and their external consequences.

Lt. Gen. (Retd) V. R. Raghavan
President, CSA

INTRODUCTION

Dr. Geeta Madhavan

The age of global trade systems and interconnectivity and the dependence of a nation on other nations for its growth and international stature have underlined the fact that the impact of internal conflict of a country is no longer confined to its territorial limits. Conflicts situations have territorial and extra territorial consequences: immediate impact upon the neighbouring countries and indirect import upon the entire region in which the country geographically exists. The conflict situations in some nations have also influenced geo politics to the extent that the world community has seen it necessary not only to be concerned and search for methods to counter or reduce the conflict situations and if possible diffuse them; also should such need arise, with international consensus, censure the ruling establishment of the country. Although the South Asian region has several countries caught in the vortex of conflict, perhaps none faces more complex challenges than Myanmar. Undeniably, Myanmar is a nation fraught with multi layered conflicts which has resulted in instability, reflected not only within its own territory but the consequences of which have deep resonance in its neighbouring countries and the entire region of South Asia.

Consequences of the long lasting internal conflict in Myanmar were examined by ten experts and their studies were presented at a Seminar in Singapore conducted by the Centre for Security Analysis on 26 and 27 May, 2010. The papers presented and the discussions amongst the informed participants highlighted a range of consequences of the conflict which are not widely known. This volume includes the papers and the ensuing discussions for the use of scholars and policy makers.

The conflict in Myanmar which is complex and multi layered has been variously seen as; (a) a conflict between the Tatmadaw and the pro democracy forces, (b) a conflict between ethnic minorities and the ruling military junta of ethnic Burmese, (c) a conflict between the ceasefire groups and other ethnic armies. However, these divisions do not take into account the innumerable related issues that have made the conflict situation more complex and created deep distrust for the ruling establishment among its people. The internal conflict in Myanmar has its historical inception from the time the country freed itself from its colonial shackles. Each successive change in the ruling establishment has pushed it further and further into a deep chasm where ethnic rebels, insurgents and drug lords thrive and by their actions have drained it economically.

In recounting the gradual progression of the conflicts and their eventual crystallization in present form Dr Tin Maung Maung Than underlines two elements that have influenced the policies of the Tatmadaw (the Royal Force). The Tatmadaw sees the military rulers as the sole guardian of Burmese interest and has identified the military's interest as the core national interest, thereby justifying its existence and its policies. Therefore, the military response is seen as the legitimate and sole response to contain the internal threats of Myanmar and to deal with possible external ones. This is apparent not only in the state centric policies of the junta but also in the consequent expansion of the military forces, the acquisition of sophisticated weaponry and the constant modernization and reorganization of its defence capabilities. According to the paper, the newer challenges that the military junta may have to face are those that are the fallout of resource exploitation due to the partial opening up of the economy and the increasing demand for a role in policy making by the ethnic minorities. The elections conducted in Nov 2010 did not hold much hope in this context as it did not intend to address the core issues of ethnicity. In its dealing with the internal conflicts and possible external threats the question arises whether the Tatmadaw will pursue the policy it has followed for years and Dr. Than's conclusion is that it will have to adopt a new paradigm in view of the fact that its military prowess has not been able to crush the armed insurgent groups. He also holds the view that the elected *civilianized* executive will have to face the challenge of placating the military that has remained unchallenged so long.

Consequences of the internal conflict situation in Myanmar extend beyond its borders. The internal conflicts and their transnational consequences form the crux of Kerstin Duell's paper. The paper explains that the conflict is not just amongst the various parties pitted against the military junta but also against each other. The conflict in Myanmar has also been identified as a conflict between democratic rights and governance as well as between ethnic rights and self determination. The conflicts are further complicated because of the deadlock that has formed between the ruling military junta and the various groups. The chronology of events leading to the current status clarifies that Myanmar has three overwhelming problems which have internal and external consequences, and several serious issues that stem from those problems. The three main problems are: the prevalent ethnic disunity, economic underdevelopment and the production and distribution of drugs and narcotics. The other issues that are detrimental to the peace and growth in Myanmar are lack of governance in some areas, lack of human security, poor public health and thriving illicit border trade in drugs and humans leading to the establishment of private power lords. Taking into account the military rulers' reluctance to bring a regime change, the only possibility of easing restrictions on Myanmar is by constructive engagements through regional bodies like the ASEAN. Sanctions against Myanmar, as apparent from similar situations in other parts of the world, only heaps suffering on the people of Myanmar and does not necessarily put pressure on the military rulers. Opening up the economy will permit countries of the region to access the rich natural resources of Myanmar which in turn would rejuvenate the slow economic growth. Besides, it is clear from the paper that the military rulers, due to their historical past, are always suspicious of foreigners and tend to be seclusive in their policies. They have also used the interest of the two powers in the region viz. China and India to counter balance the excessive influence of one or the other.

Discussion about the effects of the internal strife in Myanmar upon the neigbouring countries involves country-specific studies. Effects on countries that are discussed in detail are Thailand, Bangladesh, China and India. The paper on the effects of conflicts in Myanmar on Bangladesh by Dr Iftekhar Ahmed Chowdhury records the official statement of the military government of Myanmar while according recognition to the newly formed state of Bangladesh in 1972. The statement underscores the recognition as an outcome of the desire of the military junta of Myanmar to "live fraternally as neigbours" with Bangladesh and the establishment of a Border of Peace. The paper explains that the internal conflict in Myanmar has affected Bangladesh in several ways and offers possible ways by which the two countries can co operate to reduce the effects. The crackdown in 1978 led to the exodus of 250,000 Rohingya Muslims into Bangladesh which seriously affected the demography of the country and caused economic and social imbalances. The subsequent crackdown in 1991 further exacerbated the situation with increased influx of refugees. Although ongoing efforts are being made for resettlement, it is pointed out that 21,000 still remain in Bangladesh as stateless person. These stateless people are exposed to various radicalizing influences which have resulted in major security concerns for the region. The paper also proposes that Myanmar should consider resolving the issues of the Rohingya Muslims with the help of the two major neighbours China and India playing a significant role in the resolution process; as well as the involvement of certain internationally recognized NGOs of Bangladesh who have successfully played a major role in the economic development of Bangladesh. Early implementation of the joint road building project of Myanmar and Bangladesh would also help economic growth in the Arakan region of Myanmar.

Discussions of the effect of conflict in Myanmar in the paper by Li Chenyang is specific to the conflict between ceasefire groups and the military junta in the region of Northern Myanmar abutting China and its consequence upon the specific area. The activities of the ceasefire groups (and he specifies them as five groups) controlling 50,000 square kms but having influence over 100,000 square kms and over a population of 1,750,000 range from drugs and gambling to pornography. Referring to the Kokang incident of 2009 wherein an estimated 30,000 Burmese refugees poured into China, serious threats have been posed to security and stability of southwest China. Besides, there lurks the potential of another armed conflict in Northern Myanmar which will have severe impact on the Chinese territory. Illegal activities in the region has caused major security risk and created some strains in the Sino-Myanmar relations. The overall Sino Myanmar relations and their strategic cooperation tend to get strained with each new wave of conflict. There is also a negative impact of conflict on alternative cultivation and alternative enterprise which have been created to counter the drug problem. The other points of discussion in the paper are the impact of the conflict on anti-drug co operation, the worsening drug situation due to illegal border trade and the loss to assets and property due to the conflict situation in Myanmar. China's current and future vital national interest in Myanmar rests on two major requirements: energy security and building access into the Indian Ocean which have greatly influenced strategic co operation between Myanmar and China.

The paper on the trans border effects of internal conflicts in Myanmar on Northeast India by K Yohme clearly enunciates the emerging concept that political boundaries should no longer be seen as lines dividing land and people; instead , borderlands should be recognized as areas of connectivity. Political boundaries should be treated as gateways for economic and social exchanges for the benefit of the regions lying on both sides of the border. Myanmar and the Northeastern states of India viz Arunachal Pradesh, Nagaland, Manipur and Mizoram have direct borders and the effect of the conflict in Myanmar is widely felt within these states. However, the policy of the governments of Myanmar and India has been to view the effect in this region only from a security perspective and this has led to negative transnational consequences. The paper points out that the effects of the conflict, in reality, go far beyond security concerns and affect the economic and social ethos of the region.

The border region between Myanmar and the Northeastern states are very porous and continuous cross border activities take place in the region. In the absence of a clear policy about the region, much of these activities are termed as "illegal" and has led to the alienation of the Northeast states of India and the border regions of Myanmar. The era of globalization and the progressive economic thinking by the governments of India and Myanmar has resulted in the launch of new policies to develop the region and support peace in the border areas. Both the governments have entered into cease fire agreement with the ethnic armed groups in the region with the aim to build social and economic infrastructure and encourage participation of the local people in the development of the region. The region is fraught with several problems: similar conditions existing on both sides of the border has created linkages among the armed groups in the region and has reinforced the culture of violence and facilitated the creation of support and the establishment of sanctuaries. Illicit drugs and gun trade have led to the proliferation of insurgent groups in the Northeastern states of India. A parallel economy system has evolved in the region creating new and complex problems in the economic and social spheres. High incidence of drug use, the rise in numbers of those afflicted by HIV has caused serious concerns. However, prohibiting cross border movements for social and economic activities would be counterproductive, resulting in the growth of criminal and anti social activities. The recommendations in the paper are effective government monitoring to reduce the negative implications of cross border trade and proper identification methods along with proper monitoring mechanisms which would reduce illegal movements. Infrastructure development in the border areas in the Northeast states should be viewed as building strategic assets.

Thailand has historical and ethnic connections with Myanmar but the unsettled border region and the continuous conflict situation in Myanmar is a cause of deep worry for Thailand. Citing the creation of the Buffer Zone by Thailand, the paper by Pavin Chachavalpong discusses the negative impact of the buffer policy pursued by Thailand. The buffer zone along the border supported the anti Rangoon ethnic minorities challenging the military regime in Myanmar. The financial and logistic support extended by Thailand to the ethnic rebels worsened the situation. Over a period of time the buffer zone that was intended to ensure the security of Thailand's border transformed into an area that has created more problems than the existing ones that it was meant to counter. It has become an impediment in the way of fostering positive bilateral relationship between the two countries and created mutual distrust. The Burmese refugees have also caused demographic changes in Thailand leading to upheavals in the societal structure of Thailand. The perception of the local population vis a vis the Burmese refugees is that of preferential treatment being accorded to the refugees by the Government. The competition between the local population and the refugees for resources has also caused problems. The illegal immigrants have created an uncontrolled labour market; creating other problems like cheap labour, bribery, increased number of sex workers and a host of public health issues. Illegal arms trade, proliferation of small arms, and drug trafficking are other major causes of worry for the Thai authorities. The other issue that is important for Thailand is energy security; therefore, it is imperative for Thailand to maintain good relations with Myanmar. Thailand requires the natural gas imported from Myanmar through pipelines and the electricity from the hydro power dams of Myanmar but their erratic policy towards Myanmar has resulted in mutual distrust.

India's commitment to democracy and human rights for a long time fashioned its policies in the Myanmar context. As pointed out in the paper of B P Routary, with the formulation of India's Look East policy, a new approach has been developed by India towards the countries in the region and specifically towards Myanmar. It became apparent that a policy based entirely on a high moral ground and based on India's own values of democracy to be made applicable to all, does not necessarily serve India's national interest. India required that it engage Myanmar in a comprehensive strategic dialogue which would deal with issues that were the common concerns of both countries. Cross border insurgency, arms smuggling and border management are vital to both. China's greater role in building infrastructure in Myanmar and China's emergence as the fourth largest investor in Myanmar are causes for serious concern to India. Besides providing economic assistance to Myanmar, China has supplied the military junta with weapons and training. China's apparent interest also extends to accessing energy and natural resources in Myanmar and it seeks to extend its strategic access to the Indian Ocean through Myanmar. Therefore, India has crafted a policy exhibiting greater patience in regime reform and not allowing the internal conflicts and human rights issues to influence its dialogue with the military junta. There are other sectors viz. power, hydrocarbon and energy, in which India has national interest. The construction for road linking the North Eastern states of India to Myanmar and India's comprehensive package for the long neglected North Eastern states fulfills both its commitment to the North Eastern states of India as well as to Myanmar.

When conjoining the conflict in Myanmar with the elements of regional integration and discussing the responses, three broad questions have to be addressed: to what extent does Myanmar's military mindset interfere with the concept, what investments can the countries in the region make to ensure peace in Myanmar and do such opportunities exist and if they do what are the challenges that they will have to overcome. Anna Louis Strachtan lays great emphasis on regional integration identifying Myanmar as having great potential to be a trading partner between neighbouring countries of the region. A greater responsibility is prescribed for the countries especially Thailand, Bangladesh, India and China by which they can play a positive albeit diverse roles in facilitating conflict resolution. The main factor that is seen as possibly achieving this goal is fostering economic prosperity in Myanmar. The countries in South and Southeast Asia need to pursue greater regional co operation not only as part of national interest but also as part of fulfilling the desire to maintain stability and security in the region. Economic integration in the form of physical connectivity through trade by countries of the region in their individual capacity as well as through the regional organizations would be a positive step in achieving the mentioned goal. ASEAN, SAARC, BIMSTEC, and a progressive ASEAN Economic Community have all been invested with the opportunity of increased engagement with Myanmar. The example of neighbouring countries investing in building infrastructure to promote stability and economic growth in Afghanistan exhibits how such enterprise can be successful. There have been setbacks in Afghanistan and specifically for India, which has had to face destruction of property and death of its personnel engaged in infrastructure building from the elements opposed to bringing peace. Despite that, a proactive role in the movement to stability and peace through investment is a better option than political pressure in Myanmar. A change is desired in the isolationist attitude of the military junta and their mindset of being distrustful of any foreign influence which has resulted in the partial segregation of Myanmar in the region.

Echoing that benefits will accrue by economic development in Myanmar through increased trade and foreign investment, Larry Jagan envisages a movement that will create ethnic integration. Myanmar's military junta places high emphasis on territorial integrity and therefore they see themselves as the single unifying force in the country. The protective isolationist ideology of the military junta has not benefited the country; therefore, there should be sincere efforts to integrate the ethnic minorities groups into the political mainstream. Unfortunately, the election of Nov 2010 did not move towards this. The indicators that set out the military junta's agenda for retaining control was apparent in the election process that has been formulated, therefore, subsequent to the election no real solution has emerged in Myanmar. A federal structure which would include ethnic minorities has greater chance of ushering transition on the socio-political level. Permitting the ethnic minorities to retain their identity by allowing education to be carried out in their own language is also suggested.

Ramu Mannivanan underlines another aspect of the dialogue and reconciliation process. Referring to the Seven -Phase Roadmap, the paper draws attention to the first step of the fulfillment of such a plan which is the holding of free and fair elections. Questions do arise regarding the true commitment of the military junta to this end and whether elections would lead to the other steps that are mentioned viz. step-by-step implementation towards a democratic system, convening the Hluttaw (legislative body) and the drafting and adoption of a new constitution. The unwillingness of the military junta to prune its powers and the Proposal for Reconciliation in Burma (2009) which seems to address the apprehension of the military junta regarding the transition to democracy rather than address the concerns of the ethnic minority groups are some primary concerns. Undoubtedly, rejection of the military's junta's right to rule will not solve the present conflict; creation of an environment for dialogue through protracted engagement could be the key to economic and social transformation in Myanmar.

Two events of significance have recently transpired in Myanmar. First, the nationwide elections which were held in November 2010 , and the other the release of Ms Aung San Suu Kyi, the leader of the National league for Democracy held in house arrest since July 1989. The elections were held in tightly controlled conditions wherein political activity was denied to certain parties and individuals. However, the party formed by the military junta was provided with overwhelming facilities leading to total lack of credibility about the fairness of the election and subjecting it to sever criticism from several countries. Although the international community welcomed the release of Ms Aung San Suu Kyi, there is yet much speculation as to her future political role in Myanmar. Meanwhile, the ongoing clashes between the armed dissidents and the military forces continue resulting in thousands of refugees fleeing from Myanmar to Thailand.

Internal conflict in Myanmar had resulted in wide ranging external consequences in several countries in the region. These consequences have themselves become driving forces in the continuation of the conflict as have been discussed in detail in the papers of this volume. It is therefore, important that policy makers inside and outside Myanmar have a clear insight of the situation and evolve a series of options in the areas of economic and foreign policy which influence the social and human spheres.

Overview of Internal Conflicts in Myanmar

TATMADAW IN TRANSITION: DEALING WITH INTERNAL CONFLICT

Tin Maung Maung Than

Myanmar after gaining independence from Britain in January 1948 has been beset by insurgencies, some of which began even before it became a sovereign state.[1] Soon after gaining independence the state was in turmoil as ideological and ethnic rebellions broke out in succession[2]. The Communist Party, sections of the People's Volunteer Organization (a paramilitary force composed of nationalist veterans of World War II), and major elements of two army battalions rebelled in quick succession. The Karen National Defence Organization (KNDO) rebellion began in January 1949 and some dissident ethnic minorities also took up arms.[3] Thus, right from the beginning of its formation, security challenges to the Myanmar state took the form of hard security threats posed by armed rebellion that warranted robust military responses. As such, Myanmar's state leaders have been fixated on military strength in responding to perceived threats emanating within its border or from abroad.

Throughout the first four decades of Myanmar's independence, the *Tatmadaw* (literally; royal force) or Myanmar Armed Forces (MAF)

---

[1] Rakhine (Arakan) separatists and the Trotskyite faction of the Communist Party (popularly known as Red-Flag Communists) initiated armed insurrection in 1947.

[2] For accounts of the 'civil war', see, e.g., Martin Smith, *Burma: Insurgency and the Politics of Ethnicity* (London: Zed, 1991), pp. 106-22, 125-54. For the government's view, see *Burma and the Insurrections* (Rangoon: Ministry of Information, 1949); and *Is it a People's Liberation? A Short Survey of Communist Insurrection in Burma* (Rangoon: Ministry of Information, 1952).

[3] For a summary, see Smith, *Burma: Insurgency and the Politics of Ethnicity*, pp. 44-48, 50-53, 62-64, 71-87, 110-18. See, also, KNDO Insurrection (Rangoon: Gov ernment Printing and Stationary, 1949). F or a di fferent perspective, see, e.g. , Smi th Dun, *Memoirs of the F our-Foot Colonel*, Cornel l Univ ersity, S outheast Asia Pr ogram Data P aper no . 113 (Ithaca: Southeast Asia Progr am, Cornell Univ ersity, 1980).

had been continually engaged in military operations against ideological and ethnic insurgencies as well as remnants of the Kuomintang (KMT) army that had fled to the Thai-Myanmar border after losing control of China to the Chinese Communist Party (CCP).[4] Given the continual military threat posed by domestic rebellions, MAF was, until the 1990s, largely geared towards counter-insurgency (COIN) operations. The result was an infantry-heavy army dominating the force structure and the defence posture based on COIN doctrine remained unchanged without much upgrading or modernization of the armed forces.[5]

However, after the State Law and Order Restoration Council (SLORC) came to power in a coup on 18 September 1988, there has been a significant expansion in the size of the armed forces as well as substantial modernization through reorganization and acquisition of more potent weapons and new equipment. This trend continues under the present State Peace and Development Council (SPDC formed in 1997) even as it prepares itself to transfer power to a constitutional government by end 2010. On the other hand, since 1989 seventeen major armed groups (perhaps 80 per cent of the armed opposition) had made ceasefire agreements with the junta and only some Shan and Kayin ethnic insurgents remain to pursue armed struggle.

Tatmadaw's National Security Perspective and Threat Perceptions

Lon-Choan-Yei (Myanmarese term for the word 'Security') implies a sense of safety through an enveloping impermeability. For various reasons associated with Myanmar's historical experience with colonialism, World War II, the civil war (in the first decade of independence) and the Cold War, as well as the multi-ethnic nature of

---

[4] Maung Maung, *Grim War Against KMT* (Rangoon: n.p., 1953); and Robert H. Taylor, *Foreign and Domestic Consequences of the KMT Intervention in Burma,* Cornell University Southeast Asia Program, Data Paper no. 93 (Ithaca: Cornell University Southeast Asia Program, 1973).

[5] However, there had been some organizational changes and steady expansion of combat infantry units from the mid sixties to the late-seventies to counter the growing strength of armed insurgents; especially the Communists (Tin Maung Maung Than, "Burma's National Security and Defence P osture," *Contemporary Southeast Asia [CSEA]* 11, no. 1 (1989), pp. 44-45.

its polity (135 ethnic nationalities in eight major ethnic groups)[6], successive Myanmar government's have always adopted a state-centric national security policy approach with much emphasis on national sovereignty, territorial integrity and national unity (among all ethnic nationalities).[7] Apparently, the ruling elites, whether they are parliamentarians or military commanders, like their counterparts in many Asian states have always "felt that states were the best (and perhaps only) providers of security and.... ferociously guarded the principles of absolute sovereignty and non-interference in domestic affairs". It follows that the "state, usually referred to as *naing-ngan-daw* (literally, royal state) has been the primary referent for 'national' security" and a reification of the state.[8] Moreover, the conceptualization and scope of national security in Myanmar since its independence in 1948, "have essentially been determined by a small elite [dominated by the military] who, for all practical purposes, seem to be insulated from societal" concerns.[9] All along, Myanmar's security outlook has been preoccupied with domestic threats, the most serious being armed challenges from a variety of ethnic and ideological insurgencies that constitute a distinctly military threat.

On the other hand, notwithstanding a professed neutralist and non-aligned foreign policy augmented by regional and sub-regional cooperation since the late 1990s[10], external aggression has also been a major feature in the threat spectrum envisaged by military leaders, not

---

[6] Hla Min, "Political Situation in the Union of Myanmar and Its Role in the Region" (Yangon: Ministry of Defence, April 2004).

[7] This section draws heavily from Tin Maung Maung Than, "Myanmar: Preoccupation with Regime Survival, National Unity, and Stability" in Muthiah Alagappa, "Rethinking Security: A Critical Review and Appraisal", in *Asian Security Practice: Material an I deational Influences*, edited by Muthiah Alagappa (Stanford: Stanford University Press, 1998), pp. 390-416. See, also, Mary P Callahan*Making Enemies: War and State Building in Burma*(Ithaca; Cornell University Press, 2003) for the historical roots of Myanmar's state security concerns.

[8] Tin Maung Maung Than, "Myanmar: Preoccupation with Regime", p. 394.

[9] Ibid., p.391.

[10] For a summary, see N. Ganesan, "Myanmar's Foreign Policy towards Its near Neighbours", *International Studies Review* 11, No. 1 (2010): 1-24.

only because some neighbours did have ideological and logistic links with internal insurgencies (at times even supported them)[11] but also due to the fact that the United States together with its Western allies had until recently[12] supporting calls for regime change and had imposed sanctions and arms embargos to punish the military junta for what they deem as suppression of democracy and violation of human rights.[13] Even the United Nations (UN) has been critical of Myanmar government's handling of the domestic political situation.[14] On the global front, Myanmar's military leaders saw the unipolar post-Cold War situation as threatening. This was evident in the speech by the (then) SLORC Chairman and Commander-in-Chief of the MAF Senior General Than Shwe at the graduation ceremony of the 36th intake of the Defence Services Academy, on 7 April 1995. He said that "the concept of the balance of power is non-existent today with the collapse and disintegration of some big nations. Thus small countries like ours are in a situation where serious consideration must be given to security."[15]

---

[11] The Chinese Communist Party had supported the Burma Communist Party rebellion for nearly three decades until Deng Xiopeng put a stop to it (Maung Aung Myoe, "The Counterinsurgency in Myanmar: The Government's Response to the Burma Communist Party", PhD dissertation, A ustralian National Univ ersity, Canberra, 1999). Thailand used ethnic rebel groups straddling its border with Myanmar as a buffer for decades until the late 1990s.providing opportunities for soliciting logistic support and using the Thai side of the border as a safe haven (see Maung Aung Myoe, Neither Friend nor Foe, Myanmar's Relationship with Thai land Since 1988: A View f rom Yangon (Singapore: Institute of De-fence and Strategic Studies, 2002), chapter 2. Others had harboured dissidents and rebels vowing to overthrow the military government (see, David Steinberg, "Prospects for Democratisation in Myanmar: Impact on India", Indian Defence Review, 3 December 2009, in BurmaNet News(online news group), 3 December 2009, http://www.burmanet.org/news/2009/12/03/indian-defence-review-prospects-for-democratization-in-myanmar-im-pact-on-india-%E2%80%93-david-i-steinberg/, Accessed 16 June 2010

[12] The New Obama administration, after reviewing its Asia policy decided to engage Myanmar diplomatically without lifting sanctions. See, e.g., "US renews hand to My anmar", AFP, 30 December 2009.

[13] See Andrew Selth, "Even Paranoids Have Enemies: Cyclone Nargis and Myanmar's Fears of Invasion", CSEA, 30, no . 3 (2008): 379-402.

[14] See, e.g., "U.N. Assembly Condemns My anmar Rights Recor d", R euters, 24 December 2009, in BurmaNet News, 23-26 December 2009, http://www.burmanet.org/news/2009/12/26/reuters-u-n-assembly-condemns-myanmar-rights-record/,Accessed 16 June,2010

[15] The New Light of Myanmar, 8 April 1995.

Security and State Building

In the larger context of state-building, one can say that Myanmar under the military junta had been an exemplar of a typical 'national security state' in which the military leaders seem to have conflated national interest with the armed forces' corporate interests defined and represented by them.[16] To them nation and state become interchangeable and regime and state are conflated. The MAF professed to uphold the national interest in the form of three "Main National Causes" expounded as "non-disintegration of the Union, non-disintegration of national i.e. multi-ethnic solidarity", and "perpetuation of national sovereignty".[17] These three tenets together with the following slogans are seen in huge billboards all over Myanmar and are printed on the front page of every authorized publication in Myanmar (including area maps and business directories).

People's Desire

- Oppose those relying on external elements, acting as stooges, holding negative views.
- Oppose those trying to jeopardize stability of the state and progress of the nation.
- Oppose foreign nations interfering in internal affairs of the State.
- Crush all internal and external destructive elements as the common enemy.

National unity, with connotations of consensus and harmony, is also portrayed as the paramount national interest and security is the overriding factor in all spheres of human activity in Myanmar.

Meeting the Challenges of Armed Conflict

"War fighters, first and foremost"[18] the military leaders expect even the non-combat supporting units (like the medical corps) to fight when

---

[16] See, e.g., Callahan, *Making Enemies*, on the mi litary's state bui lding r ecord in My anmar history.

[17] Nawrahta, *Destiny of the Nation* (Yangon: News and P eriodicals Enterprise, 1995).

[18] Callahan, *Making Enemies*, p. 2.

necessary.[19] The present SPDC regime (and its predecessor SLORC) seems to believe that the security challenges threatening to displace the regime and destroy the state of Myanmar could only be countered by modernizing and strengthening the MAF and allowing it to play a vital role in governing Myanmar, even after transferring power to a constitutional government from direct military rule.[20]

MAF: Modern and Strong

At the Armed Forces Day commemoration on 27 March 2009 in Naypyitaw (new capital of Myanmar), Senior General Than Shwe, Commander-in-Chief of MAF and SPDC chair, in his speech, reiterated the oft-repeated adage that "the immediate task before us is the building of a strong and capable modern patriotic Armed Forces that can ensure total all-round defence ...We must be combat-ready forever to defend the nation and protect the life and property of the people.[21]

The building of a strong and modern MAF has been a continuing task for the MAF leadership since it began in the early 1990s with initial Chinese assistance following the visit to China by (then) Deputy Chief of Staff of MAF Lt. General Than Shwe in October 1989. The most significant move was the 1990 deal with the PRC involving weapons and military equipment worth an estimated value of some US$ 1.2 billion.[22] This indicates Myanmar's intention to follow the path of force modernization taken by other Southeast Asian countries since the early 1980s.[23] Another agreement with PRC to supply additional weapons and equipment worth US$ 400 million was reported in 1994.[24] Taken at face value, such deals

---

[19] In his speech to medical doctors at the graduation parade of the 11th *Tatmadaw* in Transition intake of the Def ence Services Medical Academ y, Than Shwe exhorted them "to keep pursuing studies in ever changing military tactic[s] so that you will be able to lead your troops in the battle fields [sic] in time of need", *The New Light of Myanmar*, 26 December 2009

[20] Senior General Than Shwe's speech on the Armed Forces Day commemoration parade at Naypyitaw on 27 March 2009, *The New Light of Myanmar*, 28 March 2009

[21] Ibid.

[22] See, e.g., the report by Yindee Lerchar oenchok in *The Nation*, 27 November 1990.

[23] Cf. Ami tav Ar chaya, *An Arms Race in P ost-Cold W ar Southeast Asia? Pr ospects f or Control*, Pacific Strategic Papers, no. 8 (Singapore: Institute of Southeast Asian Studies, 1994), pp.66-71.

[24] Bertil Lintner's report in *Jane's Defence Weekly*, 3 December 1994, p. 1.

struck between 1988 and 1994, had contributed considerably to expanding the capability of Myanmar's armed forces.

Weapons and equipment were procured not only from China but also from Israel, North Korea, Pakistan, Poland, Russia, Singapore, (then) Yugoslavia, and Ukraine. They may be classified into three categories. The first involved acquisition of similar or improved versions of current equipment, either to replace obsolete ones or to supplement the existing stock. This type of procurement—comprising ammunition, light and crew-served weapons, communications and transport equipment— was essentially aimed at building up the military's war stocks to counter the threat posed by the upsurge of insurgency in the aftermath of the 1988 upheaval and also to accommodate the overall expansion of manpower.[25] The second category comprises armaments that represent a substantial upgrading in terms of force multiplication and enhanced capability. It comprises armoured personnel carriers, artillery, anti-aircraft (AA) weaponry, helicopters and light attack aircraft.[26] Their procurement, in contrast to that of the first category, was not a short-term COIN-oriented measure but constituted an attempt to modernize the armed forces in preparation for the eventuality of conventional conflict. As such, those weapons and equipment ostensibly represent a vast improvement over the pre-1988 inventory in terms of technology and firepower. Major acquisitions include K-8 jet trainers that could also serve as light attack aircraft and large-calibre artillery pieces like 122 and 155mm long range guns.[27] The last category is concerned with the introduction of new classes of weapons hitherto absent in Myanmar's inventory. These include modern corvettes, a frigate (built locally), missile armed patrol craft, helicopter gunships, supersonic fighters, multiple rocket launchers (MRL), air-to-air missiles (AAMs), and surface-to-air missiles (SAMs) and perhaps even short-range

[25] Maung Aung Myoe, *Building the Tatmadaw: Myanmar Armed Forces since 1948* (Singapore: Institute of S outheast Asian Studies, 2009), pp . 106-107.

[26] Ibid. chapter 4 for details.

[27] Ibid., p. 109. There were reports that MAF had recently bought some 50 units of Chinese K-8 K arakorum tr ainers, also known as Hongdu JL -8 (jointly dev eloped b y China and Pakistan), in addition to a f ew bought in the late 1990s (www .defensrindustrydaily.com/ Chinas-K-8-Jets-A-Killer-for-Myanmar-06457/).

surface-to-surface missiles (SSM).[28] The most prominent purchases were 12 MiG 29 fighters from Russia in 2001 that were augmented by another order for 20 in 2009, worth US$ 570 million.[29] In fact, the opposition groups even accused the SPDC of pursuing a nuclear weapon programme through uranium enrichment with North Korean assistance. As evidence, they cited public-domain satellite imagery; classified documents and photographs supplied by a defector from one of the MAF research and development facilities.[30] All such allegation were refuted by the government with its resident representative to the IAEA stating that "no activity related to uranium conversion, enrichment, reactor construction or operation has been carried out in the past, is

---

[28] Maung Aung Myoe, *Building the Tatmadaw*, chapter 4, "Opposition media have reported that North Korea supplied Hwasong-6 (SCUD C variant) ballistic missiles that could reach 700 kilometres with a 800 kilogrammes warhead (Min Lwin and Wai Moe, "Junta form Missile Force to Guard Against External thr eats", *Irrawaddy* 13 July 2010,http://www.irrawaddy.org/article.php?art_id=18960 Accessed 13 July 2010; specifications ar e from www.deagel.com/Ballisitc-Misiles/Hwasong-6_a000854001.aspx, Accessed 14 November 2010)

[29] Wai Moe, "Junta B uys 230 Mili tary Air craft in 21 Y ears",*Irrawaddy* online, 26 December 2009, ht tp://www.irrawaddy.org/article.php?art_id=17475, Ac cessed on 5 June 2010

[30] Only circumstantial evidence based on accounts of secret facilities equipped with dual-use precision machinery, sk etches and photogr aphs of a v essel simi lar to a container f or chemical reactions to produce metallic uranium and a test bed for producing UF6 as well as an experimental laser enrichment device for UF6 were provided by Major Sai Thein Win (a missile engineer trained in Russia) whose anecdotes described the work of "nuclear battalions" and demonstrations of a CO2 laser and reactor control rod movement to the military top brass. See, Bertil Lintner, "Myanmar's Nuclear Bombshell",*Asia Times* Online, 5 June 2010, http://www.atimes.com/atimes/Southeast_Asia/LF05Ae01.html, Accessed on 5 June 2010 and "Expert says Burma Planning Nuclear B omb" DVB (Democratic Voice of Burma; a Norway-based opposition radio/TV station) Interview, 4 June 2010, . For technical analysis of the evidence by R obert Kelly, a f ormer IAEA director and U. S. nuclear weapons expert, see R obert E. Kelly and Ali F owle, Nuclear Related Activities in Burma", May 2010, online at www.devb.no/burma-nuclear-ambitions-dvb-reports. See, also, David Albright, *Peddling Peril: How the Secret Nuclear Trade Arms America's Enemies* (New York: Free Press, 2010), pp. 159-60, 244.For a skeptical view questioning the conclusions and the veracity of a defector's account, see Andrew Selth, "Does Burma have a WMD pro-gram?" *The Lowy I nterpreter* Onl ine, Lowy Institute for International P olicy, http://www.lowyinterpreter.org/post/2010/06/07/Does-Burma-have-a-WMD-program.aspx, Accessed 7 June 2010

ongoing or is planned for the future".[31] Although the U.S. State
Department expressed concern over these allegations China, Russia
and ASEAN (Association of Southeast Asian Nations) member states
remained ambivalent or unconvinced while the EU took a wait-and-see
stance.[32]

Factories for producing light weapons, mortars and associated
ordnance were also constructed and the military's C4I (command,
control, communications, computers and intelligence) capabilities were
upgraded and expanded. Military infrastructure, including naval docks
and a multitude of large tunnels (apparently for storage, shelter and
communications), had been constructed, presumably with North
Korean assistance.[33] The bulk of the weapons and equipment acquired
were imported and the scale of arms and equipment purchased for the
force modernization effort since 1989 was much larger, at US$ 2.1 billion,
than the US$ 350 million spent during the 1969-88 period.[34]

---

[31] "Resident Representative of Myanmar to IAEA Ambassador U Tin Win sends reply to
Director Mr. Marco Marzo of Division of Oper ations A, Department of Saf eguards, IAEA",
New Light of Myanmar, 19 June 2010. See, also , "Press Statement of Ministry of F oreign
Affairs on unf ounded allegations against My anmar regar ding nuclear progr amme",
Naypyitaw, Ministry of Foreign Affairs, 11 June 2010. For the opposition's reaction, see,
Bertil Lintner, "Deception and Denials", *Asia Times* online, 1 July 2010, http://
www.atimes.com/atimes/Southeast_Asia/LF30Ae01.html, Accessed on 30 June 2010

[32] "Myanmar Nukes Would Pose Stability Threat, U .S. Says", Global Securi ty Newswire, 11
June 2010, online at http://gsn.or g/siteservices/print_friendly.php?ID=nw_
20100611_5649; "Neighbours Hesitant in Addr essing Myanmar Nuclear Allegations", Global Security Newswire, 20 July 2010, online at http://gsn.org/siteservices/
print_friendly.php? ID=nw_20100720_ 6554; "Nuclear Pipe Dream", *Irrawaddy*, July 2010,
pp. 10-14; and "Russia, EU: Mor e study needed on My anmar's alleged nuclear activity",
Deutsche Presse-Agentur, 23 July 2010.

[33] For details, Maung Aung Myoe, Building the Tatmadaw, chapter 4; and unauthorized copy
of a secret draft report of the MAF delegation, led by Chief of Joint Staff General Thuya
Shwe Mann, to North Korea and China from 21 November to 2 December 2008 (in author's
possession; hereafter referred to as Secret Trip Report). The authenticity of this r eport is
attested by the fact that the alleged perpetrators were recently sentenced to death (Wai
Moe, "New Enemies of the State in B urma", *Irrawaddy* online, 9 January 2010).

[34] The figures were derived from the international arms transfer data (*World Military Expenditures and Arms T ransfers* [Washington, D.C.: Arms Control and Disarmament Agency]
various issues; *SIPRI Yearbook* [Oxf ord: Oxf ord Univ ersity Pr ess], 1994 , 1997, 2001,
2005, and 2009).

While the state was expending substantial amounts of relatively scarce foreign exchange on arms purchases, the manpower and combat units of the MAF were also being expanded considerably from pre-1988 levels. It had been estimated that the number of infantry combat battalions increased from 168 in early 1988 to 504 in 2007[35], divided between 13 regional commands, 10 light infantry divisions (LIDs of brigade strength), 10 regional operation command (ROC, under regional command) and 20 military operation commands (MOC). Furthermore, other combat arms were also expanded with the formation of air defence, artillery and armoured divisions as well as a missile command. Support units in signals, logistics, engineering, transport ordnance and medical fields were also augmented with manpower and modern equipment. Training facilities were also upgraded and expanded while new training institutions for engineering, computing, nursing and medicine were established. The navy was expanded in line with acquisitions of new naval vessels with longer range and greater firepower thereby allowing better coverage of Myanmar's EEZ (extended economic zone). The air force saw the formation of new fighter and helicopter squadrons, support units and radar stations that presumably enhanced its capacity for interception and close air support. As a result, the total strength of the MAF in 2002 was estimated to have been around 400,000 with 16,000 in the navy and 15,000 in the air force. The current strength may have declined to about 350,000, probably due to desertions and inability to recruit enough replacements.[36]

Whether MAF's expansion of armaments and manpower over the last two decades had actually resulted in raising its capabilities to the level of an effective fighting force on par with other professional armed forces in the region is still a subject open to debate and speculation. War-fighting capability is difficult to measure *ex ante* even in the aftermath of actual combat operation but it is obvious that its assessment requires more than just the tallying of troops and weapon platforms in the order of battle.[37] Such quantitative information, though

---

[35] Many are believed to be operating at less than half strength. See Maung Aung Myoe, *Building the Tatmadaw*, p. 78.

[36] Andrew Selth, "Known Knowns and Known Unknowns: Measuring Myanmar's Military Capa- bilities", in *CSEA* 31, no. 2 (2009), pp . 282-83.

[37] For an example of one appr oach, see James F. Dunnigan, *How to Make War* (New York: William Morrow, 1993).

not completely irrelevant is inadequate to gauge the ability of a particular armed force to achieve victory or deter the potential enemy. A multitude of factors such as morale, discipline, leadership, command and control protocols and procedures, operational readiness, quality and frequency of training and exercises, logistics, technical proficiency, doctrine and tactics must be considered and weighed to arrive at an informed judgement. Moreover, in the case of Myanmar, the secretive nature of the military regime and its tight control over information gathering and dissemination make it even more difficult to gauge the capabilities of the MAF. On the other hand, observers had pointed out the apparent problems of "doctrine, training, integration, logistics and maintenance", associated with "rapid expansion and acquisition of so many weapon systems from so many different" sources.[38] There are also issues relating to the poor quality of some weapons and equipment and lack of indigenous technological base to keep Myanmar's "modernized armed forces operational without external assistance".[39] Possible factors that could substantially degrade MAF's ability to prevail in high intensity modern warfare are likely to be: shortcomings in system integration, lack of skilled manpower, inadequacies in spares and supplies, logistic bottlenecks and technological deficiency as well as financial constraints that restrict fuel consumption, live-firing exercises, large scale manoeuvres and compromise alert status of combat units. With many imponderables and lack of hard data, one tends to concur with Selth's conclusion that "known unknowns vastly outnumber the known knowns" and the MAF's newfound strength in numbers is deceptive as far as its conventional war-fighting capabilities are concerned.[40]

Institutionalizing Tatmadaw's Leading Role in Myanmar

According to the military's vision, a firm constitution that avoids the pitfalls of both the 1947 and 1974 constitutions is necessary for a stable political environment in which indigenized rules of "multi-party democracy" can be "formulated". As such, SLORC envisaged a political configuration

---

[38] Selth, "*Known Knowns*", p. 288.

[39] Ibid.

[40] Ibid., p. 290.

institutionalizing the military's role in "national politics" as a solution to the problem of dysfunctional "party politics".[41] The junta initiated a process in 1992 to hold a national convention (NC) that would lay down "the basic principles for the drafting of a firm and stable Constitution".[42] The resulting deliberations that began in 1993 were concluded only in 2007 after a long recess between 1996 and 2004. The results of the NC were distilled and formulated into a draft constitution by a committee in February 2008. The draft constitution drew harsh criticism and calls for rejection by the National League for Democracy (NLD) and other opposition groups, student activists, human rights and democracy advocacy groups and Western governments who accused the SPDC of perpetuating military control under the guise of a civilianized political regime and skewed electoral rules.[43] Unfazed by criticisms from home and abroad, the SPDC conducted a constitutional referendum in May 2008 that reportedly endorsed the new constitution by over 92 per cent of the voters. The MAF will have a major role to play in the post 2010 Elections constitutional government in accordance with the following provisions in Myanmar's third constitution since independence:

- The military's complete autonomy to manage its own affairs (Chapter 1, Basic Principles, article 20);

- Designation of the military Commander-in-Chief (C-in-C) as supreme commander of all armed forces (Chapter 1, Basic Principles, article 20);

- Reserved seats for the military in the form of C-in-C's nominees amounting to 25 per cent of the seats in both house of the national parliaments (Chapter 4, The Legislature, articles109 and 141);

- Reserved seats for the military in the form of C-in-C's nominees amounting to one-third of the elected representatives in the

---

[41] Lt. Gen. My o Nyunt's speech, *New Light of Myanmar,* 8 June 1993.

[42] SLORC Declaration No. 11/92, 24 April 1992 (*Working People's Daily* [WPD], 25 April 1992).

[43] For a summary of reactions to the new constitution see, R obert H. T aylor, *The State in Myanmar* (London: Hurst, 2009), pp. 503-4.

parliaments of the (14) States and Regions comprising the Union (Chapter 4, The Legislature, article 161);

- Reserved positions for the nominees of the C-in-C as ministers and deputy ministers for defence, home affairs and border areas (Chapter 4, The Executive, articles 232 and 234);

- Exemption for military personal to remain in military service while serving as ministers and deputy ministers whereas civilians have to resign from their positions as parliamentarians or civil servants or suspend their party affiliations (Chapter 4, The Executive, articles 232 and 234);

- The President, after coordinating with the National Defence and Security Council, may declare a national emergency and then hand over executive, legislative and judicial powers to the C-in-C in situations "if there is sufficient reason for a state of emergency to arise that may disintegrate the Union or that may cause the loss of sovereignty, due to acts or attempts to take over the sovereignty of the Union by insurgency, violence and wrongful forcible means" (Chapter 11, Provisions on State of Emergency, articles 417 and 418);

- Requirement for the powerful executive President to be "well acquainted with the affairs of the Union such as political, administrative, economic and military", have 20 years continuous domicile, and be born of full citizen parents. Moreover, the candidate, one of the parents, the spouse, any of the children or his/her spouse must not be a subject or citizen of a foreign country or has sworn allegiance to a foreign country, or enjoy the same privileges and benefits bestowed by the foreign country to its subjects and citizens (Chapter 3, Head of State, article 59)[44];

---

[44] This article effectively excludes the candidature of DASSK for President due to her marriage to an Englishman and her son's foreign nationality. However the constitutional provisions do not rule out her eligibility for becoming a member of parliament (article 120) or even a minister (article 232)

- All the armed forces in the Union shall be under the command of the Defence Services (Chapter 7. Defence Services, article 338);

- Amendment of any of the major provisions in the constitution could only be made if it secures more than 75 per cent of the votes in the national parliament (a combined upper and lower house) together with more than 50 per cent votes of all eligible voters in a national referendum (Chapter 12, Amendment of the Constitution, article 436);

- An 'immunity' clause that protects the junta and all government personnel from being persecuted for any act carried out "in the execution of their respective duties" (Chapter 14, Transitory Provisions, article 445).

As such, the military appears to have all its cards in place to ensure its continued dominance of Myanmar's politics and society in the name of upholding the three main national causes designed to overcome security challenges to the regime and state.

Leadership Transition in the MAF: Ensuring Unity and Loyalty

Though the current leaders project the image of the military as a monolithic institution with a united officer corps there have been several instances of rifts and tensions within the command hierarchy in the past. As such, the present SPDC leadership has been taking measures to ensure a smooth transition in the MAF in preparation for the eventual transfer of state power to an elected government. The SPDC chairman Senior General Than Shwe himself closely manages the opaque leadership transition within Tatmadaw hierarchy and it is highly likely that the military, which had seen five Commanders-in-Chief since independence, will be led by a new generation of commanders in the post-election period. The first generation led by the late General Ne Win could be identified with the anti-fascist struggle and the birth of the Tatmadaw while the second generation that came into power after the 1988 coup advanced their careers during the Socialist era under the ruling Burma Socialist Programme Party (BSPP) and were cadres of that party. On the other hand, the third generation leaders who are expected to take over the reins of post-elections Tatmadaw would, in all probability, be those who were born a decade or so after independence and had learnt the ropes under SLORC/SPDC tutelage. They neither have the "revolutionary" credentials of a patriotic independence struggle accorded to the first generation leaders nor the absolute authority of a military junta and may have to rely more on military professionalism to prove their mettle in a new setting of civil-military relations.[45] The current hierarchy of Tatmadaw seems to be as shown in the Table 1 on next page:

---

[45] Andrew Selth, " 'Civil-Military Relations in B urma: Portents, Predictions and P ossibilities', Griffith University Regional Outlook Paper No. 25, 2010

Table 1

Army Command Hierarchy (March, 2010)

Name	Designation	Rank
Sen. Gen. Than Shwe	C-in-C (SPDC Chair)	OTS-9
Vice Sen. Gen Maung Aye	Dy. C-in-C & Army C-in-C (SPDC Vice Chair)	DSA-1
Gen. Shwe Mann	Joint Chief of Staff	DSA-11
Gen. Tin Aung Myint Oo	(SPDCSecty.-1, QMG)	DSA-12
Lt. Gen. Tin Aye	Chief OP	DSA-9
Lt. Gen. Tha Aye	BSO-1	DSA-16
Lt. Gen. Min Aung Hlaing	BSO-2	DSA-19
Lt. Gen. Ko Ko	BSO-3	DSA-19
Lt. Gen. Khin Zaw	BSO-4	OTS-49
Lt. Gen. Myint Swe	BSO-5	DSA-15
Lt. Gen. Ohn Myint	BSO-6	DSA-17
Lt. Gen. Thura Myint Aung	Adj. G	DSA-18
Lt. Gen. Thein Htaik	IG	DSA-16
Lt. Gen. Hsan Hsint	MAG	DSA-15
Lt. Gen. Myint Hlaing	Chief Air Defence	DSA-17
Lt. Gen. Ye Myint	Chief MAS	DSA-15
Lt. Gen. Hla Htay Win	Chief Training	DSA-20
Lt. Gen. Maung Shein I	IAG	DSA-20

Notes: non-SPDC member; the second group's rank ordering protocol is not known. OP = Ordnance Production; QMG = Quartermaster-General; Adj.G = Adjutant-General; BSO = Bureau of Special Operations (territorial); IG = Inspector-General; MAG = Military Appointment-General; MAS = Military Affairs Security; IAG = Inspection and Auditor-General; OTS = Officers Training School; DSA = Defence Services Academy.

Currently, General Shwe Mann appears to be in charge of all the three services. Age-wise, he is nearly a generation behind Senior General Than Shwe and a decade behind Vice-Senior General Maung Aye in terms of graduating cohort from the DSA (Defence Services Academy). Moreover, most other officers in the command hierarchy (see Table 1) are several years behind Shwe Mann's cohort and Than Shwe is like a father figure to them. These young army generals in their early fifties owed their rapid promotions to the current leadership's patronage and are believed to be particularly beholden to Than Shwe. In a similar manner those down the line from the current crop of regional commanders through divisional and tactical commanders to battalion commanders as well as senior staff officers and commanders of supporting arms (armour, artillery, supply & transport, signals, engineers, medical and training units) have all benefited from rank-upgrading exercises and manpower expansion. Officers from the navy and the air force have also enjoyed similar benefits from the modernization trend and have neither the resources nor the inclination to challenge the dominant army leadership.

Preparations for the leadership transition MAF seems to has reached a crucial stage where a new team to lead the MAF in 2010 and beyond are being groomed for the eventual transition. All top generals in the current SPDC lineup are unlikely to remain in the MAF after the elections and most of the other senior officers depicted in the aforementioned command hierarchy are expected to retire as well.[46] The new crop of MAF leaders is likely to be chosen from the cohort of DSA 19-20 or later.[47]

---

[46] It was reported in early May 2010 that Prime Minister General Thein Sein and all cabinet minsters as well as deputy ministers holding military ranks had shed their uniforms in anticipation of participating in the forthcoming elections (Nayee Lin Let, "Naypyidaw: No More 'Military Government'", *Irrawaddy* online, 6 May 2010, www .irrawaddy.org/print_article.php?art_id=18401)., Accessed 6 May, 2010

[47] The conventional wisdom suggests that the next C-in-C and his deputy should be able to serve for at least the full five year term of the electoral cycle before reaching the supposed mandatory retirement age of 60, f or apparent reasons of stability and continuity. They should also be junior to the executive President who is most likely to be a retired General.

Moreover, the major concern of the military leadership since the coup of 1988 has been the perpetuation of corporate solidarity within its ranks ostensibly in the national interest. As such, the leadership transition of the *Tatmadaw* must ensure that potential cleavages will not be realized and tensions between the various cohorts jostling for power will not be exacerbated once the current paramount leader leaves the scene and more importantly that the SPDC chairman's legacy remains intact and his interests well protected. To this end, dire warnings of catastrophic consequences arising from disunity have been repeatedly issued by the leadership together with a reference to internal and external threats posed by communists, ethnic insurgents, neo-colonialists, neo-imperialists, Western media, self-serving expatriates, meddling NGOs, hypocritical proponents of human rights and democracy, and a hostile superpower.[48] The ratification of the *Tatmadaw* as the "parent" of the armed forces members exploits Myanmar traditional values and culture and serves as a constant reminder to maintain corporate loyalty and group solidarity within the armed forces. Nevertheless, there had been purges in the upper echelons of the MAF and persistent rumours of factionalism between graduates of the prestigious DSA and OTS (Officer Training School) as well as between the intelligence arm and the combat arms as well as tensions between the chair and vice-chair of the SPDC. The MAF as an institution has withstood the test of time thus far and had not broken out into open confrontation at the top. [49] Soliciting patronage and jostling for promotions and coveted positions do occur but everybody appears to be contented with maximizing gains within the system while working to avoid the ire of the top leaders. Plugged into the patronage network they are likely to have considerable vested interests in maintaining the status quo and remain intensely loyal to the military leadership. The Senior General at the apex of the Tatmadaw hierarchy appears to have a firm grip over his

---

[48] This theme is present in almost all speeches made by military leaders in their addresses at graduation ceremonies for military cadets, commemorative speeches on Independence Day, Armed Forces Day and other national commemorative events as well as in addresses to military commands and units during tours and field trips.

[49] Win Min, "Internal Dynamics of the Burmese Military: Before, During and After the 2007 Demonstrations", in Monique Skidmore and Trevor Wilson (eds.) *Dictatorship, Decline and Disorder in Myanmar* (Canberra: ANU Press, 2008), pp. 29-47

subordinates through a combination of patronage, personalized rule, and unpredictable behaviour.[50]

Nevertheless, the transition from direct military rule with absolute power and authority to indirect control of the Myanmar state could turn out to be unpalatable for some of those who have been enjoying the power and privileges associated with SPDC rule, as well as others who aspire to take their turn. That may foster factionalism and cleavages that could stall the leadership succession process and in the worst case lead to a split in the leadership and the spectre of a palace coup could manifest.[51]

Internal Conflict: Old and New

It is unlikely that internal conflicts will cease upon the institution of electoral rule under the 2008 Constitution and may even intensify in the coming months as the political temperature rises as the military regime's seven-step "Road Map" enters the final stages leading to the general elections. The SPDC and its successor regime will, in all probability, have to contend with daunting security challenges from old and possible new conflict situations related to contentious issues involving resource exploitation, socio-cultural and economic aspirations of local communities, and identity polities. Potential adversaries include insurgents, political dissidents, advocacy groups, ethnic ceasefire groups and even disenfranchised elements within the military who may resort to violence or mass protests.

Resource Exploitation and Allocation Conflicts

Large scale national development projects like hydro-electric power production and influx of foreign labour in mining and timber concessions have apparently led to localalized conflicts resulting from grievances over displacement of affected populations and disenfranchised communities. These could become confrontational if and when political

---

[50] Benedict Rogers, *Than Shwe: Unmasking Burma's Tyrant* (Chiang Mai: Silkworm B ooks, 2010). This unauthorized biography contains anecdotal and circumstantial information on the Senior General's modus operandi.

[51] Bertil Lintner, "The Staying P ower of the Burmese Mili tary Regime", in *Between Isolation and Internationalization: The State of Burma* (Stockholm, SIIA, 2008), p.243.

dissidents take them up as a *cause celebre* and mobilize opposition. Some examples are the opposition to the Myitsone Dam project sited at the confluence of the two parent rivers of the mighty Ayeyawady (Irrawaddy) and apprehensions about Chinese mining projects in the Kachin state involving thousands of Chinese labourers.[52]

At the national level, conflict over issues of power and governance, usage of natural resources, distribution of resource rents and budgetary allocations could arise between natural-resource rich regional governments (of seven [Bamar majority] regions and seven [ethnic] states) and Naypyidaw as well as among the regions.[53]

Political Violence and Terror Attacks

A recent spate of bombings in Yangon and elsewhere indicate that there are radical elements willing to use terror tactics to destabilize the SPDC rule and derail the electoral process-in-making. With the National League for Democracy (NLD; the winning party in the 1990 elections) boycotting the elections and its incarcerated leader Aung San Suu Kyi virtually barred from taking political office, some frustrated political activists who refused to accept the 1988 Constitution and the resultant electoral process could go underground and may resort to violence, especially during the election period. One also cannot rule out the infiltration of international terror networks into Myanmar to support the extreme faction of the "Rohingaya" movement who claimed to represent hundreds of thousands of dispossessed and disenfranchised Muslim migrants and communities in the Rakhine (Arakan) State.[54]

---

[52] Kachin News Group, "Fresh Batch of Chinese Workers Arrive in Myitkyina", 20 May 2010, in BurmaNet News, 20 May 2010; AKT, "60 Arrested Over Kachin Dam Bombs", DVB, 26 May 2010, http://www.dvb.no/news/60-arrested-over-kachin-dam-bombs/9176, Accessed 26 May 2010.

[53] Martin Smith, "Ethnic Politics in Myanmar: A Year of Tension and Anticipation", in *Southeast Asian Affairs 2010* (Singapore: Institute of Southeast Asian Studies, 2010), p. 227; "Burma in 2010: A Critical Year in Ethnic Politics", Burma Centrum Nederland, Burma Policy Briefing No. 1, June 2010

[54] For a summary of the plight of the Rohingya people see, e.g., Yeni. "Unwanted Anywhere", the lead story in *Irrawaddy* (March-April 2009), pp. 18-20 and accompanying cover stories in pp. 21-27.

The Continuing Insurgency

Despite the apparent success of the junta's strategy in securing ceasefire arrangements with major armed ethnic groups, remnants of the decades old ethnic insurgency linger on mainly at the eastern border regions adjacent to Thailand. Apart from several minor armed groups (Chin National Front or CNF and the Arakan Liberation Front or ALF on the Indian border[55] and the armed wing of the Karenni National Progressive Party or KNPP near the Thai border) there are two significant insurgent groups to contend with. One is the breakaway faction of the MTA (Mong Tai Army led by narco-warlord Khun Sa that surrendered in 1996), led by Yawd Serk (Ywet Sit) known as the Shan Sate Army-South (SSA-South) which is ensconced in Eastern Shan States with a force reportedly numbering several thousand fighters. Another is the Karen National Liberation Army (KNLA, the military arm of the Karen National Union or KNU; fighting since 1949) with some 2-4,000 troops.[56] These two armed groups have been under constant pressure from the MAF and are basically on the defensive.[57] The KNU/KNLA is at *nadir* after six decades of fighting, plagued by attrition, factionalism, depleted resources and weak leadership.[58] However, some troops or even whole units from the Shan and Kayin ceasefire groups who do not accept the junta's demobilization plan could break away and defect to the SSA (South) and KNU camps respectively.[59]

---

[55] There are also anti-Indian insurgent groups belonging to the United Liberation Front of Assam and the National Socialist Council of Nagaland that create problems in Myanmar-India relations. Lately the MAF had stepped up pressure on them as well as the Rakhine and Chin insurgents. See, Nyein Chan, "Army Expands Outposts Near Indian Border", *Mizzima News*, 7 May 2010, http://www.mizzima.com/news/inside-burma/3913-army-expands-outposts-near-indian-border-.html, Accessed 7 May 2010; and K. Yhome, "India-Myanmar Relations (1998-2008): A Decade of R edefining B ilateral Ties", ORF Oc casional P aper No . 10, New Delhi, Observer Research Foundation (January 2009), pp. 14-15.

[56] International Institute for Strategic Studies (IISS), *The Military Balance 2009* (Abingdon, Oxon.: Routledge, 2009), Table 47, p. 474. It is likely to be at the low end of that estimate, due to further factionalism and attrition.

[57] Lt. Gen. Yawd Serk, "The Weak Points of Burma's Ethnic Resistance Groups", *The Nation*, 29 June 2010, in BurmaNet News, 29 June 2010.http://www.burmanet.org/news/2010/06/29/the-nation-thailand-the-weak-points-of-burmas-ethnic-resistance-groups-lt-general-yawd-serk/, Accessed 30 June 2010

[58] Smith, "Ethnic Politics", pp. 221-22.

[59] Hseng Khio F ah, "Will Ceasefire Shan Army Sp lit into Two Factions?", S.H.A.N., 26 April 2010, on Burma News International, http://www.bnionline.net/news/shan/8395-will-

The Ethnic Ceasefire Groups: Demobilization Dilemma

The instituting of a constitutional arrangement that allows pluralistic electoral participation could be interpreted as a means to ensure continuity and sustainability in realizing the military's vision of national security. However, the very constitutional provision (article 338) that was meant to anoint the MAF as the sole armed organization with a monopoly on the use of force has created a security dilemma for the SPDC with respect to the armed wings of the ceasefire groups (CFG). When they entered into ceasefires with the government all CFGs except the Kachin Independent Organization (KIO) had only verbal agreements that allowed them to keep their arms and engage in business activities with some localized autonomy and authority. The larger CFGs like the KIO (Kachin Independence Army or KIA, its armed wing, has about 5-6000 troops) and those on the Chinese border (Wa, Kokang and Mong La groups comprising a majority of ethnic Chinese inhabitants) were allowed greater autonomy to administer and control their designated areas officially known as "special regions". Among them the Wa CFG led by the leaders of the United Wa State Army (UWSA, 15,000 to 25,000 strong and reputedly armed with heavy mortars, artillery and modern anti-air weapons) was given wide latitude to run its area with almost no intervention by the central government. Even the MAF had reportedly refrained from entering Wa territory without prior arrangement. The three CFGs whose territories are adjacent to the Yunnan province of China have had extensive socio-economic and quasi-political links with China, set their own judicial and administrative rules and are believed to have engaged in illegal border trade, including drug production and trafficking.[60]

---

ceasefire-shan-army-split-into-two-factions.html, Accessed 27 April 2010; and Joseph Allchin, "DKBA Commander's Defiance Nudges K aren State T owards W ar", DVB, 26 July2010, http://www.dvb.no/news/dkba-commanders-defiance-leads-karen-state-to-gear-up-for-war/10890, Accessed 26 July 2010.

[60] See International Crisis Gr oup (ICG), "China's Myanmar Dilemma", Asia R eport No. 177, Brussels, 14 September 2009, pp. 0-13; and Mary Callahan, *Political Authority in Burma's Ethnic Minority States: Devolution, Occupation, and Coexistence*, East-West Center Policy Studies 31 (W ashington D.C.: East-West Center, 2007). F or an in-depth r eport on dev el-opments along the Sino-My anmar border, see Hélène Le B ail and Abel T ournier, "From Kunming to Mandalay: The New 'B urma R oad,' Asie Visions 25, P aris, Centre Asie If ri (March 2010).

In accordance with the Constitutional rule forbidding armed forces independent of the MAF, the SPDC, in early 2009, had demanded that the CFGs either turn their armed forces into a border guard force (BGF) with reduced strength and truncated command structure or local militia (lower status and smaller units than the BGF) before the new constitution comes into force. This goes against the grain of most CFGs, which had repeatedly expressed their preference to keep their forces intact and negotiate the terms and conditions of the demobilization with the new elected government after 2010. The SPDC, on its part, had also refused to change the terms of its demands for transforming the CFG's armed wings into units under its direct command. Consequently, the larger CFGs, the KIA, USWA, MNDAA (Myanmar National Democratic Alliance; popularly known as the Kokang group estimated at 2000 strong) and NDAA (National Democratic Alliance Army; popularly known as the Mong La group with several thousand troops) all refused to comply. In fact, the BGF format requires the CFGs to downsize their combat formations (brigades and divisions in the case of Wa) into 326-men battalions embedded with MAF personnel who would control supplies and logistics and apparently devoid of heavy weapons. Tensions had been rising between those four major CFGs and the military on account of this BGF issue and were exacerbated when the MAF subdued the defiant Kokang group in August 2009 by supporting an internal revolt by pro-junta leaders following violent clashes as the army enforced the indictment against the group leader Pheung Kya-Shin for illegal weapon production. Though these four CFGs had formed an alliance called Myanmar Peace and Democratic Front (MPDF) in March 2009, the alliance failed to act in support of the Kokang group. Nevertheless the remaining three CFGs pose a formidable challenge to the MAF if it had to use force to make them comply with the SPDC's plan for transforming them into a fragmented BGF under direct MAF control. The New Mon State Party (NMSP) with a few thousand men-at-arms also declined the military's offer to demobilize its troops into a smaller BGF.[61] Even the DKBA

---

[61] "The Kachin's Dilemma-Become a Border Guard Force or Return to Warfare", EBO Analysis Paper No.2/2010, Brussels, Euro-Burma Office, 2010; Lawi Weng, "Mon Reject Militia Plan", Irrawaddy., 23 April 2010, http://www .irrawaddy.org/article.php?art_id=18309, Accessed 24 Apri l 2010; and B rian Mccartan, "My anmar Ceasefir es on a T ripwire", Asia Times, 30 April 2010, http://www.atimes.com/atimes/Southeast_Asia/LD30Ae01.html, Accessed 30 April 2010.

(Democratic Kayin Buddhist Army; a breakaway Buddhist faction of the Christian-dominated KNLA), seen as the military's staunch ally against the KNU, was sending mixed signals, at times indicating that it would maintain the *status quo* instead of conforming to the military's BGF scheme.[62]

Up to five deadlines, beginning with October 2009, had passed and the impasse continues to date. There were some indications that the junta had stopped pressing for immediate transformation and might defer the issue until after the elections.[63] All in all, the problem of CFGs intransigence in refusing to play by the SPDCs rules to demobilize their armies has become the most acute security challenge for the SPDC and the successor regime that would be sworn in after the elections.[64]

Coping with Internal Conflict: A New Paradigm?

Despite all the efforts expended on force modernization and expansion over the two decades of direct military rule at great expense, the *Tatmadaw* may find itself wanting in dealing with the conflict situations depicted above. Even in the case of the traditional military confrontation with the remaining armed insurgent groups the fact is that the MAF has thus far been unable to militarily crush them. In the event that the impasse with the CFGs over the issue of demobilization through the

---

[62] Lawi Weng, "DKBA, KNU held   Secret Peace Talks", *Irrawaddy*, 2 July 2010,   http://www.irrawaddy.org/article.php?art_id=18864, Accessed 2 July 2010; and Saw Thein Myint, "DKBA Brigade 5 R efuses to T oe Junta's BGF Line", Kachin Information Center, 23 July 2010, in BurmaNet News, 23 July 2010, http://www.burmanet.org/news/2010/07/23/kachin-information-center-dkba-brigade-5-refuses-to-toe-juntas-bgf-line-%E2%80%93-saw-thein-myint/, Accessed 27 July 2010

[63] Hseng Khio Fah, "Junta Sets no New Deadline ór BGF Program at Latest Meeting", S.H.A.N., 24 June 2010, http://www.shanland.org/index.php?option=com_ content&view=article&id=3076:junta-sets-no-new-deadline-for-bgf-program-at-latest-meeting&catid=86:war&Itemid=284, Accessed 26 June 2010.

[64] "The Kokang Clashes-What Next?", EBO Analysis Paper No. 1/2009, B russels, Euro-Burma Office, September 2009; Maximilan Wechsler, "No United Army for Us, Rebels Vow", *Bangkok Post,* 13 December 2009; and "No K owtowing by Dissident Ceasefire Armies", S.H.A.N/, 28 December 2009, http://www.shanland.org/index.php?option=com_ content&view=article&id=2874:no-kowtowing-by-dissident-ceasefire-armies&catid=85:politics&Itemid=266, Accessed 27 January 2010. F or a summary, see Smith, "Ethnic P olitics", pp. 217-20.

BGF process led to the resumption of hostilities there is no assurance that the MAF could quickly achieve total victory. Given the proximity to China and Thailand, both of which are concerned not only with protecting their substantial investments and trade in the affected regions but also with border security and stability, the viability of a military option is questionable. Moreover, international repercussions of a violent confrontation with ethnic CFGs is also another factor working against a military solution. Furthermore, military's actions will also be constrained by the rules and procedures of constitutional government.

Civil-military relations under the envisaged power sharing arrangement between the elected civilianized executive (in all likelihood led by retired generals) and the virtually autonomous military may also generate unforeseen tensions in the state's authority structure at the centre and also in the provinces where the almost omnipotent authority of regional commands would be confined to military matters in contrast to the executive powers of the newly installed post-election regional governments.

Finally, in line with the pluralism brought about by the political transition in Myanmar, the *Tatmadaw* must find a new paradigm to deal with conflict situations instead of the usual unilateral practice employing force and coercion as in the past. This may turn out to be the most difficult challenge facing the new generation of generals in charge of the post-election *Tatmadaw.*

NON-TRADITIONAL SECURITY THREATS, INTERNATIONAL CONCERNS AND THE EXILED OPPOSITION

Kerstin Duell

Burma[1] has been witnessing decades of conflict and civil war before the backdrop of centuries of a no less tumultuous history. The contemporary conflict is characterised by multi-layered, complex, shifting dynamics set within a deeply divided society and fought out between numerous state and non-state conflict parties, most of them pitted against the military government but also against each other. Persisting strife has resulted in chronic socio-political, economic, humanitarian and environmental[2] crises.

Domestic Conflicts and Internal Crises

After Burma's independence from British colonial rule in 1948, disagreements between Burman and ethnic nationality politicians, and the military triggered ethnic and communist rebellions which carved out "liberated areas" from the Burmese polity. Thus, a number of opponents have challenged the rule and legitimacy of successive, military-dominated governments: First, the armed ethnic nationality movements for self-determination, second, the armed communist movement, which eclipsed in 1989, and third, the predominantly

---

[1] In an attempt to accommodate diverse political camps with regards to the highly polarised issue of naming the country, this author applies "Myanmar" to the military government and official actors, i.e. the "Myanmar Government", the "Myanmar Army" or *Tatmadaw* (literally "royal force"), and "Burma" for non-state actors as well as the pre-1988 state.

[2] Environmental degradation is fuelled by deforestation; pollution from extensive mining; dams for hydropower; and general lack of environmental policies.

unarmed urban population led by university students and Buddhist monks.[3] Armed and non-violent opposition to military rule have co-existed, while an internal dynamic of violent action and counter-reaction has emerged, peaking in three major confrontational waves – post-1948, post-1962, and post-1988.[4] Neither the various opponents nor the governments can be seen as monolithic entities. On the contrary, all have contained at times competing or opposing factions and subgroups. It is this politico-historical heterogeneity compounded by Burma's ethnic jigsaw, and by external influences that create today's political conundrum.

Since 1994 the United Nations General Assembly has passed annual resolutions calling for tripartite dialogue and encouraging "the Government of Myanmar to engage in a substantive political dialogue with Aung San Suu Kyi and other political leaders, including representatives from ethnic nationality groups."[5] The international community has in this way identified the military government, Aung San Suu Kyi and the National League for Democracy (NLD), and leaders of a number of ethnic nationalities[6] as the three main conflict parties. The military, however, only held talks with the NLD or individual ethnic nationality leaders, thus foregoing inclusive and transparent three-party negotiations. Repeated attempts to break the political deadlock through dialogue stopped short of mutually acceptable agreements addressing political key concerns. Instead, the military has followed its own "Seven-Step Roadmap" to disciplined democracy.

Contention has always centred on the core unresolved questions pertaining to the form of government[7], and the organisation of the

---

[3] The 1988-founded All Burma Students' Democratic Front (ABSDF) is an exception.

[4] Martin Smith, *State of Strife: The Dynamics of Ethnic Conflict in Burma.* (Singapore: Institute of Southeast Asian Studies, 2007), p 4.

[5] United Nations General Assembly, Resolution 49/197, 23 December 1994.

[6] "Burmese" refers to all citizens of Burma, as opposed to ethnic "Burman" (the demographi-cally and politically dominant group), and "non-Burman" or "ethnic nationalities" (the eth-nic" minorities").

[7] Historic precedents include monarchy, colonial rule, democracy, socialist one-party system, indirect and direct military rule.

state – centralism versus federalism determining centre-periphery relations; in other words, who exercises in what manner and to which degree control over territories, resources and peoples.

This results in two struggles, the one for democratic rights and governance, and the one for ethnic rights and self-determination. Prior to the 1988 uprisings, these issues and their defenders remained separate. What is more, the two struggles were detrimental to each other. The ethnic nationalist struggle for local autonomy and group rights, for example, was a significant contributor to the failure of democracy in the 1950s and the emergence of an all-dominant military, and continues to complicate civil-military relations today. Conversely, the struggle for democracy has complicated the ethnic struggle, most notably by raising questions about which Burmese to negotiate with.[8]

After 1988, these two struggles merged within the pro-democracy movement in exile whereas domestic politics offered fewer opportunities to do the same. A number of factors then contributed to the post-1988 increase in political resistance but decrease of armed conflict.

Competing Ideas of Nationhood, and Self-determination: The Enduring Challenges of Ethnic Conflict

One of the most ethnically diverse countries in the world, the "Union of Myanmar" is mainland Southeast Asia's largest country and home to approximately 53 million people. In the absence of reliable statistics or a census more recent than 1983, exact population figures or a binding ethnic breakdown remain highly contested.[9] It is generally agreed that the politically dominant Burman ethnic group constitutes about two thirds of the population. The remaining third is divided into seven principal ethnic nationality groups and over one hundred ethno-

[8] Timo Kivimäki and Morten B. Pedersen. *Burma: Mapping the Challenges and Opportunities for Dialogue and Reconciliation,*(Brussels and Helsinki: Crisis Management Initiative, 2008), p 11.

[9] Estimations range from 47-58 million people, a substantial variation that is characteristic for statistics on Burma. Similarly, the figure 57,504,368 announced on 15 May 2008 appears spurious. David I. Steinberg, *Burma/Myanmar: What Everyone Needs to Know* (New York: Oxford University Press, 2010), p- xxivf.

linguistic groups and subgroups. The traditional ethnic homelands cover more than half of the national territory surrounding central Burma like a horseshoe along the international borders. Incidentally, most of the country's natural resources stem from these areas.

While resource wealth buttresses the post-1988 political economy of military rule, Burma's ethnic struggles should not be seen as contemporary "resource wars" for four reasons: First, ethno-political violence does not result from contemporary grievances but dates back to pre-independence times; second, ethnic nationality movements are extremely diverse in their respective histories, identities, and legitimacies; third, legacies of international linkages and "regional conflict complexes" continue to linger on from the Cold War; fourth, deep humanitarian and social crises have built up over six decades, making it impossible for any stakeholder to solve them in the complexity and scale required.[10] In sum, rather than being an example for "greed and grievance" Burma is a case of a "conflict trap" where no single issue can be considered the root cause of conflict but a complex set of dynamics.[11]

Historical Legacies and Territorial Divisions

Contemporary ethnic leaders consider the ongoing political and armed conflicts as a constitutional problem because the issues of ethnic rights, the extent of self-determination, and the right to secession have not been solved. The protracted conflicts between the military and numerous ethnic nationalities can only be understood before the backdrop of a history of centre-periphery frictions, mutual distrust, and unmet expectations.

This starts with divergent interpretations of pre-colonial history. The military regime portrays the pre-colonial state as a unified Burman kingdom broken up by British colonial rule to support its claims for Burman domination, while ethnic nationalities insist on distinct ethnic territories, and legacies of dynastic or tribal rule underscoring their historic independence.

---

[10] Smith, *State of Strife,* p 3.

[11] Ibid., 3-4.

During colonial times, the British interfered little in the ethnic nationalities' "frontier" or "excluded areas" in contrast to direct colonial rule over central "ministerial Burma". When Aung San's delegation negotiated independence from the British in January 1947 in London, no ethnic nationality leader was invited, provoking several leaders to cable threats of boycotting the "Atlee-Aung San Agreement"; Britain demanded consultation with the ethnic nationalities.[12] Aung San hence attended an ethnic nationality conference in February 1947. The historic "Panglong Agreement" guaranteed "full autonomy in internal administration for the Frontier Areas in principle", including financial autonomy.[13] Unfortunately, only Shan, Kachin, and Chin leaders attended and signed the agreement. Panglong has since been constructed in various ways suitable for the agendas of the *Tatmadaw*, the NLD and ethnic nationalities respectively; while the 12 February became a national holiday as "Union Day".[14]

Within the federal framework of the 1947 constitution, the traditional Shan and Karenni principalities were amalgamated into one state and constitutionally guaranteed a right of secession after ten years. The Kachin also received a state but no secession rights. The Chin, representing less than one percent of the country's population, were granted fewer rights and a "special division". Territorial authority of the three other major ethnic groups—the Mon, Karen, and Arakanese - was left open in the constitution and to be decided after independence.[15]

Ethnic homelands were placed under the control of the capital Rangoon after independence in 1948. Thwarting ethnic expectations, the government refused to grant secession rights while political centralism prevented a truly federal structure. The new national army soon started fighting against ethnic nationality armies and civilians.

---

[12] Martin Smith, *Burma: Insurgency and the Politics of Ethnicity* (London: Zed Books, 1991), p 77-78.

[13] Panglong Agreement, 12 F   ebruary 1947 . http://burmalibr ary.org/docs/panglong_agreement.htm, Accessed December 2009.

[14] Mathew J. W alton, "Ethnicity, Conflict, and History in Burma: The Myths of P   anglong", *Asian Survey*   48(6) (2008):889–910.

[15] Mary P . Cal lahan, "Democr acy in B urma: The Lessons of History".   *NBR Analysis* 9(3) (1998a):9.

Thus, "minority" socio-political grievances rose dramatically with independence. Ethnic nationality leaders answered the civilian and military administrations with revolt, a heightened sense of a distinct identity, and a desire for political separation.

Ethnic as well as the ideology-based insurgencies soon controlled territories complete with people, infrastructure and natural resources.[16] During the Cold War, rebel groups enjoyed support from foreign states. Thus, some British supported the Karen, China the Communist Party of Burma, the Naga, and the Kachin, and Thailand a variety of rebel groups; East Pakistan (later Bangladesh) backed the Muslim Rohingyas with Middle Eastern funding; and India was said to be involved with the Kachin and Karen; the US and Taiwan assisted the 16,000 Kuomintang troops as a bulwark against the spread of Communism until a Chinese incursion with the aid of Burmese troops eliminated the KMT in 1961.[17]

Since the 1974 Constitution, the country has been administered through seven Burman "divisions" and seven ethnic nationality "states" – Arakan, Chin, Kachin, Shan, Karenni, Karen and Mon (clockwise from southwest to southeast). This does not imply, however, government control over the entire national territory.

A further administrative reorganisation to include previously unrepresented ethnic nationalities will be put into practice after the 2010 elections. The seven divisions (taing) will be renamed "regions", while the seven "states" retain their names. The six new "self-administered areas" are the Naga Self-Administered Zone in Sagaing Region as well as the Danu, Pao, Palaung, Kokang Self-Administered Zones, and the Wa Self-Administered Division in Shan State.[18]

---

[16] See Bertil Lintner's numerous books and articles on the ethnic nationalities' "parallel administrations" at the height of their power in the late 1970s, and 1980s.

[17] Steinberg, *Burma/Myanmar: What Everyone Needs to Know* , 44-45.

[18] Tom Kramer, *Neither War nor Peace: The Future of the Cease-fir e Agreements in Burma* (Amsterdam: Transnational Institute, 2009), p-4

Ethnic Nationality Responses to post-Cold War Changes

In the past as today, complex, fluid configurations characterise the numerous ethnic nationality movements with their armed, political, women's, youth wings, and other sub-organisations. Usually, the armed and political wings link at the apex of pyramid-like power structures. Leaders within the traditional armed groups are not elected, but the groups have started to address the problematic issue of representation. Infighting has occurred within, and clashes between various armed groups while a number of factions and splinter groups emerged, some of which allied with the *Tatmadaw*. Simultaneously, new alliances were formed, building on the largest, the National Democratic Front (NDF) of 1976.

In 1990, thirty-six political parties representing ethnic groups contested. Among them the largest to win were the Shan Nationalities League for Democracy (SNLD) with 23 constituencies, and the Arakan Democracy League with 11 constituencies. The ethnic coalition United Nationalities League for Democracy (UNLD) controlled 66 constituencies (including the Arakan NLD but not the SNLD constituencies). All ethnic nationality NLDs cooperated with the NLD but most were subsequently banned, and continued in exile.[19]

The contemporary ethnic political landscape comprises still fighting (non-ceasefire) ethnic armies as the remainders of the NDF, as well as post-1988 ceasefire groups, ethnic nationality political parties, ethnic organisations in exile and new coalitions. In addition, the rise of community-based organisations such as the prominent *Metta, Shalom*, and *Karen Development Network*, suggests that civil society may play an increasingly important socio-political role albeit the scope and space for civil society remains highly contested (this applies to Burman and non-Burman civil society organisations alike). In line with the ceasefire groups, these civic organisations focus on peace-building through development as opposed to the political parties' strategy of reaching political solutions first.[20]

---

[19] Camilla Buzzi, *Burma: Twelve Years After 1988. A Common Future?* (PD Burma/ Worldview Rights, 2002), http://www .ibiblio.org/obl/docs/CB-Web.htm , Accessed 1 July , 2007.

[20] N. Ganesan and Kyaw Yin Hlaing, *Myanmar: State, Society and Ethnicity* (Singapore: Institute of Southeast Asian Studies, 2007); Kyaw Yin Hlaing, "Burma: Civil Society Skirting

On the domestic political scene, over 20 ethnic armies, including the two largest groups United Wa State Army (UWSA), and Kachin Independence Organisation (KIO), have agreed to ceasefires with the *Tatmadaw*.[21] The main groups have all been given formal autonomy over areas defined as Special Regions, together with varying levels of financial support and business opportunities for the development of their areas; in return they have pledged to cease hostilities against the government, and avoid any cooperation with the remaining insurgent groups, but remain under arms. Smaller groups, mostly breakaway factions from the larger armies, "exchanged arms for peace", economic support, and land to resettle but they retain no or little autonomy.[22] There are several reasons, why ethnic leaders entered truces, however imperfect, with the regime: First, war-wariness after decades of civil war; second and related, the need to address the longstanding socio-economic hardship of the population; and third, the intent to re-enter the legal realm facilitating the participation in national politics and negotiations with the *Tatmadaw*. Ethnic leaders see more prospects in dealing with the Burman leaders in power, than with the NLD curtailed by the detention of some of its leaders.[23] Considering the fact that ceasefire groups still command standing armies (in contrast to the unarmed democratic opposition), they do have some leverage vis-à-vis the government. In the decade that has passed since most of the ceasefires, the ethnic movements have maintained their core demands for self-determination and equal rights within the federal union, while frustration set in over the lack of political and constitutional solutions.

The Karen National Union (KNU) and a few other armies continue their armed resistance against the state and have aligned themselves with the pro-democracy organisations on the Thai-Burmese border. Following the post-1988 exodus of activists into NDF-controlled areas,

---

Regime Rules" in Muthaiah Alagappa (ed.) *Civil Society and Political Change in Asia: Expanding and Contracting Democratic Space* , (Stanford, California: Stanford University Press 2004) , 389-418.

[21] Smith, *State of Strife,* p67-69.

[22] Kivimäki and Pedersen,*Burma: Mapping the Challenges and Opportunities for Dialogue and Reconciliation,* (Brussels and Helsinki: Crisis Management In itiative, 2008)10f.

[23] Smith, *State of Strife,* 41.

ethnic nationality and Burman leaders have sought to identify common aims in their opposition to the *Tatmadaw*, and have created common fronts such as the National Coalition of the Union of Burma (NCUB). Most Burman and non-Burman movement organisations state their objectives as (1) establishment of a genuine federal union; (2) abolition of all types of totalitarianism, including military dictatorship; (3) promotion of democratic governance; and (4) guarantee of human and civil rights, political equality, and self-determination. Important to note is that non-Burman leaders have come to espouse some form of federal government as opposed to earlier demands for the right to secession.

In addition to bridging the gap between the Burman and non-Burman opposition, ethnic leaders also need to overcome the substantial differences between the various non-Burman ethno-religious-linguistic groups with their diverse historic narratives and traditions of governance. In exile, ethnic nationalities have initiated the drafting of "alternative" constitutions for their respective states within a federal framework, an endeavour outlawed by the SPDC. Parallel to Burman-non-Burman coalitions, the nationalities have formed their exclusive coalition groups, the Ethnic Nationalities Council (ENC), and the United Nationalities Alliances (UNA).

Competing Visions of Modernity, Institutions, and Role of the State: The Conflict between Democratic Forces and the Military Regime

The antecedents of the contemporary democratic opposition as well as the armed forces, the *Tatmadaw*, date back to the anti-colonial struggle for national independence. University students were the vanguard of the anti-colonial "Thirty Comrades" or *Thakin* movement and supplied the nation with some of its most dynamic leaders across the political spectrum.[24] Thus, erstwhile comrades became civilian politicians, military leaders, and communist insurgents after independence and soon faced each other from opposing camps.

Since the nation's legendary founding father Aung San, a student union leader-turned-nationalist politician and military hero, and long-term dictator Ne Win were *Thakin,* both, the military government and the NLD lay claim on the independence movement and the military

[24] Michael W.Chamey, *A History of Modern Burma*. (Cambridge:New York,CUP,2009) 115.

institution. The historical role in the fight for independence holds the key for contemporary political identity, rhetoric, and the contest over legitimacy, and national symbols. On the one side, the military government justifies its preponderance over Burmese politics in terms of its historic role of safeguarding the nation's unity against internal and external enemies. On the other side, the NLD frames its democratic political programme as "the second struggle for independence" – independence that was won in 1948 and lost to the *Tatmadaw* in the 1962 coup.

The quasi-mythical martyr Aung San, who was assassinated at the eve of independence in 1947, still looms large over Burma. The *Tatmadaw* used to celebrate Aung San as the founder of the military but drastically downgraded references to him once his daughter Aung San Suu Kyi emerged on the political scene in 1988.[25] Suu Kyi derives a part of her appeal and legitimacy from her father, whom she resembles physically as well. Aung San continues to be one of the symbols of today's pro-democracy movement, and his portrait appears, next to images of the Buddha, during demonstrations.

Student Activism

University students inherited a strong tradition of political leadership and identity from the anti-colonial movement, and were at the forefront of most political events in Burma. Burma's first student union, the Rangoon University Students' Union, was founded by Aung San and other Thakin[26] in 1931 and renamed into All Burma Federation of Student Unions (ABFSU) in 1951. ABFSU initiated several boycotts and strikes during the democratic period in 1949, 1953, 1956 and 1958. Demands consisted primarily in changes in the education system, while the 1958 demonstration called for an end to the civil war.[27]

---

[25] For instance, Aung San's portrait was removed from banknotes. Houtman terms this policy "Aung San Amnesia". Gustaaf Houtmann, *Mental Culture in Burmese Crisis Politics: Aung San Suu Kyi and the National League for Democracy*, Monograph Series No 33, (Institute for the Study of Languauges and Culture of Asia and Af rica, Tokyo: University of Foregin Studies, 1999), 15

[26] Burmese Nationalist Group

[27] Htun Thaung, *Student Activism in Burma: A Historical Perspective*   . Australia: Lawyers' Information Network, 1997 , www.link.asn.au/downloads/papers/burma/p_bm_05.pdf, Accessed 1 December, 2007

Student activism continued during the period from 1962-1987 despite harsh government reprisals, while political demands moved from educational matters to broader socio-political issues. Students and other urban opponents of the military had little contact with the ethnic or communist rebel movements or external players prior to 1988, except for the few students who left for insurgent-controlled areas to join the armed opposition. Whenever political opportunities arose, students mobilised Buddhist monks, workers, and the public to participate in anti-government action. Major protests were organised in 1963 (calling for a dialogue between military, students, and ethnic rebels); in 1969 (demanding the restoration of democracy and the end of military dictatorship); in 1974 and in 1975 (voicing general discontent with the BSPP rule); in 1976 (demanding democracy, the re-establishment of student unions, and the release of previously arrested demonstrators), and in 1987 (against the demonetisation).[28]

During the 1990s, university students again organised a number of protests; in 1991 (recognising the Nobel peace prize awarded to Suu Kyi, and calling for her release, the transfer of power to the elected civilian government, and the legalisation of student unions); in December 1996 (calling for the right to form student unions, and for national reconciliation – this indirectly sparked a workers protest in January 1997 and a monks protest in March 1997), and in 1998 (against military dictatorship, for the release of political prisoners).

The ABFSU continued to operate underground in the form of small cells often organised as "book clubs" or discussion groups and resurfaced during the 1988 and 2007 uprisings when it was officially re-established, on 28 August 1988 by Min Ko Naing and other student leaders, and on 28 August 2007 by Kyaw Ko Ko respectively.

The student movement's flag, a fighting peacock, derived from a national symbol for the Burmese monarchy that students appropriated during their anti-colonial struggle. The flag continued to symbolise the Burmese students' resistance to any ruler suppressing the rights of

---

[28] ABFSU, *Burmese Student Movement* (compiled by Myint Zaw).http://abfsu.net/?page_id=3, Accessed 1 May, 2010; Aung Sa w Oo, *Burma's Student Movement:A Concise History*, 3rd edition, 1993, http://abf su.net/?page_id=2, Accessed 1 Ma y, 2010.

students and the people.[29] Therefore, the ABFSU initially objected when the NLD adopted the symbol in its party flag in 1988 but the students supported the NLD and the fighting peacock soon became the NLD's emblem. In 2010, two newly registered political parties using the student's movement symbol provoked a letter of complaint to the election commission.[30]

The 1988 Student-led Uprisings

The waves of protests from 16 March to 18 September 1988 for a multi-party democracy presented a domestic political watershed in Burma. They triggered the birth of the pro-democracy movement, the emergence of Min Ko Naing as student movement leader, and of Aung San Suu Kyi as opposition leader, the formation of the political party "National League for Democracy" (NLD), and the ensuing mass exodus of students and other dissidents into exile.

The movement irreversibly changed the political landscape by ending the "Burma Socialist Programme Party's" one-party rule, its ideological underpinnings the "Burmese Way to Socialism", and (at least officially) the dictatorship of General Ne Win, and lastly, by gaining the concession to hold free multi-party elections.

Students initiated the uprisings; their mobilisation was greatly facilitated by the physical environment of the university campus, and the ABFSU's popularity. The students then mobilised virtually every sector of society, even some civil servants and soldiers; spontaneous, nation-wide uprisings in major cities and smaller towns ensued. The protests triggered the BSPP's collapse and the virtual breakdown of the state, vividly showing the regime's incapacity to run the country. The students, unfortunately, lacked the capacity to step into the power vacuum to swiftly take full control of the situation, while veteran politicians and Aung San Suu Kyi failed to convince high-ranking serving military officers to side with the pro-democracy groups. As a consequence, the military staged a coup on 18 September, and, at the

---

[29] Thaung, *Student Activism in Burma* , www.link.asn.au/downloads/papers/burma/ p_bm_05.pdf

[30] Htwe Ko, Feathers Fly Over Use of Fighting Peacock Image. *The Irrawaddy*, 7 May 2010.

cost of thousands of lives, re-took control as a new military junta named "State Law and Order Restoration Council" (SLORC).

The movement became known as the "8888 movement" after one of the largest demonstrations was held on 8 August 1988 in memory of the 1938 uprising seen as the beginning of the end of British Colonial rule.[31] Since 1988, activists have commemorated the 8 August; for instance in 2007 over 1,000 people including former students, NLD members, and foreign diplomats attended a memorial in Rangoon.

The Domestic Democratic Opposition

1. Aung San Suu Kyi and the National League for Democracy (NLD)

Previously unknown in Burma, Aung San Suu Kyi immediately became the icon of the pro-democracy movement following her first public speech at the Shwedagon Pagoda on 26 August 1988, which attracted a crowd of over half a million people. As the daughter of national hero Aung San and Khin Kyi, former MP and first Burmese ambassador to India, Suu Kyi sprang from a family inextricably linked to national history, endowing her with legitimacy, and broad public admiration. Her charisma and exceptional oratorical skills enabled her to transform inherited moral authority into personal authority.[32] Despite the student leaders' efforts and successes in initiating the uprisings, the movement had lacked an overarching leader until Suu Kyi emerged. Her principled stance, a rhetoric evolving around Gandhian non-violence, Buddhism, democratic ideals, and anti-corruption provided direction and played "a crucial role in transforming the Burmese uprising into a sustained and remarkably co-ordinated movement."[33] Several veteran politicians and former military leaders, including former Defence Minister Tin Oo, a former close associate of Ne Win, Aung Gyi, and U Nu publicly supported Suu Kyi.

---

[31] Megan Clymer, "Min Ko Naing, "Conqueror Of Kings": Burma's Student Leader", *Journal of Burma Studies* 8 (2003):45.

[32] Oo Z aw, "Aung San Suu K yi: Gandhian Dissident Democr at" in John K ate et.al (ed.), *Dissident Democr ats: The Chal lenge of Democr atic Leadership in Asia* , (New Y ork: Palgrave,Macmillan,2008) 252.

[33] Bertil Lintner, *Aung San Suu Kyi and Burma's Unfinished Renaissance*, (Clayton, Australia: Centre of Southeast Asian Studies, Monash University , 1990) 3.

In later years, her defiance in spite of harassment and years under house arrest since 1989 earned her high domestic and international respect. This translated into numerous prizes, most notably the Nobel Peace Prize in 1991. Thus, Aung San Suu Kyi has been Burma's only truly recognisable figure within the international community until today.

The NLD was founded by Aung San Suu Kyi, Tin Oo, and Aung Gyi on 27 September 1988, and won over 80 percent of the 1990 vote. Faced with the regime's curtailment of freedoms, and the refusal to recognise the election result, the NLD could neither form a government, nor function as a political party most of the time. Suu Kyi devised the tactic of deliberately observing the regime's regulations, and thus unmasking their flaws. For instance, she challenged the SPDC through legal means, exposing the very lack of an independent judiciary and a legal framework.[34] Strictly adhering to non-violence provided the means to sustain domestic democratic opposition in the long-term despite rash oppression.[35]

Insisting on transfer of power to the parliament-elects, the NLD issued several deadlines to the military: The Gandhi Hall Declaration of 29 July 1990 (demanding the convening of parliament and the transfer of power),[36] the letter to Than Shwe of 26 March 1996 (again demanding the convening of parliament),[37] and the Shwegondaing Declaration of 29 May 2009 (calling for a review of the controversial 2008 Constitution, political dialogue and the unconditional release of all political prisoners).[38] The NLD also boycotted the regime's roadmap whenever a process was seen as falling short of democratic and representative requirements, such as the National Convention in 1995 or the 2010

---

[34] The 1974 constitution was abolished in 1988, and the military ruled by decree. The proposed 2008 constitution would be Burma's third.

[35] Zaw, "Aung San Suu Kyi: Gandhian Dissident Democrat", 253

[36] Gandhi Hall Declaration, National League for Democracy,8th Waxuing Day of Wagaung BE 1352, 29 July 1990, http://www .burmalibrary.org/docs/Gandhi_Hall_Declaration.htm

[37] Letter of U Aung Shwe dated 25 March 19996, http://www.burmalibrary.org/reg.burma/archives/199604/msg00017.html

[38] National League for Democracy, Statement on 29 April 2009, http://wwwburmalibrary.org/docs07/NLDStatement2009-04-29.pdf

elections. In defiance of the military's claim to power, the NLD formed the Committee Representing the People's Parliament (CRPP) in 1998. During times between the years of house arrest, Aung San Suu Kyi and the NLD leadership held weekly political meetings in front of Suu Kyi's house in Rangoon, and toured the country, in particular ethnic nationality states, to rebuild the party's grassroots support.

The United Nations became involved through various offices in reconciliation efforts, most notably the "secret talks" between Suu Kyi and the government from 2000 to 2003 mediated by UN special envoy Tan Sri Razali Ismail, and the 2007-2009 meetings mediated by UN special envoy Ibrahim Gambari. Nevertheless, all dialogue since 1994 between Aung San Suu Kyi or other NLD leaders, and the military failed to bring about sustained and substantial political change.

In protest against the laws for the 2010 elections, the NLD decided unanimously on 29 March against registering as a party with the Election Commission – and thus automatically ceased to exist on 6 May 2010. To the shock of many pro-democracy movement participants and observers, the NLD effectively disbanded after having been the movement's flagship for two decades.

2. The 88 Generation (or Min Ko Naing) Group

Many students who participated in the 1988 uprisings either went into exile or were arrested and served lengthy prison terms. In 2006, some of those who were released, including the prominent student leader Paw Oo Htun, known under his nom-de-guerre Min Ko Naing "conqueror of kings"[39], formed the "88 Generation Group" inside Burma. Composed predominantly of former political prisoners, the "88 Generation Group" is no political party but a movement without formal leadership or organisational structures. Its key participants were at the forefront of the 88 protests and have become some of the most prominent dissidents in the country such as Ko Ko Gyi, Htay Kywe, Pone Cho and Min Zeya. In 2006, the group declared they saw Aung San Suu Kyi as

---

[39] Min Ko Naing received numerous prizes, including the John Humphrey Award (1999), Homo Homini Award (2000), Student Peace Prize (2001), Civil Coverage Award (2005), Gwangju Human Rights Award (2009). He was imprisoned from March 1989-November 2004, from September 2006-January 2007, and since August 2007 .

their leader "She is the one person that can bring about reconciliation and lead us into a new, democratic future."[40] Min Ko Naing stated that "The people of Burma must have the courage to say 'no' to injustice and 'yes' to truth."[41] The public holds the group in high regard, while the government is apprehensive of the group's political potential and has re-arrested Min Ko Naing and key people on several occasions. Despite their arrest, the 88 Generation initiated some of the most significant acts of political defiance since 1988, leading up to the 2007 protests.

In October 2006 the 88 Generation organised the "White Expression Campaign" (supporters dressed in white, the symbol of Burma's many martyrs, to demand the release of political prisoners); the "Multiple Religious Prayer Campaign" (worshippers dressed in white at Buddhist, Christian, Hindu and Muslim holy sites); and the "Signature Campaign" (535,580 signatures demanding the immediate release of political prisoners and the initiation of genuine national reconciliation were collected and sent to the Burmese government and the UN headquarters in New York). This was followed by the "Open Heart Campaign" (over 25,000 letters expressing hardship and grievances were collected and sent to Senior General Than Shwe) in January 2007; the "Sunday White Campaign" (supporters dressed in white visit families of political prisoners on Sundays) in April 2007. The group also called on the government to stop suppressing calls for democratic change, and urged the United Nation's Security Council to pass an effective resolution on Burma's political crisis.[42]

The American Federation of Teachers gave its 2008 President's International Democracy Award to the 88 Generation students.

At the time of writing, a number of political parties covering the political spectrum from military, ethnic nationalities, former NLD

---

[40] Bertil Lintner, "Burma's Warrior Kings and the Gener ation of 8.8.88". *Global Asia* 2 no. 2 (2007):78.

[41] Bertil Lintner, "The Burmese Way to Fascism", *Far Eastern Economic Review*, October 2007

[42] "88 Generation Students' Timeline", *Mizzima News*, 11 November, 2008; Lintner, "Burma's Warrior Kings", 78f.

members, to the so-called third force (which includes students from
the 88 generation) had registered for the 2010 election process.[43]

3. The 2007 Monk-led Uprisings

The demonstrations between 19 August and 31 October 2007 were the
most significant since 1988 and thus the next watershed after nearly 20
years of pro-democracy struggle in Burma and in exile. In contrast to
1988, communication technologies played a crucial role in mobilising
people in Burma, and in the immediate distribution of images and short
videos via youtube, facebook, media and other websites inside Burma
and worldwide, causing international condemnation. Thus the
international community followed events closely until the Myanmar
Government shut down the internet, effectively isolating the country.
In line with the colour revolutions of Eastern Europe, the international
media quickly coined the term "Saffron Revolution" although the
demonstrations had little in common with those colour revolutions.

Similar to 1988, economic grievances triggered the outburst of
longstanding public discontent. On 15 August, the SPDC withdrew
subsidies causing an overnight price increase of 100 percent for diesel
oil and 500 percent for compressed natural gas; this made transport and
the generators for electricity unaffordable while food became more
expensive.[44]

The 88 Generation Group played an important role in organising
the first demonstrations in August, but Min Ko Naing and other
prominent veteran activists were immediately arrested, depriving the
movement of direction. Buddhist monks then took the initiative in the
street marches that led to a renewed mass movement. However, monks
could only take the moral high ground and mobilise people but hardly
serve as outright political leaders. Thus, unlike in 1988 when a number
of political leaders emerged, the 2007 movement was leaderless and

---

[43] For the expanding l ist of candidates and parties see http://www .irrawaddy.org/election/
and http://www.mizzima.com/election2010.html and http://euro-burma.eu/
elections_32.html

[44] Donald S eekins, The Geopoli tics and Economics of Burma' s Military Regime, 1962-2007.
Understanding SPDC T yranny. *Japan Focus*, 11 November 2007

rudderless.[45] Notwithstanding theological controversies regarding the participation of fully ordained Buddhist clergy in any political activities, the Alliance of All Burmese Buddhist Monks (AABBM) issued statements and deadlines to the military. AABBM demanded (1) an apology to the monks for the Pakkoku incident (in which soldiers had desecrated a monastery, beaten, disrobed, and arrested monks); (2) the reduction of fuel price; (3) the release all political prisoners including Aung San Suu Kyi; and (4) dialogue with democratic forces.

Hundreds of thousands of monks, nuns, and citizens participated in over 200 protests spread across most states and divisions until the "Saffron Revolution" was ended by military might. The government met none of the demonstrators' demands, hence prices remained high and inflation soared. What was more, when the UN country chief Charles Petrie issued a statement concerning the deteriorating humanitarian crisis, he was expelled from the country.

Nonetheless, the 2007 protests had several important consequences. First, the dominant presence of Buddhist monks deprived the government of its crucial tool for legitimising its rule (as protectors of Buddhism and Buddhist nationalism); second, the SPDC somewhat rekindled dialogue with Aung San Suu Kyi through the meditation of a UN special envoy; third, the unprecedented level of international attention and condemnation fostered diplomatic initiatives and some alignment of diverse international policies.[46]

Mass Grievances: Mismanagement in a Failing State

Burma's alarming record of low humanitarian, as well as human and civil rights indicators has made the government target of persisting condemnation in the post-Cold War era. The people struggle daily with the consequences of economic underdevelopment, insufficient health care, and minimal opportunities for education and employment that leaves younger generations without a future inside the country. Endemic poverty persists with half of the population living below the

---

[45] Bertil Lintner, The Burmese Way to Fascism. *Far Eastern Economic Review* October 2007

[46] Zaw, "Aung San Suu Kyi: Gandhian Dissident Democrat", 264.

poverty line at a per capita income of US$ 290.[47] The cyclone Nargis of May 2008 worsened malnutrition, child mortality, and life expectancy, and caused food shortages because the affected Irrawaddy Delta area previously produced 65% of the country's rice, 50% of its poultry, and 40% of its pigs.[48] Poverty fuels conflict, and public discontent erupts when long-standing grievances suddenly increase further, as the large-scale demonstrations in 1988 and 2007 have shown. An increase of per capita income, in contrast, would reduce conflict potential.

The military government lacks the capacity and arguably also the political will to redress these multiple crises (although some observers argue that hierarchies and fear prevent negative information to reach the SPDC's top echelons, leaving Myanmar's leaders in the dark as to the crises in the country[49]). In its defence, the leadership cites sanctions and limited humanitarian aid as obstacles to overall improvement. The SPDC is failing in all of the five overarching categories used to measure state failure: (1) safety and security, (2) rule of law and transparency, (3) participation and human rights, (4) sustainable economic development, and (5) human development.[50] Burma ranks among the world's top twenty failing states.[51]

At the same time, a mistaken conflation of the regime's power and state efficacy conceals that fact that the Myanmar state remains inherently weak despite or rather *because of* its strong rulers. Typically, weak states tend to be ruled by despots, elected or not, who rigidly control dissent and harass civil society but provide very few political goods.[52] A strong state regime tends to be detrimental to state capacity

---

[47] Poverty line defined by the Worldbank.

[48] Steinberg, *Burma/Myanmar: What Everyone Needs to Know* , 2.

[49] Ibid.

[50] Robert I. Rotberg, "Disorder in the Ranks", *Foreign Policy*, 22 June, 2009

[51] Foreign policy and The Fund f or Peace, *The Failed States Index 2009* . Washington: FP, 2009, http://www.foreignpolicy.com/articles/2009/06/22/2009_failed_ states_ index_interactive_map_and_rankings, Accessed 30 November , 2009. Burma deterior ated from rank 18 in 2006 to rank 13 in 2009 among the most critical states.

[52] Robert I.Rotberg, "Failed States, Collapsed States, W eak States: Causes and Indicators", in Robert I Rothberg, *State Failure and State Weakness in a Time of T error*, (Cambridge, MA: World Peace Foundation; Washington: Brookings Institution Press, 2003), 4-5.

resulting in weak state effectiveness in key policy areas. "The elite appear to make no distinction between what serves the regime and what serves the nation. This view ignores the important differences between state control and state effectiveness."[53] Finally, the inability to solve three of Burma's most intractable problems – ethnic disunity, economic underdevelopment, and drug production - demonstrates the military regime's weakness.[54]

1. 1962-1987 Economic Nationalisation and Politico-Economic Isolation

Burma's developmental failure derives largely from the leadership's ideology, idiosyncrasies, and being cognitively trapped the past. The same generation of nationalistic leaders ruled the country from 1948 to 1988, and their conservative nationalism continues to influence their younger followers.[55]

Experiences of British colonialism, Japanese imperialism and the Asia-Pacific War followed by the Cold War produced a deep distrust against foreign "meddling in internal affairs", an obsession with self-sufficiency, and an anti-modern, xenophobic attitude. Seeking control over all aspects of domestic and international issues, Ne Win's "Revolutionary Council" introduced a self-reliant, socialist-type state-planned economy and followed policies of economic centralisation and nationalisation. Burma was insulated from foreign, especially Western influences by expelling foreign companies, and institutions, by relinquishing foreign aid, and by adhering to strict political neutralism.[56] Therefore, the elite's "developmentalism" was highly nationalistic, inward-looking, and extremely averse to integration with the

---

[53] Emily Rudland and Morton B. Pederson, "Introduction", in Morten B. Pederson et al. (ed), *Burma/Myanmar: Strong Regime, Weak State?* (Adelaide: Crawford House; London: Hurst, 2000) 7.

[54] Ibid. 9.

[55] Tin Maung Maung Than, *The Political Economy of Burma's (Myanmar's) Development Failure 1948-1988*, (Singapore: ISEAS, 1999), 22.

[56] David I. Steinber g, "Burma in 1982: Incomplete T ransitions", *Asian Survey* 23 no.2 (1982):165-171; David I. Steinberg, "Burma in 1983: The Dilemmas of Neutralism and Succession", *Asian Survey* 24 no .2 (1984):195-200.

international capitalist economy thus leaving little room for developmental initiatives.[57] This hindered the emergence of an entrepreneurial class and modernisation. Instead, the state sought to extract revenue only for the system's privileged, aversely affecting production and distribution.[58]

The black market evolved into a parallel economy while the official economy neared collapse, and the population struggled with a spiralling inflation, several demonetisations,[59] exploding rice prices, and fuel shortages. By 1985, about 40% of the population lived below the absolute poverty level.[60] The spectacular downfall from "Asia's rice bowl" and one of the potentially richest nations to "least developed country" classification in 1987 predicated the end of the socialist era, the demise of the "Burma Socialist Programme Party's" rule, and the 1988 uprisings.

2. Post-1988 Partial Economic Opening and Exploitation of Natural Resources

The dirigiste economy and socialist doctrine were abolished in July 1988, and a foreign investment law promulgated in November the same year. The ensuing albeit military-controlled and limited opening of the country to foreign investors has invited the large-scale exploitation of the country's wealth of natural resources - gas and oil, precious stones, timber, and minerals. Foreign and multinational companies profit from the advantage of a low-wage, complying, and literate labour force, and from the government's provision of infrastructure, often through the use of corvée labour. The absence of a legal framework protecting the rights of local workers, and the environment are of further advantage

---

[57] Maung Than, *The Political Economy of Burma's,* 13.

[58] Peter J. Perry, *Myanmar (Burma) Since 1962: The F ailure of Development,* (Hants, England; Burlington, VT: Ashgate, 2007)

[59] 1. Demonetisation in 1964 covered currency notes of 50 and 100 kyats,

    2. Demonetisation in 1985 notes of 20, 50, and 100 kyats,

    3. Demonetisation in 1987 notes of 25, 35, and 75 ky ats respectively.

[60] UNICEF, *The State of the W orld's Children1988.* Oxford: Oxf ord University Press, 1988

for companies, but not the population. When transnational activist campaigns for divestment on the grounds of human rights, and sanctions from Western governments from 1997 onward discouraged Western companies from engaging with the military, Asian companies quickly filled the gaps.

What is more, following the end of the "Burmese Way to Socialism", and the ceasefires between armed groups and the *Tatmadaw*, competition increased in all commercial fields, and many more players such as government departments, companies, ceasefire and non-ceasefire organisations engaged the exploitation of natural resources. The lion-share of profits went to the *Tatmadaw*, military-linked businesses, and Asian states.[61]

Yet, outside of the extractive industries, foreign investment remained nevertheless limited due to the country's volatile, unpredictable business environment subject to the leadership's arbitrary top-down decisions.[62] The economy was further crippled by an incompetent, inflated bureaucratic structure that was never thoroughly reformed after the end of the socialist system. Widespread corruption, patron-client relations, rent-seeking civil and military officials, and cultural notions of hierarchy, loyalty, and personal power hamper the state machinery.[63]

Finally, although the government's foreign exchange reserves has increased from about US$30 million in 1988 to US$3.1 billion in 2008,[64] the lack of distribution prevents the trickling-down of wealth from the top echelons of the military and associated business tycoons to the general population. High inflation and poverty continues.

---

[61] Martin Smith, 43.

[62] Steinberg,2010,101.

[63] Mutebi, Alex M. 2005. "Muddling through" past Legacies: Myanmar's Civil Bureaucracy and the need for reform. In *Myanmar: Beyond Politics to Societal Imperatives* , ed. Kyaw Yin Hlaing, Robert H. Taylor, Tin Maung Maung Than, 140-160. Singapoe: ISEAS; and Steinberg 2010.

[64] Steinberg, David I. 2010. *Burma/Myanmar: What everyone needs to know* . New York: Oxford University Press, 14.

Policies Adopted by Successive Governments

Centralisation of Power and Militarisation of the State

Since independence, Burma has been governed by direct military rule under "Caretaker Government (1958-1960), and the "Revolutionary Council" (RC, 1962-1974) and by constitutional military rule under the "Burma Socialist Programme Party" (BSPP, 1974-1988), both led by General Ne Win. After the 1988 uprisings and demise of the BSPP, direct military rule was reinstalled under a junta that first named itself "State Law and Order Restoration Council" (SLORC, 1988-1997) and then, at the suggestion of a Western PR firm, "State Peace and Development Council" (SPDC, 1997-). This makes the *Tatmadaw* (armed forces) the historically most resilient and durable military regime worldwide.

After the coup in 1962, the military sought to build its legitimacy around its contribution in the independence struggle. Similar to cases in Africa and Latin America, the military portrayed itself as the only organised, structured institution able to hold the country together. This hegemonic narrative is still employed today.

Under the leadership of Commander-in-Chief General Ne Win (and since 1992 Than Shwe) the *Tatmadaw* has attempted to unify the country through military coercion. As a consequence, the once respected institution founded by Aung San deteriorated from being a solution to foreign invasion and domestic centrifugal forces to one of the root causes of the contemporary malaise.

Paradoxically, it was precisely the strong opposition the early post-colonial state faced from its outset that transformed the Burmese army into such a powerful and largely autonomous force. Domestically, the government faced communist and separatist ethnic rebellions as well as army mutinies. External threats included incursions by the US-backed Chinese nationalist Kuomintang into Northeastern Burma, where they prepared for retaking mainland China from the Chinese Communists. Hence, "discrete historical circumstances... established a state predicated on, constructed around, and ultimately held hostage to organized violence."[65] War and crises engendered powerful coercion-

---

[65] Mary P. Callahan, *Making Enemies: War and State Building in Burma,* (Singapore: SUP, 2004), 2.

intensive institutions and provoked a recursive relationship between state building and warfare that has produced the most durable incarnation of military rule in history.[66] Accordingly, post-war Burmese regimes were made up of professional soldiers who never mastered the art of politics enough to win a single election but who, in contrast to politicians, did not fear the costs of repression and hence endured despite electoral defeat.[67] "War fighters who are not adept at politics. But they are war fighters, first and foremost."[68]

These early post-war developments conditioned the military elite's mindset and ideology for decades to first, focus on military expansion for new tasks, second, devise strategies for counter-insurgency that included people auxiliary forces, third, distrust and spy on its own citizens perceived to support insurgency, fourth, be suspicious of if not hostile to any outside forces.[69]

It is crucial to understand that the military has practically supplanted the state, leaving state institutions inherently weak. It has co-opted most branches of society, and has reached into many families, creating a militarised society. Despite vilification of the military's top echelons, the military as an institution provides the only avenue for upward social mobility and thus most [ethnic Burman] families have at least one member in the armed forces.[70] Finally, it is widely agreed that the contemporary Myanmar Government wields more power and territorial control than any previous regime, including the colonial administration.

---

[66] Ibid., 3.

[67] Ibid., 8.

[68] Ibid., 2.

[69] Maung Aung Myoe, *Building the Tatmadaw: Myanmar Armed Forces Since 1948.*(Singapore: ISEAS, 2009)

[70] Mary P. Callahan, Cracks in the Edifice: Military-Society Relations in Burma Since 1988, in Morten B. Pederson et. al. in *Burma/Myanmar: Strong Regime, Weak State?* , (Adelaide: Crawford House; London: Hurst, 2000), 22-51

Dramatic Expansion of the Armed Forces

From a small and rather insignificant force consisting of a few thousand former anti-colonial guerrillas in 1948, the *Tatmadaw* increased to about 198,600 personnel by 1988.[71] The 1988 uprisings and the creation of the SLORC then set in motion a massive increase and modernisation. With an estimated 350,000 personnel the *Tatmadaw* has become the world's 15th largest military and uses an estimated 40% of the national budget; although official figures are unreliable they reflect the government's spending priorities, notably the proportionately highest annual defence expenditures in the entire Asia-Pacific region.[72]

Strict arm embargos by the US and EU to Burma do not prevent a wide range of other states supplying arms, missiles, and military hardware to the SPDC. Bent on self-preservation, the regime purchases mostly from China but also from a range of other countries including, Russia, Serbia, Ukraine, Singapore, India, Pakistan, North Korea, South Korea, and Israel. In fact, the "acquisition of so many different weapon systems from so many different countries have apparently contributed to difficulties with doctrine, training, integration, logistics and maintenance."[73] There is a discrepancy between costly, sophisticated military equipment and combat units' poor training to actually use it, as well as a gulf between *Tatmadaw* officers and the rank-and-file.[74]

Persistent indications for and recent evidence of the SPDC's nuclear ambitions abetted by North Korea and Russia cause international concern.

Neutralisation and Cooptation of the Ethnic Nationalities

1. Counter-Insurgency Strategies

From the outset, the military regarded insurgencies as the most serious security threat to state and nation, and only in the late 1980s this threat

---

[71] Maung Aung Myoe, *Building the Tatmadaw: Myanmar Armed Forces since 1948,*(Singapore: ISEAS, 2009) 91.

[72] Andrew Selth, "Known Knowns and Known Unknowns: Measuring Myanmar's Military Capabilities", *Contemporary Southeast Asia* 31 no. 2 (2009):282-285; Andrew Selth, *Burma's Armed Forces: Power Without Glory*, (Norwalk, Connecticut: EastBridge, 2002)

[73] Selth, "Known Knowns and Known Unknowns", 288.

[74] Selth, *Burma's Armed forces, 87-101*

perception became a bit more external.[75] Therefore, three main counter-insurgency strategies were devised: A Mao-style "people war", the "Four Cut" strategy, and a three-phase-counter-insurgency plan.

To involve the population in the "people war" against insurgency, mobile and residential militias (Ka Kwe Yay or KKY) were formed in the 1960s in government-controlled areas with the objective to strengthen cooperation among the BSPP, the *Tatmadaw* and the people.[76] In return for their cooperation, local militia were allowed to rule their areas relatively undisturbed. In Shan State, militia leaders soon became heavily involved in the opium trade; the most well-known being Lo Hsinghan in the Kokang region, and Khun Sa in northern Shan State.[77] When Ne Win abandoned the scheme in 1973, these leaders went underground, teamed up with their former adversaries from the armed Shan resistance and built up large armies and drug syndicates.[78] In this way, *Tatmadaw* counter-insurgency strategies directly fuelled the narcotics trade.

Later, the "People's War" doctrine was modified in accordance with emerging threat perceptions in the military' strategic and political environments. To the battle space (land, sea, air, space) "cyberspace" was added as a new dimension[79] - obviously in response to the exiled activists' intense use of the internet.

Ne Win also devised the "Four Cuts" (Pya Ley Pya) in the mid-1960s to separate armed opposition groups from their civilian support bases by cutting off the four main links – food, funds, recruits, and intelligence.[80] This went hand in hand with a change in official rhetoric

---

[75] Maung Aung Myoe, *Building the Tatmadaw: Myanmar Armed Forces since 1948,* (Singapore: ISEAS, 2009), 42.

[76] Ibid, 30f.

[77] Bertil Lintner, *The Rise and fall of the Communist Party of Burma*, (Ithaca: Southeast Asia Program, Cornell University, 1990), 52.

[78] Ibid.

[79] Maung Aung Myoe, *Building the Tatmadav,* 196f.

[80] For variations with regards to the four elements see Maung Aung Myoe,   *Building the Tatmadav,* 10.

as armed rebellions were denied any political status and instead branded as "saboteurs, bandits, smugglers" and so on; albeit well documented and frequently praised in official speeches, the strategy's very existence was being denied in the early 1990s.[81] By then, large-scale relocation and flight related to counter-insurgency operations had completely transformed the human landscapes of the Mon, Karen, Karenni, and Shan areas in particular.[82] Altogether, the "Four Cut" strategy proved devastatingly effective. Its military weakness only became apparent in the remote borderlands with China, India, Thailand and Bangladesh where insurgents had a back door escape and supply lines across the borders.[83]

Finally, a three-phase-counter-insurgency warfare plan was in place to gain control over insurgency-held territories. Burma's map was divided under the *Tatmadaw's* nine regional military commands and shaded in three colours: *"Black for entirely insurgent-controlled areas; brown for areas both sides still disputed; and white was 'free'. The idea was that each insurgent-colored area would be cleared, one by one, until the whole map of Burma was white. For the black 'hard-core' areas and brown 'guerrilla' zones a standard set of tactics was developed which, after a little refinement, has remained little changed till today."[84]

Today's map contains government-controlled areas, ceasefire areas, and "free-fire" zones of ongoing conflict were insurgency and counter-insurgency operations persist to the great detriment of local populations. The zone categorisation is nevertheless somewhat misleading due to the heavy militarisation of the entire country.

2. Post-1988 Ceasefires

During the unravelling of the CPB Communist insurgency in 1989, then military intelligence chief and later Prime Minister General Khin Nyunt

---

[81] Smith, *Burma: Insurgency and the Politics of Ethnicity*, 258-259.

[82] Carl Grundy-Warr, *Geographies of the Dispossessed: The Karenni Refugees of the Myanmar's Trans-Salween*. Unpublished Photo Essay with Photos by Dean Chapman. Undated; Carl Grundy-Warr, "Lost in Sovereign Space: Forced Migrants in the Territorial Trap, *Asian and Pacific Migration Journal* 11 no.4(2002): 450f.

[83] Smith, *Burma: Insurgency and the Politics of Ethnicity*, 259.

[84] Ibid.,259; Maung Aung Myoe, Building the Tatmadav, 31.

embarked on a major peace initiative with individual ethnic rebel groups. Interestingly, the government never offered a ceasefire to any Burman group. The ceasefires afforded several advantages to the *Tatmadaw*:

- A possible coalition of the four former CPB mutinying groups with the NDF ethnic alliance forces was pre-empted;

- Troops previously occupied in fighting insurgents were freed to embark on other tasks, including along the Thai-Burmese border hosting the opposition groups as well as refugee camps;

- Ceasefire groups could not offer sanctuary to political activists any longer, especially the armed student ABSDF, while diminishing "liberated areas" impacted negatively on the growing number of activist organisations;

- Most NDF non-ceasefire groups interlinked with exile and underground fronts but were substantially weakened and not comparable to the NDF's strength of the 70s and 80s; some held unsuccessful peace talks with the *Tatmadaw*;[85]

- By extending control over areas rich in natural resources and along the international borders, the government gained access to territories of strategic importance and high economic value; major infrastructure projects to link these areas with central Burma followed suit;

Instead of multilateral talks and transparent agreements with all ethnic armies, the government followed a divide and rule tactic vis-à-vis ethnic movements by negotiating with individual groups. Most agreements resulted in non-written, verbal truces that included some economic perks to individual ethnic leaders, thus foregoing equal treatment of all. By the mid-1990s, the *Tatmadaw* had forged ceasefires with 17 groups, including major groups such as the KIO, SSA, CPB, and the Mong Tai army of "opium king" Khun Sa. Thus, ceasefire parties can be roughly divided according to three main outlooks: first, former ethnic

---

[85] Smith, *State of Strife,* 40.

resistance NDF-members; second, Communist ex-CPB and allies; and third, "new" local business-focussed militia.[86]

The ceasefires fundamentally altered the situation in the "peripheries". "By the mid-1990s, a complex change in relationships was underway between former adversaries and stakeholders on different sides of the conflict zones, and this blurred the alignments in national politics even more in the operational field."[87] Moreover, with the ceasefires, the country's political economy changed significantly. At this juncture, the case fits the criteria of modern "resource wars" insofar as ideologies were replaced by competition between leading figures of the government and armed opposition.[88] Crucially, this competition fuelled the narcotics trade (see non-traditional security below) provoking more border wars in Shan state between the ceasefire United War State Army (UWSA), a key player in the narcotics trade, and the non-ceasefire SSA-South.[89]

3. Proposal to Turn Ceasefire Groups into Border Forces

The fragility of the ceasefires became apparent in the ceasefire groups' refusal to cooperate with the government's plans for military restructuring in preparation for the 2010 elections. In April 2009 the government ordered all 17 ethnic ceasefire groups to transform their armies into "Border Guard Forces" (BGF) under the command of the Burmese army as outlined in the 2008 constitution. Most groups reject the plan except for the smaller groups unable to withhold pressure from the *Tatmadaw*. The ceasefire groups' defiance of the *Tatmadaw's* deadlines reveals the limits of the junta's political powers and its key failure to address the underlying core issues, grievances and aspirations of the cease-fire groups. The regime expects ceasefire groups to either become BGF or disarm, and to form new political parties to participate in the elections but the groups want to see their basic demands to be

---

[86] Ibid., 48.

[87] Ibid., 41.

[88] Ibid., 42.

[89] See work on drugs by Tom Kramer as well as Jelsma, and Vervest at Transnational Institute, Netherlands.

met first.[90] Ethnic nationalities criticise the constitution's shortcomings in guaranteeing minority rights, and in turn refuse to effectively give up control of the border regions with China, India and Thailand.

The tensions have escalated into *Tatmadaw* offensives against ceasefire groups in addition to ongoing offensives against non-ceasefire groups. This results in increased militarisation along Burma's international borders. The Kokang conflict in Shan state in mid-2009 was widely seen as a precursor to mounting instability during and after the elections. It also served as a warning of the international ramifications in case of renewed warfare as 37,000 people fled into China's Yunnan province, straining Sino-Burmese relations. China deployed more forces at this border.

The *Tatmadaw's* attack on the Kokang has clearly undermined any trust between ethnic nationalities and the regime. Ceasefire armies are on alert, recruit and train troops, and purchase arms.[91] Especially the UWSA has stocked up its arsenal, including anti-aircraft systems, from China, which aims to keep the Wa as a buffer against the Burmese.[92] Bombs and sabotage acts occur. Ceasefire and non-ceasefire groups have formed strategic alliances in case of sustained *Tatmadaw* attacks.[93]

4. Marginalisation of the Domestic Democratic Opposition

The *Tatmadaw* has come to perceive the very populace as threats to internal peace and as "barriers to the army's consolidation of political power and national sovereignty."[94] Distrust of the own citizens – be they civilian professional bureaucrats, democrats or the middle class - triggered the flight of the Western-educated class soon after 1962 and thus the first wave of the Burmese Diaspora. "The coup leaders

[90] Tom Kramer, *Neither War nor Peace: The Future of the Cease-fire Agreements in Burma,* (Amsterdam: Transnational Institute,2009), 2.

[91] BGF Developments. *Mizzima Elections 2010* database. http://www.mizzima.com/towards-elections/security-threats/bgf-developments.html

[92] Aung Zaw, Wa: The Regime's Next Target? *The Irrawaddy,* 4 September 2009

[93] Marwaan Macan-Markar, Ethnic Rebel Groups Defy Junta's Order. *The Irrawaddy,* 24 April 2010

[94] Callahan, *Making Enemies,* 206.

developed a network of informers and spies [...] and set about refolding the thought and behavior of the people through control of education, media, and the normal contact between individuals."[95]

Strategies for neutralising the unarmed political opposition include intimidation, defamation in the state-controlled media, and detention[96] as well as tight control of the civil sphere.[97] The post-1988 increase of paramilitary forces such as the *Swarrn Ashin* and others have serious implications for democratic and civil society activities.[98] Acts of harassment are often perpetuated by members of the regime-sponsored Union Solidarity and Development Association (USDA).

The *Tatmadaw's* own history rooted in student political activism conditioned the army to fear and suppress university students, by eliminating their leaders, symbols, as well as the spaces that facilitate mobilisation, the campuses. Soon after the 1962 coup, independent student organisations were abolished and student protests suppressed. The army occupied Rangoon University killing over 100 students, and dynamited the physical symbol of student activism and the secular sphere, the Rangoon University Student Union building where Aung San and others had held their speeches.[99] This occurred under the command of Sein Lwin who in 1988 was to become known as the "butcher of Rangoon".[100] Thus military-student relations were characterised from the outset by control, arrests, and closure of universities.

---

[95] Josef Silverstein, "From a Political to an Administrative State, 1948-1988: Whatever Happened to Democr acy?" in Josef Sil verstein (ed.)*Independent B urma At F orty Years: Six Assessments*, (Ithaca: Southeast Asia Progr am, Cornell University, 1989), 15.

[96] The Assistance Association for Political Prisoners (Burma) lists 2,171 political prisoners detained across the country . http://www.aappb.org, Accessed 7 July , 2010

[97] Martin Smith documents censorship and lack of political freedom in his reports for Article XIX. Christina Fink analyses the impact of state contr ol over all aspects of societ y.

[98] For a further discussion see Selth, *Burma's Armed Forces*.

[99] John H. Badgley, "Burma: The Nexus of Socialism and Two Political Traditions" *Asian Survey* 3 no. 2 (1963):89-95.

[100] Bertil Lintner, *Burma in Revolt: Opium and Insurgency since 1948*, (Chiangmai: Silkworm Books, 2nd edition, 1999), 213-214.

Since 1988, universities and to a lesser extent schools have been closed down repeatedly for up to several years which has disrupted higher education for several generations of students.[101] Moreover, campuses have been relocated to the outskirts of Rangoon to disperse the student body in several locations, pre-empting communication and mobilisation among students.

Similar to students, the approximately 400,000 Buddhist monks with their own tradition of activism face restrictions. The government seeks to control the Sangha hierarchy, examinations, sermons, monks' registrations, and movements. Surveillance and infiltration with informers of the registered 45,000 monasteries has drastically increased in the aftermath of the 2007 uprisings, with authorities closing down monasteries causing monks to disrobe and leave.[102]

NLD members face most of the above, namely imprisonment or house arrest of their leaders (Aung San Suu Kyi, U Tin Oo, Htun Khun Oo a.o.) and members, closure of party offices, harassment and attacks by USDA. In what became known as the "Depeyin massacre" a USDA mob killed some of Aung San Suu Kyi's bodyguards as well as dozens of supporters. In 2009, Aung San Suu Kyi was imprisoned and tried for what observers considered fabricated charges in order to prevent her from taking part in the 2010 elections.

Transnational Consequences of Government Policies

Emergence and Partial Radicalisation of Transnational Opposition[103]

The movement-in-exile[104] began in the second half of 1988 when state repression triggered an unprecedented exodus of thousands of students

---

[101] For instance, between 1997 and 2000 universities remained shut for 3,5 years (Wall Street Journal, 25 July 2000)

[102] Bertil Lintner, *The Resistance of the Monks Buddhism and Activism in Burma*, (New York: Human Rights Watch, 2009)

[103] Kerstin Duell, *The Burmese Opposition exiled in Thailand and India, 1988-2008: Resources, Donor Agendas and Political Opportunities Negotiated within Transnational Advocacy Networks*. PhD thesis, National University of Singapore, 2010

[104] Using the term "the movement" does not necessarily imply one coherent structure, hierarchy or strict boundaries, but rather the fluidity and dynamics of a network of organisations. In fact, the Burmese pro-democracy movement-in- exile is highly heterogeneous while

as well as veteran politicians and other regime opponents into rebel-held border areas. The majority went to the Thai-Burmese border controlled by the Karen National Union and the New Mon State Party, but also initially to the borders with China (to territories of the Kachin Independence Organisation and the Shan resistance), India (where the students were assisted by Indian security personnel), and Bangladesh.

Finding shelter with the ethnic nationalities confronted activists from urban, Burman-dominated areas with the armed struggle and living conditions of ethnic nationalities for the first time. Fleeing students set up camps along most the border areas, which eventually fell under the newly founded world's largest student army, the All Burma Students' Democratic Front (ABSDF). Key developments during the exiled movement's formative years included:

- Changing perceptions between Burmans and ethnic nationalities fostered mutual understanding and mitigated some of the decade-old distrust.

- Differing political agendas were aligned into one set of overarching movement objectives. Pro-democracy activists came to regard federalism as essential for nation-building. This change ultimately influenced the wider Burman population. In return, the ethnic armies officially declared in 1990 not to break away from the country under a real federal union, forfeiting their traditional right to secession.[105] Exiled groups demanded "regime change", i.e. the immediate removal of the military government, rather then "regime reform" and strove for participatory governance.

- Many of the movement's current leaders from the 88-generation were socialised in the ABSDF. From their time in the jungle stem political values, strong personal friendships as well as enmities that still condition relationships between movement

questions of leadership , identity, and representation remain points of contention among movement participants, and observers.

[105] *Win Min*, Presentation at Burma Studies Conference, July 2006, Singapore.

entrepreneurs and ties between their respective organisations.[106]

- Among the ethnic nationalities, the Karen National Union's military strength and territory along the Thai-Burmese border were of overarching significance for the pro-democracy movement. The KNU played a decisive role in the formation and military training of the ABSDF, as a key member in all alliances[107], and in the military protection of democratic forces, internally displaced people, and refugee camps.[108]

- When students, politicians, MP-elects and other regime opponents sought refuge in KNU-controlled territories to found or re-establish political organisations, the KNU and NDF headquarters Manerplaw emerged as an alternative capital and axis of power to Rangoon.

Following the 1990 elections and the regime's refusal to transfer power, some of the parliament-elects formed the National Government of the Union of Burma (NCGUB) in Manerplaw. The elections held in 1990 allowed the pro-democracy movement to capitalise on a legitimate leadership officially elected by the people. By holding the 2010 elections, the SPDC aims to undermine this legitimacy.

Owing to persistent military pressure on the ethnic nationalities' territories by the *Tatmadaw*, most notably the loss of Manerplaw in 1995, but also to strategic and organisational differences between the armed and the non-violent groups, activists shifted from the jungles to border towns and cities. Eventually, Thailand and to a lesser extent India became the locales where student leaders and other dissidents set up a plethora of political organisations, coalitions, and umbrella

---

[106] Aung Naing Oo recounts key events of the early years in the ABSDF in his ongoing series "Beyond 1988 - Reflections" in *The Irrawaddy*, Feb 12, 2008.

[107] National Democratic Front (NDF), Democratic Alliance of Burma (DAB), National Coalition of the Union of Burma (NCUB).

[108] Interviews with KNU leaders, 2006 and 2007.

groups that together form the Burmese pro-democracy movement-in-exile.[109]

The advent of the worldwideweb in the late 1980s enabled activists to reach out to the Burmese Diaspora comprising individuals who had left for economic or political reasons during previous decades. Through the internet, activists facilitated first, contacts among the Burmese Diaspora scattered in Europe, the US, Canada, Australia, New Zealand and Asian countries; second, supplied the Diaspora with news from their homeland hardly available prior to 1988; and third, started to reach out to the United Nations, international non-governmental organisations and to transnational activists networks. Burmese dissidents benefited from the fact that their flight to exile coincided with the onset of the revolution in communication technologies that facilitated the dissemination of their voices across the globe. Crucially, the movement emerged at the end of the Cold War when changing international norms and discourses opened new political opportunities for the political agency of non-state actors.

Over time, an extensive transnational pro-democracy movement has emerged in Burma's neighbouring as well as in Western countries. The movement is organised in the "Western" (India) and the "Eastern" (Thailand) Command or Region, a term adopted from the decades of armed struggle. Political organisations are clustered around the 88 student generation, 1990 MP-elects, ethnic platforms, gender, media or specific issue areas such as human rights, environment and so on.

In addition to Burmese core political groups striving for a transformation of Burma's political system, a number of Burmese and foreign movement support groups work on subsets of home and host country issues. Moreover, the needs of growing refugee communities generate networks of INGOs, local NGOs, refugee self-help projects and other initiatives to improve the situation of Burmese in their respective host countries. Although humanitarian organisations are not

---

[109] Regarding other neighbouring countries, Bangladesh is the site of two conflicting ethnic groups from Arakan State, the Muslim Rohingya and the Buddhist Rakhine, who remain relatively isolated from the mainstream opposition. No political activists were allowed to operate from China except for some leaders of the Communist Party of Burma who received sanctuary when the CPB disintegrated.

part of the political movement, information is shared, and sites, personnel, and networks partially overlap.

From their main bases in Thailand, Burmese activists effectively frame their grievances and project their movement for distant audiences in order to campaign for a political transition. To this end, they appropriate post-Cold War discourses centring on human rights, democracy, non-violence and transitional justice. The movement has successfully galvanised a transnational network of advocacy, solidarity activism, donor agencies, research institutions, churches, the media, and many others sympathetic to its political aims.

Due to the nature of the Myanmar regime, opposition forces use transnational advocacy networks to lobby third party states and international bodies to exert pressure on the regime, thus amplifying demands internationally until they echo back into the domestic arena.[110] In this way, the pro-democracy movement has gained much more leverage over the *Tatmadaw* in the arena of world politics, than the curtailed opposition could achieve on the domestic stage. When measuring the effectiveness of transnational advocacy networks in terms of (1) information generation, issue attention, and agenda setting; (2) discursive change from states and other policy actors; (3) procedural changes at the domestic and international levels; (4) changes in policies; and (5) influence behaviour changes in target actors[111], the exiled movement has been remarkably successful on most accounts.

Entering transnational arenas, though, not only offers opportunities but also produces needs, dependencies, and constraints that impact on the movement's leadership, cohesion, strategies, and overall trajectory. Funding in particular is a core concern. Although networks are usually seen as voluntary, reciprocal, and horizontal with an inherent assumption of being non-hierarchical, in reality power tends to flow from control over resources and is usually exercised from the global north, i.e. the donors, to the global south but rarely vice versa.[112] This dilemma pits

---

[110] Keck and Sikkink, "Activists Beyond Borders", 12 and 200.

[111] Ibid, 201.

[112] Keck and Sikkink, " Activists Beyond Borders", 1997; Nicola Piper and Anders Uhlin, "New Perspectives on Transnational Activism", in Piper and Uhlin (eds), *Transnational Activism in Asia: Problems of Power and Democracy*, (New York: Routledge, 2003), 1-23

the political economy of a transnational opposition movement against that of an entrenched military regime buttressed by a wealth of energy reserves. Put differently, the exclusively Western donor countries and institutions support the pro-democracy movement in terms of diplomacy, rhetoric, and resources; they are nonetheless outweighed by the Asian powers' geo-strategic and economic stakes in the country and it's military.

As a consequence, despite successes in the international realm, activism has not substantially weakened the military's preponderance over Burmese politics. On the contrary, after the 2003 attack on Aung San Suu Kyi and her NLD entourage, and the purge of prime minister and military intelligence chief Khin Nyunt in 2004, hard-line approaches dominated all fronts – the military, segments of the domestic and exiled opposition forces, and the international community. Khin Nyunt's removal impacted very negatively on the pro-democracy movement, reconciliation efforts, and the stability of ceasefires he negotiated because the SPDC became more isolationist. In addition, the SPDC lost a key international ally for its "Seven-Step Roadmap" when former Thai Prime Minister Thaksin Shinawatra was deposed in late 2006. At the time of writing, the Myanmar Government ploughs through the roadmap and preparations for the 2010 elections regardless of the pro-democracy movement's persistent criticism and boycott.

Proliferation of Non-Traditional Security Threats

Developments in Burma threaten the *conventional security* of neighbouring countries due to the *Tatmadaw's* dramatic expansion, nuclear plans as well as the presence of guerrilla forces and warfare near the borders. Asian statesmen, however, routinely deny perceiving Burma as a threat to regional security.

In addition, decades of protracted, intrastate conflicts between the government and various non-state armed groups have produced endemic poverty, lack of human security, mass migration, illicit trades, epidemics, and environmental degradation to name the most important *non-traditional security* (NTS) threats.

NTS threats emanating from Burma not only have a destabilising impact on the direct neighbouring states but also adversely affect the long-term development of the region. Resulting from interwoven long-term, politico-economic, ethno-religious, and historical factors, Burma's NTS challenges have reached a scope and emergency that require intra-state (of all Burmese conflicting parties) and international cooperation. With regards to the Burmese borders, regional states, UN bodies, and INGOs have securitised illegal migration, drug traffic, and the HIV/AIDS epidemic in particular as urgent matters. The Havel-Tutu report on Burma's threats to regional peace and security also finds that the following UN Security Council criteria apply to the situation in Burma (1) overthrow of a democratically elected government, (2) conflict between the central government and ethnic factions, (3) widespread internal humanitarian and human rights violations, (4) substantial outflow of refugees, and (5) other cross-border problems (drug production and trafficking, HIV/AIDS).[113]

Burma's international boundaries have become security flashpoints due to the combination of ongoing conflict, an unprecedented scale of the movement of peoples, and insufficiently secured borders. Moreover, Burma's borders with Bangladesh, India, China, Laos, and Thailand remain some of the least regulated ones even by Asian standards. They are poorly patrolled and demarcated in difficult physical terrain such as mountains and jungles. Unresolved border demarcation issues persist between Burma and Thailand, India and China respectively, and with Bangladesh over maritime boundaries, including a gas field.

Borderlands with Burma are geographic peripheries of the respective nation-states with limited infrastructure, development, agricultural possibilities, and governance. They are the homelands of ethnic "minorities" who are securitised as "problems" and neglected by the elites in the respective capitals. Borders cut across ancient trade routes, weekly markets, villages and ethnic communities spanning over several states (for instance the Chin-Mizo-Zo group between Burma, India, Bangladesh). Throughout history, a host of non-state actors

---

[113] Vacláv Havel and Desmond M. Tutu, *Threat to the Peace: A Call for the UN Security Council to Act in Burma,* Report commissioned by Washington: DLA Piper Rudnick Gray Cary, 2005

competed with either state for control over territory, people, and trades in the borderlands. This engenders contemporary, contesting territorial claims and practices. Transnational organised crime such as the traffic in humans, drugs, arms, gems, timber, wildlife, contraband and counterfeit goods thrives under these conditions. People, goods, diseases, and environmental destruction all follow the same routes.

Ironically, in spite of porous borders facilitating the high (predominantly illegal) mobility of people, borderlands are often inaccessible for INGOs, UN agencies and even local NGOs due to regulations and geography. Thus, the lack of state capacity in conjunction with restricted access on both sides of the border prevents humanitarian assistance to people living in the borderlands, including hundreds of thousands internally displaced people (IDPs) inside Burma.

Table: Burmese Borders and States

COUNTRY	LENGTH [114]	BORDER STATE	BURMESE BORDER STATE
China	2,185 km	Yunnan	Shan and Kachin States (including several Special Regions)
Thailand	1,800 km	Ranong, Chumphon, Prachuap Khiri Khan, Phetchaburi, Ratchaburi, Kanchanaburi, Tak, Mae Hong Son, Chiang Mai, Chiang Rai (South to North)	Tenasserim Division, Mon, Karen, Karenni and Shan States; maritime boundary in the Andaman Sea
India	1,463 km	Mizoram, Manipur, Nagaland, Arunachal Pradesh	Chin State, Sagaing Division, Kachin State
Laos	235 km	Bokeo, Luangnamtha	Shan State
Bangladesh	193 km	Chittagong	Arakan and Chin States; maritime boundary in the Bay of Bengal

---

[114] CIA World Factbook 2008. Figures vary substantially according to source and owing to border disputes and issues of demarcation.

Large-scale Migration into Neighbouring Countries

The tremendous exodus of people from Burma across the borders poses serious challenges to neighbouring countries, especially to Thailand that receives the largest number of people. Inside Burma, a large floating population of IDPs has even further increased following the devastations of Cyclone Nargis that left 138,000 people dead and 2.5 million homeless.[115] Internal displacement induced by conflicts and development (infrastructure projects, hydropower dams, gas pipelines etc.) affect an estimated 1-3 million people, one third of them children.[116]

Once these IDPs cross an international border, they become refugees. Since none of the receiving states is a signatory to international conventions regarding refugees, the authority and protective role of the Office of the United Nations High Commissioner for Refugees (UNHCR) remains limited; host governments at times slow down or stop the registration process. Deportations, harassment from security personnel, and abuses from the population are reported in all host countries.[117] A fraction of the total number of refugees receives official refugee status enabling them to qualify for third country resettlement in Europe, North America, Australia and New Zealand.

There are 140,747 registered refugees in 10 camps on the Thai-Burma border,[118] 80,435 documented migrant workers,[119] and at least 2

---

[115] According to the Post-Nargis Joint Assessment report published on 21 July 2008, the cyclone Nargis of 2 and 3 May 2008 left 84,530 people dead, with a further 53,836 people still reported missing. Other groups claim that the death toll has passed 130,000, while 12 million are displaced.

[116] Free Burma Rangers and Partners Relief and Development, *Displaced Childhoods: Human Rights and International Crimes Against Burma's Internally Displaced Children* , (Thailand: FBR and PRD, 2010)

[117] Numerous interviews with refugees in India, Thailand, Malaysia, and from Bangladesh, 2004-2008.

[118] TBBC. *Burmese border refugee sites with population figures May 2010* . (Bangkok: TBBC, 2010)

[119] "Crackdown on Myanmar illegal Labourers Boosts Border Rackets", *DPA*, 8 July 2010.

million illegal migrants[120] in Thailand; approximately 500,000 legal and illegal migrants in Malaysia,[121] approximately 300,000 stateless Rohingya[122] in Bangladesh,[123] and at least 100,000 Burmese migrants in India, most of them in Mizoram State.[124]

Thailand is the only country where some refugee camps even predate the 1988 mass exodus. The long border is dotted with currently operating camps and as well as former camp locations that had to be shifted owing to cross-border attacks by the *Tatmadaw* and the allied DKBA. Refugees are settled in camps under the supervision of either the Thai Ministry of Interior (MOI), UNCHR or the Thai-Burma Border Consortium, a collective of international humanitarian relief agencies. In order to be registered with UNHCR and MOI, refugees must stay in the camps, are not allowed to work, and face detention if caught outside. Thai security forces police and secure the camps while the National Security Council tightly regulates access to the refugees, only allowing authorised personnel. In reality however, these rules are flaunted. After over twenty years in exile the camps have evolved into extremely basic makeshift villages. For refugees, the camp has become the fourth, inseparable element that has now added itself to the old trinity composed of the state, the nation and the land.[125]

---

[120] Aung Zaw, "Abhisit Needs to Set a New Course on Burma. *The Irrawaddy*, February 2009

[121] Fact file related to Burma and the Election, *Mizzima News*, 19 March 2010

[122] Brought from Bangladesh into Burma's Arakan State in the 1960s as labourers, the Rohingyas were soon perceived as a threat by the Burmese owing to a comparatively higher birth rate. Government propaganda constructed them as foreigners without rights or citizenship. Being stateless, the Rohingyas are totally disenfranchised. As Muslims they command no sympathy from the Buddhist Rhakine population in Arakan State; while religion generally remains a sensitive issue in Burma. Rohingya flee predominantly to Bangladesh and Malaysia (see extensive work on Rohingya by Chris Lewa).

[123] Physicians for Human Rights, *Stateless and Starving: Persecuted Rohingya Flee Burma and Starve in Bangladesh* (Cambridge, MA: PHR,2010)

[124] The approximately 100,000 Burmese in India can be divided into less than 2,000 UNHCR-registered refugees in New Delhi, about 80,000 illegal migrants in Mizoram and the remaining Burmese Manipur and Nagaland (interviews in India, 2004, 2005, 2007, 2008).

[125] Giorgio Agamben, The Camp as Nomos of the Modern, trans. Daniel Heller-Roazen. In *Violence, Identity and Self-Determination*, ed. Hent de Vries and Samuel Weber, (Stanford: Stanford University Press,1997) 113-114.

In Bangladesh's Cox Bazar area near the border, approximately 70,000 Rohingya of the total of 300,000 in Bangladesh country live in both official and unofficial refugee camps. The Government of Bangladesh and UNHCR jointly administer two official camps with a combined population of 28,000 registered refugees where a number of UN agencies provide assistance. The 41,000 unregistered refugees congregated in two unofficial camps, however, barely survive. INGOs operate without official sanction under precarious circumstances. The remaining over than 200,000 Rohingya are dispersed in the rest of the country. Bangladesh's policy towards the stateless Muslim kin has been less than welcoming. The government ceased conferring refugee status to any Rohingya arriving after 1993 and prevented improvement of the camps, stressing the "temporariness" of shelter.[126]

In India, there are no refugee camps (the initial makeshift shelters of 1988 at the border were soon dismantled) for Burmese who therefore stay in private housing. Since the Indian Constitution does not have a refugee law, the sole path to legality consists in registration with UNHCR in New Delhi. However, UNHCR has not been allowed to set up an office in the restricted Northeast where people arrive from the border. Because of the long, costly journey to Delhi Burmese refugees in the Northeast are forced to remain illegal. In contrast to Thailand's extensive humanitarian and non-governmental infrastructure focussing on Burma-related issues, there are only a handful of NGOs working to improve the situation of Burmese in India.

The situation in Malaysia resembles that of India insofar as the refugees have to fend for themselves through their modest self-help organisations. There are no official refugee camps but illegal camps throughout the country. Malaysian human rights organisations, despite being sympathetic to the Burmese, face restrictions when promoting migrants' rights. Most of the refugees' grievances stem from mistreatment by RELA, Malaysia's People's Volunteer Corps. A paramilitary force close to the government, RELA members enjoy wide powers including searches and arrests without warrants, and since 2005

---

[126] All data on Bangladesh stems from Physicians for Human Rights, *Stateless and Starving: Persecuted Rohingya Flee Burma and Starve in Bangladesh*, (Cambridge, MA: PHR, 2010)

the power to arrest illegal immigrants.[127]

Human Smuggling and Human Trafficking

In the Burmese case, it is especially difficult to distinguish between migration, human smuggling, and human trafficking.[128] Migration seen as "voluntary" originates in push factors created by the socio-economic crisis. People rely on agents, brokers or traffickers to be smuggled across international borders that they are unable to cross legally (except for the Indian border where Burmese can enter legally). Upon arrival however, they may find themselves in conditions very different from what agents promised, including debt bondage or unpaid labour. Poverty and illegality in the destination country make Burmese vulnerable to abuse, imprisonment and deportation; deportees are often caught by traffickers at the borders and re-trafficked.[129]

Burma is both a source and a transit country (from China to Thailand, and Bangladesh to Malaysia). Traffic to Thailand consists in children and young women being trafficked into sex work, begging or street selling; women into domestic work and factories; men into hard, manual, often dangerous labour in the construction, agriculture, and fishing industries. From Thailand, many Burmese are trafficked onward to Malaysia to work in the same industries.[130] Traffic to China is driven by the demand for brides and predominantly male babies (the one-child policy triggers the abortion of female foetuses, which in turn leads to a gender imbalance and shortage of women for marriage). A side aspect of trafficking is the trade in human organs because donors tend to be illegal immigrants.

While Bangkok has long been a major regional hub for trafficked humans, the (fenced) Sino-Burmese border has emerged as another

---

[127] Interviews in Malaysia, 2007; Amnest y International Malaysia, *Civilian Volunteer Corps RELA Continues to Arrest and Detain Migrants, Refugees in Malaysia*. 11 December, 2008

[128] Winston Set Aung, *Migration and Human Smuggling from Myanmar: Moving Toward Win-Win Solutions*, (Stockholm: Institute f or Security and Development P olicy, 2009)

[129] Interviews with UNHCR and local NGOs in Mala ysia, 2007.

[130] Burmese refugees in Malaysia said their fear of forced repatriation drove them to Malay- sia. If forcedly repatriated from Malaysia, they would only be driven to the Thai-Malaysian border where the traffickers were already waiting (interviews in Malaysia, 2007).

hotspot. Authorities responded by forming the "China-Myanmar Cooperation Against Human Trafficking" in the border town Ruili. Burma ranks among the eleven countries worldwide making least effort to combat trafficking although the government has ratified UN Conventions on human trafficking, and the GMS countries' COMMIT MoU, and cooperates with the Chinese and Thai authorities. Reports blame the regime for failing to remove the causes driving Burmese abroad as well as for actively engaging in internal trafficking of child soldiers and forced labourers.[131]

Production and Traffic of Narcotics

Burma is after Afghanistan the world's second largest producer of illicit opium accounting for 80% of heroin produced in Southeast Asia, as well as reportedly the world's largest producer of methamphetamine, and a significant producer of other synthetic drugs.[132] The potential value of Burma's opium production spanning over 31,700 hectares was estimated at US$ 104 million in 2009.[133] As a consequence, the drug trade receives high international attention among Burma's issues.[134]

The Kokang and Wa regions in Burma's Shan State are the traditional key opium-producing areas in Southeast Asia. The legendary "Golden Triangle" between Burma, Laos and Thailand has been the heart of Asia's narcotics trade. Since the 1990s, the border areas of Shan State have been dotted with small, mobile labs producing methamphetamines and synthetic drugs, sometimes co-located with heroin refineries. Production amounts to several hundred million methamphetamine tablets annually for markets in Thailand, China, and India, as well as for onward distribution beyond the region.[135]

---

[131] US Department of State, *Trafficking in Persons Report,* (Washington: US Department of State, 2010); See also reports by the ILO, UN and NGOs.

[132] Liana Sun Wyler, *Burma and Transnational Crime*, (Washington: Congressional Research Service, 2008)

[133] UNODC. 2009. *Opium Poppy Cultivation in South-East Asia Lao PDR, Myanmar.*

[134] McCoy, Alfred and Bertil Lintner are regarded as experts on Burma's narcotics, while the regional media closely follows the issue.

[135] Anthony Davis, Southeast Asian Crime Syndicates Turn to 'Ice'. *Jane's Intelligence Review, 21* August, 2006

The political economy of Burma's narcotics has been inextricably intertwined with politics in Shan State and its players over time – Burma's largest insurgency, the Communist Party of Burma, the Shan resistance, Kuomintang troops, drug lords and their troops, Chinese triads and new militias. Ne Win's anti-insurgency people militia in the 1960s facilitated the emergence of militia leaders engaging in the narcotics trade. Thus, Lo Hsing-han and later Khun Sa became the "King of Opium" reigning in the Golden Triangle. By the mid-1980s, Khun Sa's Mong Tai Army was among the strongest armed groups along the Thai border.[136]

After 1988 the two key armies that had dominated the drug trade and territories in Shan State for decades, disintegrated: First, the collapse of the Communist Party of Burma in 1989 due to an internal revolt triggered the split along ethnic lines into several ethnic Chinese militias – the Myanmar National Democratic Alliance Army (MNDAA) in the Kokang region, the United Wa State Army (UWSA) in the Wa region, both in Northern Shan State, and the National Democratic Alliance Army (NDAA) in eastern Shan State. Second, the surrender of drug warlord Khun Sa in 1996 caused the dissolution of his Mong Tai Army, while MTA breakaway groups became heavily involved methamphetamine production.

In all cases, the Myanmar Government accommodated the respective leaders. The new, ex-CPB militias (which are no ethnic resistance groups but ethnicity-based) concluded separate ceasefire agreements with the *Tatmadaw* in return for business opportunities and "Special Regions" for the main players. "Special Regions" in the Shan and Kachin States along the international borders enjoy a considerable degree of autonomy. The ethnic Kokang MNDAA control Special Region No. 1, the Wa UWSA Special Region No. 2, the ethnic Shan NDAA-ESSA Special Region No. 4 and so forth. The UWSA has risen to one of the largest heroin producing and trafficking organisations worldwide whose senior members control an army of approximately 16,000-20,000 troops and large segments of Eastern Burma. The United

---

[136] Tom Kramer, Martin Jelsma, and Tom Blickman, *Withdrawal Symptoms in the Golden Triangle: A Drugs Market in Disarray*, (Amsterdam: Transnational Institute, 2009) 13.

States government indicted the UWSA as "drug kingpins" in 2003 and individual leaders prior to that.[137]

As for the drug lords, both Khun Sa (1933-2007) and Lo Hsing-han (born in 1938) lived in Rangoon. Despite being wanted in the US for very high awards leading to their capture, none of the narcotic syndicate leaders was ever extradited to the US by the regime.[138] Instead, drug lords make substantial investments and enjoy close links to the military. In particular Lo Hsing-han founded Burma's largest conglomerate Asia World Co Ltd., currently managed by his son Tun Myint Naing, a.k.a. Steven Law. The fact that the Myanmar Government has granted all major narcotics syndicates "Special Regions" after concluding ceasefires, and that former drug lords are able to set up major economic empires indicate that drug money fuels Burma's economy with the military's tacit complicity. The trade could not proceed without at least the involvement, if not active participation, of the SPDC.[139]

Burma's narcotics production and traffic has severe implications for its direct neighbours, and the region. Worst affected has been Thailand were "yaba" and other synthetic drugs have affected the general population, including the middle-class youth (in contrast to heroin). The general trend is that all provinces neighbouring Burma show the highest number of internal drug users paralleled by the highest HIV prevalence rate of the respective country.

Heroin and methamphetamine is trafficked overland and via the Mekong River, primarily through China, Thailand, India, Laos and, to a lesser extent, via Bangladesh, and within Burma. Traffickers are also increasingly using maritime routes from ports in southern Burma to reach trans-shipment points and markets in southern Thailand, Malaysia,

---

[137] US Drug Enforcement Agency, "Eight High-Ranking Leaders Of Southeast Asia's Largest Narcotics Trafficking Organization Indicted By A Federal Grand Jury In Brooklyn, New York" News release 24 January, 2005, URL: ht tp://www.justice.gov/dea/pubs/states/newsrel/nyc012405.htm

[138] Leaders of drug syndicates are under travel bans in the US, targeted sanctions on the US Treasury Department sanctions l ist, and indicted b y the Drug Enforcement Agency .

[139] Bertil Lintner and Michael Black, *Merchants of Madness: The Methamphetamine Explosion in the Golden T riangle,* (Chiangmai: Si lkworm Pr ess, 2009) R eports issued b y the US Government and INGOs criticise the SPDC for its compli city.

Indonesia, and beyond.[140] There are dozens of routes to Thailand via Chiang Rai, Chiang Mai, Mae Hong Song, Tak Provinces; routes to Western Laos through Eastern Shan State into Bokeo Province, through Laos into Cambodia, to Southern China via Yunnan, and to Northeast India via Manipur.[141] Supplies of the precursor chemical from China, Thailand, and India follow the same routes.

Infectious Diseases and Drug Resistance

Burma faces a high burden of infectious diseases, notably HIV/AIDS, Tuberculosis, and Malaria, as well alarming health indicators for life expectancy, child and mother mortality, deaths from preventable diseases, malnutrition etc. In addition, inappropriate practices in supply and use of medicines, poor drug quality and counterfeiting drive the development of drug-resistant, mutating strains of major diseases; resistance to drugs thrives when a country has insufficient or poorly trained health professionals, a weak health system infrastructure, and poor regulation and enforcement.[142]

International humanitarian assistance that could substantially alleviate the public health crisis is severely hampered by official denial, red tape, and prohibition of access. For instance, the existence of HIV in Burma was not publicly admitted until 2001, while several ministries were involved in the screening and approval of HIV/AIDS-related information materials and programmes carried out by INGOs.[143] Finally, severe restrictions to the humanitarian programmes of INGOs and UN bodies, in particular access to ethnic nationality and border areas provoked the withdrawal of the Global Fund in 2005, and the downgrading of activities by the International Red Cross in 2006.

---

[140] US Department of State, "2010 International Narcotics Control Strategy Report", Washington: US Department of State, 2010

[141] See maps by Pierr e-Arnaud Chouvy at ht tp://www.pa-chouvy.org or http://www.geopium.org

[142] Rachel Nugent, Emma Back, and Alexandra Beith, The Race Against Drug Resistance, (Washington: Center f or Global Development, 2010), 23f .

[143] Interviews with UN and INGO representatives, Rangoon 2000 and 2001.

In border areas and the sites of internal conflict, the large presence of displaced populations and military personnel, and non-existent health care exacerbate the precarious health situation. Migrants' high mobility and poverty increase their vulnerability to infectious diseases on either side of the border. Beyrer et al clearly establish the nexus between lack of governance, internal strife, lack of human security and public health – they also repeat the longstanding criticism that the Myanmar Government spent less than three percent of the national budget on health vis-à-vis forty percent on the military.[144]

Pandemics also thrive in the shadows of transnational organised crime, including the unsafe industries of the organ trade and the procuring and selling of blood products.[145] Particularly HIV and its co-infection TB spread along the trafficking routes of heroin and humans. The scope of the region's production and consumption of drugs as well as the sex industry pose huge challenges to HIV/AIDS prevention.[146]

Uncontrolled disease in border areas serves as a reservoir for continued infection. Neighbouring countries record the highest infection rates of various epidemics in their respective provinces bordering Burma – in Northern Thailand, Yunnan, and Nagaland. After Africa Asia is most affected by HIV/AIDS worldwide with the serious pandemics occurring in India, China, and in Southeast Asia in Cambodia, Burma, and Thailand.[147]

Split of International Community over approach to Myanmar Government

During the Cold War Burma (similar to Afghanistan and Turkey) functioned as an *insulator* or zone of weak interaction bordering several

---

[144] Chris B eyrer, Mathieson, and Suw anvanichkij et al. , *The Gathering Storm: I nfectious Diseases and Human Rights in Burma* , (Open Society Institute, University of California, Berkeley and John Hopkins Bloomberg School of Public Health, 2007)

[145] Beyrer, Chris. 2001. Acceler ating and Disseminating acr oss Asia. *The Washington Quar-terly* 24(1):214.

[146] Ibid.

[147] HIV prevalence rates in 1999: Cambodia 4.04, Burma 2-5.00, Thailand 2.15, India 0.70, China 0.07. Beyrer, Chris. 2001. Acceler ating and Disseminating across Asia. *The Washington Quarterly* 24(1):211–225.

regional security complexes (RSC), namely the South, Southeast, and East Asian RSCs.[148] Beijing's cultivation of the *Tatmadaw* since the late 1980s however began to erode Burma's role as an insulator, prompting ASEAN and India to engage with Burma, and India to balance Chinese military presence.[149] Increasingly a point of linkage, Burma is succumbing to larger dynamics encompassing all of Asia.

Amid these post-Cold War reconfigurations, Burma's strategic location and resources have gained increased geopolitical significance. Situated as a geographical bridge linking South, Southeast and East Asia as well as offering naval access to one of the world's most strategic water passages, the Straits of Malacca, heavily impacts on Burmese relations within the region and beyond.

Among the regional multilateral groups, Burma joined ASEAN, BIMSTEC, the Greater Mekong Subregion, the Ganga-Mekong Cooperation, and related trans-regional infrastructure projects such as the Asian Highway, Trans-Asian Railway, India-Burma-Thailand Trilateral Highway (under BIMSTEC), BCIM Forum *Kunming Initiative* (Bangladesh, China, India, Myanmar), Stillwell Road renewal (Burma, China, India), and APIBM Corridor *New Silk Road* (Afghanistan, Pakistan, India, Bangladesh, Myanmar).[150] In May 2008, Burma also applied for membership in SAARC, apparently in an effort to counterbalance influence and criticism from ASEAN.

Cross-national infrastructure projects are nevertheless a double-edged sword. Improved connectivity not only benefits development, trade and regional cooperation, not last in dealing with cross-border problems, but at the same time enables the very problems that need to be addressed – the influx of narcotics, militias, illegal immigrants and

---

[148] Barry Buzan and Ole Wæver, *Regions and Powers: The Structure of International Security*, (Cambridge: CUP, 2003), 41.

[149] Ibid., 164.

[150] Infrastructure projects and the heavy exploitation of natural resources are officially portrayed as benefiting economic development of all parties concerned. Numerous reports by Burmese and regional environmental and human rights organisations though document the local populations' loss of livelihoods, environmental degradation and abuses by security personnel "clearing" and policing the respective sites.

so forth. Such concerns impede for instance the proposed Trilateral Highway project linking Moreh in Manipur, Northeast India, to Mae Sot at the Thai-Burmese border via Bagan in Burma.[151]

Asia's fast industrialising giants China and India compete for Burmese natural resources, especially oil, gas, hydroelectric power and for access to Southeast Asian markets via land and water, not last to develop their respective landlocked regions bordering Burma. As both powers seek to increase their respective spheres of influence, their strategic interests clash in Burma. In an attempt to draw Burma into their respective orbits, China and India have reached bilateral agreements on a range of issues with the Myanmar Government, including infrastructure and pipeline projects.

China eyes the vital access to the Indian Ocean to circumvent the Strait of Malacca carrying its energy supplies from Africa and the Middle East and follows a "Go West" development policy. As part of its larger "String of Pearls" strategy to counter US maritime power along the sea lines of communication, China supports the Myanmar Government's modernisation of military facilities, ports and airfields. In historic antagonism China also watches Indian actions, fearing economic competition, and Western plots to incite the two powerhouses against each other.[152] As a result, Beijing has emerged as Naypyidaw's main trade partner, political ally and major supplier of arms.[153] As Burma's third largest investor China has made substantial investments across the country, in particular in Kachin State's high-priced jade mines, hydropower projects and real estate development along the Yunnan-India Highway. A joint Yunnan-Kachin State development will moreover allow Beijing greater influence over northern Thailand and Laos.

---

[151] Tanvi Pate, "India-Myanmar-Thailand Trilateral Highway", *Eurasia Review*, 6 May, 2010. http://www.eurasiareview.com/2010/05/india-myanmar-thailand-trilateral.html

[152] Sreeram Chaulia, "Argumentative Chinese Step Forward". *Asia Times Online*, 18 May, 2010

[153] The latest arms-for-natural-resources agreement involves the exploitation of a copper mine by leading Chinese weapons manufacturer China North Industries (*Wall Street Journal*, 23 June 2010).

China is widely regarded as wielding the most influence over the Myanmar Government but this view neglects first, the troublesome past when China supported the Communist Party of Burma's insurgency, and second, the SPDC's aversion to dependencies especially on one powerful neighbour. Moreover, limitations to Chinese influence have surfaced in recent years, when Chinese efforts to nudge the *Tatmadaw* towards economic and political stabilisation were frustrated. Beijing supports the generals in the UN Security Council and elsewhere but at rising diplomatic costs.

China has used the era of international sanctions to increase its strategic and economic influence in Myanmar by helping the junta to weather sanctions. As a veto-wielding permanent member of the UN Security Council, China has shielded the military regime from international collective action on more than one occasion. Thus, China is well entrenched in the country and dominates the nation's economic development, trade and commerce.

India seeks to prevent Chinese encirclement along its land and maritime boundaries and to counterbalance Chinese influence in Southeast Asia. In particular, China's de-facto control over Kachin State bordering the Northeast Indian state of Arunachal Pradesh which China claims to be "Southern Tibet" and hence part of occupied Tibet, is a point of contention. Adjacent to the Indo-Burmese border, the stretch of Indo-Chinese border is the site of Chinese military build-up and incursions into Indian territory.[154]

New Delhi's other high priority consists in developing India's insurgency-riddled Northeast characterised by endemic underdevelopment, lack of infrastructure, energy supply and communication technology. The seven (or eight) Northeastern states are only connected to the rest of India by a narrow stretch of land, the Siliguri Corridor. Crucially, Northeast India's ethno-nationalist autonomist or secessionist movements enjoy Chinese, Pakistani and Burmese support, fuelling a vicious circle of insurgency and counter-insurgency. Burma has emerged as a safe haven, training ground and

---

[154] Vijay Sakhuja, "Military Buildup Across the Himalayas: A Shaky Balance" *China Brief*, 9 no. 18, (10 September, 2009): 8-10.

arms market for ethnic resistance fighters from India. Several dozen Indian rebel camps are believed to be on the Burmese side while insurgents travel through Burma to China to buy arms.[155]

Designed to address these concerns, India's early 1990s "Look East" strategy has engendered a dramatic policy shift vis-à-vis the Myanmar Government away from outspoken, principled, pro-democracy support towards realism and cooperation. This translates into joint military operations along the border against ethnic resistance groups and highly controversial Indian deliveries of arms and military vehicles to Burma.[156] To improve access, trade and general bilateral relations, India has constructed the India-Burma friendship bridge in Zokhawthar, Mizoram, finances roads on both sides of the border, and plans an alternate route for the transport of goods into the Northeast via roads and inland riverine transport through the Kaladan Multi-Modal Transport Project.

Despite promises, the Myanmar regime has shown little inclination to evict Indian rebels from its soil. Similarly, India's rapprochement has not diminished Chinese influence over the regime. Lastly, the Myanmar Government has awarded contracts for gas exploitation to China and South Korean companies. In sum, Look East has failed to achieve the planned results. Although "Look East" has improved bilateral relations substantially, the Indian Government faces criticism from the Indian intelligentsia for departing from Gandhian and Nehruvian values (ostensibly upheld by Aung San Suu Kyi and the Burmese opposition), and from Northeastern and Burmese activists for human rights violations related to the large presence of military and paramilitary forces.[157] India was also slammed for sending its Petroleum Minister to sign agreements at the height of the 2007 Saffron Revolution. Unable to match Beijing's clout over the *Tatmadaw*, New Delhi continues to

[155] Bertil Lintner, "Northeast India: Bo iling Pot of International Riv alry: Bangladesh was a Conduit for Anti- India Insurgency", *Yale Global Online*, 17 February, 2010

[156] Amnesty International and Saferworld, *Indian Helicopters for Myanmar: Making a Mockery of Embargoes? A report by European Union Non-governmental Organisations* , London: AI and Saferworld, 2007

[157] Raj Shekhar, Why India is silent over extension of Da w Suu Kyi's House Arrest? *Burma Review*, 29 May, 2007; Diptosh Majumdar, On Myanmar, Govt tells Left to Get Real. *Indian Express*, 29 October, 2004

compromise some of India's core political values and credibility while being led on by Naypyidaw. If India supported the ushering in of Burmese democratic forces instead this would give it a competitive advantage over China.[158]

Thai-Burmese relations are characterised by historic animosity. Among all neighbouring states, Thailand arguably suffers most from Burmese conventional and non-traditional security threats. As a host to hundreds of thousands of Burmese and refugee camps close to the border, Thailand faces cross-border incursions of the *Tatmadaw*, shelling, and landmines. Thai perceptions of threat have increased with the prospect of ceasefire groups being turned into border guard forces after the 2010 elections. This would diminish the last buffer zone between the two countries (a policy Thailand followed during decades). With a keen interest in Burma's energy and other resources, Thailand is Burma's largest investor and buys the largest legal export of natural gas. Thailand's frequently changing governments have often taken opposite approaches ranging from strong support to critics of the Burmese regime. As the primary member to be affected by the crises in Burma, Thailand has often stirred ASEAN's stance towards Burma.

ASEAN accorded membership to Burma in 1997 in line with its policy of "constructive engagement" - promoting trade, economic, and diplomatic ties to encourage socio-economic liberalisation and stability.[159] Other reasons included countering Chinese influence over the country, gaining greater leverage over the junta in order to address pressing security issues, and, not last, benefiting from Burmese resources. Yet, as different as their leadership styles are the diverse approaches to and interests in Burma within the association. For instance Thailand and Singapore, the first countries to resume relations with the regime after the 1988 crackdown, are Burma's largest investors today.[160] The SPDC's rationale for joining ASEAN in turn was the veneer of political legitimacy, an alliance vis-à-vis the UN and major powers to

---

[158] C.R.Hariharan, "Myanmar: Developments in Myanmar and the Security of North East", *South Asia Analysis Group,* 1 November 2009

[159] Stephen McCarthy, "Burma and ASEAN: Estranged Bedfellows", *Asian Survey* 48 no. 6 (2008):917.

[160] Lily Zubaidah Rahim, "Fragmented Community and Unconstructive Engagement", *Critical Asian Studies* 40 no.1(2008) :67-88.

offset diplomatic isolation and sanctions from Western countries, as well as access to regional and extra-regional economic opportunities.

ASEAN strives for regional integration, intramural harmony, a careful balance between China and India and good international trade relations. The Myanmar Government as a stumbling block to these objectives in general and to ASEAN-EU relations in particular has tested the limits of policies of "non-interference in internal affairs". Despite face-saving measures offered by ASEAN and its habitual deflection of ASEAN-external criticism on Burma, the Myanmar regime has become a liability, embarrassing the regional body on many occasions and tarnishing its international credibility.[161] In fact, since the Depeyin attack on Aung San Suu Kyi and her entourage in May 2003, the expulsion of the country from ASEAN has been repeatedly suggested.[162] In 2005, Burma had to forfeit its turn in chairing ASEAN in 2006. Criticism following the regime's brutal handling of the "Saffron Revolution" in 2007, an official rebuke during the ASEAN Ministerial Meeting of July 2008 for extending Aung San Suu Kyi's house arrest present a novelty. ASEAN's desire to deflect attention from the failure of its decade-long quiet diplomacy certainly fuels such unprecedented criticism.

As a result, the military regime has turned more towards China and other countries such as Russia and North Korea, effectively reducing ASEAN's possibilities to influence the SPDC. This new orientation is not last reflected in the move of the capital to newly built Naypyidaw hundreds of kilometres away from the sea. Whereas the location is isolated from the West and many ASEAN states, it is much closer to the Asian continental powers playing key roles in Burma's economic and military survival.[163]

In contrast to Western states, Asian countries have high stakes in resources located in the country and in conventional and non-traditional

---

[161] On diminishing credibilty, in particular following the Saffron Revolution see Mely Cabalero-Anthony, "The ASEAN Charter: An Opportuni ty Missed or One that Cannot B e Missed?", *Southeast Asian Affairs* , (2008): 71-85.

[162] McCarthy, "Burma and ASEAN", 920.

[163] Ibid., 926.

security threats emanating from its borders. The problems associated with an international pariah as well as a failing state in the neighbourhood loom large not only over ASEAN. The current (re-) militarisation of the borders, increasing military clashes between *Tatmadaw* and ethnic nationality forces, and the possibility of an armed ethnic front against the government over the elections raise concerns.

This conditions the respective cautious, accommodating or cordial approaches towards the Myanmar Government. Except for India's initial open support for democracy, all Asian countries have followed policies of constructive engagement although the autarkic and xenophobic military leadership remains an unpredictable partner for long-term bilateral and multilateral commitments.

Western countries in contrast voice strong criticism that is fuelled by Burmese activists operating from their new countries of residence. The EU and US imposed the most comprehensive sanction regimes, while Australia, New Zealand, Canada hold up partial sanctions. After years of following a tough principled stance, there is a growing recognition that isolating and punishing the regime has diminished the scope and avenue for influencing it. Notably, the Obama administration is re-evaluating its approach towards the country.

Conclusion: Consequences of Burma's Conflicts and Crises

Burma's conflicts date back to pre-independence times and have no single root cause. Instead, elite choices, historical legacies, outside interventions, and developments in the international politico-economic system combined produce a "conflict trap".

Problems stem from or have been exacerbated by the *Tatmadaw's* policies, priorities, or negligence. There are obvious correlations between the military's expansion into "a state within a state" and the current crises, largely a man-made disaster. The alarming lack of state capacity, and the crippled economy drag the country and its population into a downward spiral while the military elite and business tycoons gain from selling natural resources. Policies or negligence are largely the causes of poverty, the lack of human security, educational and employment opportunities, and the presence of internal conflict. Such grievances, aggravated by arbitrariness and corruption, drive millions of Burmese out of the country.

Yet, the crucial fact remains that neither the Myanmar Government nor any other stakeholder alone will be able to solve the problems of a failing state built up over decades. This will hold true regardless of the 2010 election results. Unfortunately, the conflict parties – the military, diverse ethnic movements, domestic opposition, and exiled movement – will not work together on alleviating the crises as long as the issues of democratic, participatory governance, federalism, and human rights remain unresolved. In the meantime, a limited number of agencies seek to slow down a ticking time bomb of NTS issues.

Meanwhile, decades of political stalemate, ungoverned space, demand for resources, and the black market have produced a situation where illicit trades are thriving in particular along Burma's borders. This attracts different sets of actors who greatly benefit from the status quo and who by extension have no interest in Burma's peace, stability or democratic opposition.

The deep, multi-layered politico-economic, humanitarian, and environmental crises have tremendous implications for the region's stability. Thus, mismanagement has long ceased to be an "internal affair" of Burma. There is a pressing need for concerted efforts of domestic, regional and international players. Asian states have the highest stakes in Burmese security and geo-strategic issues and should therefore play a key role in fostering lasting political solutions. Unfortunately, none of the regional powers shows a sustained commitment to the Burmese opposition. Activist pressure and the regime's lack of legitimacy seem insufficient to outweigh resource wealth buttressing the political economy of military rule. It remains to be seen whether the 2010 elections exacerbate or improve Burma's overall situation.

References

Agamben, Giorgio. 1997. The Camp as Nomos of the Modern, trans. Daniel Heller-Roazen. In *Violence, Identity and Self-Determination*, ed.

Hent de Vries and Samuel Weber, 106 -118. Stanford: Stanford University Press.

Amnesty International and Saferworld. 2007. *Indian helicopters for Myanmar: Making a mockery of embargoes? A report by European Union non-governmental organisations.* 2007. London: AI and Saferworld.

Aung Saw Oo. 1993. *Burma's Student Movement: A Concise History.* 3rd edition. http://abfsu.net/?page_id=2 (accessed 1 May, 2010).

Badgley, John H. 1963. Burma: The Nexus of Socialism and Two Political Traditions. *Asian Survey* 3(2):89-95.

Beyrer, Chris. 2001. Accelerating and Disseminating across Asia. *The Washington Quarterly* 24(1): 211–225.

Beyrer, Chris, Mathieson, and Suwanvanichkij et al. 2007. *The gathering storm: Infectious diseases and human rights in Burma.* Open Society Institute, University of California, Berkeley and John Hopkins Bloomberg School of Public Health.

Buzan, Barry and Ole Wæver, Jaap de Wilde. 1998. Security: A new framework for analysis. Boulder, CO: Lynne Rienner.

Buzzi, Camilla. 2002. *Burma: Twelve Years After 1988. A Common Future?* PD Burma and Worldview Rights. http://www.ibiblio.org/obl/docs/CB-Web.htm (accessed 1 July, 2007).

Callahan, Mary P. 1998. Democracy in Burma: The Lessons of History. *NBR Analysis* 9(3):9.

— 2000. Cracks in the Edifice: Military-Society Relations in Burma Since 1988. In *Burma/Myanmar: Strong regime, Weak state?* ed. Morten B. Pederson, Emily Rudland, Ronald J. May, 22-51. Adelaide: Crawford House; London: Hurst.

— 2004. *Making enemies: War and state building in Burma.* Singapore: Singapore University Press.

Charney, Michael W. 2009. *A history of modern Burma.* Cambridge; New York: Cambridge University Press.

Clymer, Megan. 2003. Min Ko Naing, "Conqueror Of Kings": Burma's Student Leader. *Journal of Burma Studies* 8:33-63.

Fink, Christina. 2001. *Living Silence: Burma under the military rule*. New York: Zed Books.

Free Burma Rangers, and Partners Relief and Development. 2010. *Displaced Childhoods: Human Rights and International Crimes Against Burma's Internally Displaced Children*. Thailand: FBR and PRD.

Ganesan, N. and Kyaw Yin Hlaing, ed. 2007. *Myanmar: State, Society and Ethnicity*. Singapore: Institute of Southeast Asian Studies.

Grundy-Warr, Carl. *Geographies of the dispossessed: The Karenni Refugees of the Myanmar's Trans-Salween*. Unpublished photo essay with photos by Dean Chapman. Undated.

— 2002. Lost in Sovereign Space: Forced Migrants in the Territorial Trap. *Asian and Pacific Migration Journal* 11 (4):437-61.

Hariharan, C. R. 2009. Myanmar: Developments in Myanmar and the Security of North East. *South Asia Analysis Group,* 1 November.

Keck, Margaret and Kathryn Sikkink. 1997. *Activists Beyond Borders: Advocacy Networks in International Politics.* Ithaca: Cornell University Press.

Kivimäki, Timo and Morten B. Pedersen. 2008. *Burma: Mapping the Challenges and Opportunities for Dialogue and Reconciliation*. Brussels and Helsinki: Crisis Management Initiative.

Kramer. Tom. 2009. *Neither War nor Peace: The Future of the Cease-fire agreements in Burma*. Amsterdam: Transnational Institute.

Kramer. Tom, Martin Jelsma, and Tom Blickman. 2009. *Withdrawal Symptoms in the Golden Triangle: A Drugs Market in Disarray*. Amsterdam: Transnational Institute.

Kyaw Yin Hlaing. 2004. Burma: Civil Society Skirting Regime Rules. In *Civil Society and Political Change in Asia: Expanding and Contracting Democratic Space*, ed. M. Alagappa, 389-418. Stanford, California: Stanford University Press.

Lintner, Bertil. 1990. *Aung San Suu Kyi and Burma's unfinished Renaissance*. Clayton, Australia: Centre of Southeast Asian Studies, Monash University

— 1990. *The Rise and fall of the Communist Party of Burma*. Ithaca: Southeast Asia Program, Cornell University

— 1999. *Burma in Revolt: Opium and Insurgency since 1948*. Chiangmai: Silkworm Books, 2nd edition

— 2007. Burma's Warrior Kings and the generation of 8.8.88. *Global Asia* 2 (2):78.

— 2009. *The Resistance of the Monks Buddhism and Activism in Burma*. New York: Human Rights Watch.

Lintner, Bertil and Michael Black. 2009. *Merchants of Madness: The Methamphetamine Explosion in the Golden Triangle*. Chiangmai: Silkworm Press.

Maung Aung Myoe. 2009. *Building the Tatmadaw: Myanmar armed forces since 1948*. Singapore: Institute of Southeast Asian Studies.

McCarthy, Stephen. 2008. Burma and ASEAN: Estranged Bedfellows. *Asian Survey* 48(6):911–935.

Mutebi, Alex M. 2005. "Muddling through" past Legacies: Myanmar's Civil Bureaucracy and the need for reform. In *Myanmar: Beyond Politics to Societal Imperatives*, ed. Kyaw Yin Hlaing, Robert H. Taylor, Tin Maung Maung Than, 140-160. Singapore: Institute of Southeast Asian Studies.

Nugent, Rachel, Emma Back, and Alexandra Beith. 2010. *The Race Against Drug Resistance*. Washington: Center for Global Development,

Perry, Peter J. 2007. *Myanmar (Burma) since 1962: The failure of development*. Hants, England; Burlington, VT: Ashgate.

Piper, Nicola and Anders Uhlin. 2003. New perspectives on transnational activism. In *Transnational activism in Asia: Problems of power and democracy*, ed. Piper and Uhlin, 1-23. New York: Routledge.

Physicians for Human Rights. 2010. *Stateless and Starving: Persecuted Rohingya Flee Burma and Starve in Bangladesh*. Cambridge, MA: PHR.

Rahim, Lily Zubaidah. 2008. Fragmented Community and Unconstructive Engagement. *Critical Asian Studies* 40(1):67-88.

Rotberg, Robert I. 2003. Failed States, Collapsed States, Weak States: Causes and Indicators. In *State failure and state weakness in a time of terror*, ed. Robert I. Rotberg, 1-25. Cambridge, MA: World Peace Foundation; Washington: Brookings Institution Press.

Rudland, Emily and Morton B. Pederson. 2000. Introduction. In *Burma/ Myanmar: Strong regime, Weak state?* ed. Morten B. Pederson, Emily Rudland, Ronald J. May, 1-21. Adelaide: Crawford House; London: Hurst.

Sakhuja, Vijay. 2009. Military Buildup Across the Himalayas: A Shaky Balance. China Brief 9(18):8-10.

Selth, Andrew. 2002. *Burma's armed forces: Power without glory*. Norwalk, Connecticut: EastBridge.

— 2009. Known Knowns and Known Unknowns: Measuring Myanmar's Military Capabilities. *Contemporary Southeast Asia* 31(2):282-285.

Silverstein, Josef. 1989. From a Political to an Administrative State, 1948-1988: Whatever happened to democracy? In *Independent Burma At Forty Years: Six Assessments*, ed. Josef Silverstein, 7-18. Ithaca: Southeast Asia Program, Cornell University.

 Smith, Martin. 1991. *Burma: Insurgency and the Politics of Ethnicity*. London: Zed Books.

— 2007. *State of strife: The dynamics of ethnic conflict in Burma.* Singapore: Institute of Southeast Asian Studies; Washington: East-West Center.

Steinberg, David I. 1982. Burma in 1982: Incomplete Transitions. *Asian Survey* 23(2):165-171.

— 1984. Burma in 1983: The Dilemmas of Neutralism and Succession. *Asian Survey* 24(2):195-200.

— 2010. *Burma/Myanmar: What everyone needs to know*. New York: Oxford University Press.

Thaung Htun. 1995. *Student Activism in Burma: A Historical Perspective*. Australia: Lawyers' Information Network. www.link.asn.au/downloads/papers/burma/p_bm_05.pdf (accessed 1 December, 2007).

Thai-Burma Border Consortium. 2010. *Burmese border refugee sites with population figures May 2010*. Bangkok: TBBC.

Threat to the Peace: A Call for the UN Security Council to Act in Burma. 2005. Report commissioned by Vacláv Havel and Desmond M. Tutu. Washington: DLA Piper Rudnick Gray Cary.

Tin Maung Maung Than. 1999. *The political economy of Burma's (Myanmar's) development failure 1948-1988*. Singapore: ISEAS, 22.

Winston Set Aung. 2009. *Migration and Human Smuggling from Myanmar: Moving Toward Win-Win Solutions*. Stockholm: Institute for Security and Development Policy.

UNODC. 2009. *Opium Poppy Cultivation in South-East Asia Lao PDR, Myanmar*.

US Department of State. 2010. *2010 International Narcotics Control Strategy Report*. Washington: US Department of State.

— 2010. *Trafficking in Persons Report 2010*. Washington: US Department of State.

US Drug Enforcement Agency. 2005. *Eight High-Ranking Leaders Of Southeast Asia's Largest Narcotics Trafficking Organization Indicted By A Federal Grand Jury In Brooklyn, New York*. News release 24 January.

Wyler, Liana Sun. 2008. *Burma and Transnational Crime*. Washington: Congressional Research Service.

Zaw Oo. 2008. Aung San Suu Kyi: Gandhian dissident democrat. In *Dissident democrats: The challenge of democratic leadership in Asia*, ed. John Kane, Haig Patapan, Benjamin Wong, 241-270. New York: Palgrave Macmillan.

Internal Conflicts in Myanmar: Effects on Neighbouring States

EFFECTS OF CONFLICTS IN MYANMAR AND THEIR CONSEQUENCES ON BANGLADESH*

Iftekhar Ahmed Chowdhury

Geographically Bangladesh is 'India locked' which means India on all sides except for the Bay of Bengal in the South and Myanmar on the right. Like other countries in the region Bangladesh is also adopting a policy of 'looking east' which makes Myanmar important in terms of foreign policy.

There are broadly three ways in which countries relate to the world. If one is small and weak and surrounded by powerful countries, one adopts the "Pilot Fish Behavior", in other words you tack close to the shark in order to avoid being eaten. Surrounded by India and China, Bangladesh takes a position of creating linkages with the rest of the world in a way that she meshes herself in a web of external linkages so that the power gap between the other neighbors and her reduces. The second approach is that of deterrence where one develops a sizable deterrent capability in order to give the bloodiest possible nose to any potential adversary. The third option is what Ralph Pittman calls "opting out of the international system" like Burma. He said that Burma decided to opt out of the international system. However, Burma is yet to get there and follows an interesting foreign policy as it remains just about engaged to strengthen its sense of security.

---

* This paper is based on the author's presentation at the seminar on Internal Conflicts in Myanmar and Trans Border Consequences held on 26-27 May 2010 at Singapore.

Bangladesh has always tended to "look west" in the past. The economic foreign policy was almost post colonial; the economic and intellectual linkages were with the West. The exports of garments, which is the country's main export, was to the West and even the migrant workers went towards the West. Bangladesh's global position was endeavoring to shape international norms to its best advantage which required a very active role in the UN and the WTO for instance. Active diplomacy and engagement in the world affairs became necessary with the net result that it had to maximize its external interactions. This was not the case with Myanmar although it did initially provide a UN Secretary General. Given Myanmar's traditional pattern of opting out of the international system its involvement in various multilateral and bilateral forums has been an interesting change. It is involved in BIMSTEC, ASEAN as well as bilaterally with India, China, North Korea and Russia. It is also an observer in SAARC seeking a full membership and is also a part of a group of 50 least developed countries called the LDCs although this is not played up much by Myanmar. The greatest advantage of LDC's is that one gets benefits in terms of market access in trade, which Myanmar would not get for a variety of reasons.

The structure of civil and political organization in the two countries is also very different. Bangladesh is pluralist liberal democracy, albeit noisy and at times chaotic. Home grown ideas like Micro-Credit and non formal education for girls have helped alleviate poverty, have empowered women, and marginalized extremist thoughts and actions. Bangladesh also has one of the most vibrant civil societies including some of the world's largest NGOs like BRAC or Grameen Bank. The founder of the Grameen Bank, Mohomad Yunus was also awarded the Nobel Peace Prize. The Army has been involved in politics on and off but its role has been far more subdued than the original country Pakistan. Bangladesh has been developing and the growth has been equitable. The World Bank has called it the so called Bangladesh Paradox, a paradigm of silent revolution. The Constitution provides for a Westminster type of parliamentary government but unicameral legislature with 330 members, 30 of which are reserved for women. In the case of Myanmar, the country has been run by the military for over four decades. Its Constitution was approved just two years ago. The Constitution provides for a bicameral legislature and in the national assembly out of 224 seats, 56 are reserved for the military. In the House of Nationalities which is elected by regions and states, 110 of 440 seats are reserved for the military.

Bilateral Relations

Myanmar was by the way sixth country and the third in Asia to recognize Bangladesh. Myanmar's government made an interesting statement, "the government of Myanmar does not accept in principle the solution of a country's internal problems by direct help and intervention of foreign country's armed organization. However due to existence of questions requiring immediate comments on actions and inactions and also due to a desire to lift fraternally as neighbors the government of Burma has recognized the state of Bangladesh." The first part of the statement reflected the wariness about India's role in the independence of Bangladesh. The second part demonstrated sheer pragmatism. Relations between the two countries- Bangladesh and Myanmar- were good and they called it the border of peace. However, in 1978 problems crept into this relationship. Myanmar initiated a program called Operation Dragon King, which was started to upgrade the demographic information and classify residents and foreigners. This was the time when the Rohingyas who were Muslims on the borders were not accorded recognition as citizens. Consequently, there was an influx of 250,000 into Bangladesh who came in with complaints of atrocities perpetrated by Burmese authorities. Initially there was a lot of diplomatic effort which resulted in the return of many Rohingyas. Again a big push occurred in 1991 and by April 1997 Bangladesh and UNHCR had repatriated all but 21,115. Today there are 13,582 are being processed out of which 7,500 have been recognized by Myanmar and there are about 21,000 Rohingyas still in Bangladesh in a stateless kind of form.

The regions bordering Bangladesh are extremely rich in minerals and forest resources, 16,000 cubic feet of gas reserves have been identified in Rakin state. In spite of all this there has not been much trade between the two countries. This comes as a surprise also largely because Bangladesh is focused on the West. In October 2008, Maung Aye who is believed to be second in the military hierarchy, came to

Bangladesh and talked of raising the trade levels five times and there were some interesting proposals in order to strengthen the bilateral relations. When I was in charge of the portfolio of foreign affairs, Myanmar was the first country I visited and immediately we contracted an agreement to build a road through Myanmar seeking to link up with the Myanmar communications system and eventually link up with China. Myanmar has no problem with the road provided Bangladesh funds it. About 100 kms stretch remains to be linked to the Myanmar internal system. Obviously Bangladesh has to touch the Chinese for possible support and a couple of months ago when Prime Minister Sheikh Haseena visited China a joint agreement proposed a quadrilateral arrangement called BCIM- Bangladesh, China, India and Myanmar. The Chinese were very enthusiastic about it, Bangladesh signed on and India understandably would rather have it at track two level.

With regard to the elections in Myanmar, this seems to be a succession strategy for Than Shwe. He looks after the day to day running of the country and ensures that no single person consolidates power and threatens his preeminence. Many argue particularly in the West that the elections will only legitimize the process. However, others feel there are three reasons why this may be a positive step. First, any change is better than status quo. Second, the elections will create more political space even though it is a relative concept in a controlled society and finally to the extent that it is an exit strategy for senior General Than Shwe, the proponents of change argue that the process must be encouraged. The glimpse of some opportunities however few is probably encouraging to a number of ethnic groups to participate if not at the national levels at least at the provincial level. There could be two pragmatic reasons for this. One reason could be that this is one way to use minority languages, schools and local government departments to have a say on the proceeds of natural resource extraction and the use of government funds. The second reason could be the need to create a greater political space to encourage long term bottom up democratization along with a vibrant civil society. It is noteworthy that Bangladesh provides an excellent model for such civil society based endeavors. For instance in Afghanistan, BRAC is involved in the development of Afghanistan in 22 out of the 34 provinces. It is already doing peace building work in places where even the NATO fears to venture. Wherever BRAC has worked the societal landscape itself has been changed. There have been several instances of kidnapping and BRAC has been involved negotiations for the release of hostages. Our impression is that they are positively seen even by Taliban.

The Rohingya Problem

As mentioned earlier about 21000 Rohingya remain in a stateless form in Bangladesh. This problem has spread beyond Bangladesh as some many of them have started moving into Thailand. Leaders in the region have sought to take up this problem at the ASEAN level. Some Some Rohingyas have been shifted to Canada and some to the Middle East. This connection is not necessarily a very positive connection. There are some particularly in the intelligence community who worry about these stateless Rohingyas. They are exposed to many Islamist influences, links to the Middle East as well as links within even Bangladesh based Islamist and Islamic groups. This is important because they are getting involved with issues like Afghanistan etc. which radicalizes them has implications for both Myanmar and Bangladesh.

The elections in Myanmar can also provide an opportunity to enfranchise the Rohingyas in some form, at least in the Arakan region if not centrally. It could help erode some of the negative consequences mentioned earlier. There has to be some thinking out of the box that serves the interests of both Bangladesh and Myanmar. I suggest the following six steps:-

1. Active encouragement by the Myanmar government to get Rohingyas involved in the political process, at least regionally if not federally, even with a modicum of tokenism if necessary. Some of them can be involved in the new leade3rship that is taking shape.

2. Bangladesh and Myanmar could jointly undertake border development projects to improve economic conditions in the region which will support the region and include border trade, establishment of markets, jointly run bazaars Etc.

3. Early implementation of the road building project mentioned earlier which would help integrate Arakan region with the rest of Myanmar.

4. Myanmar might accord Bangladeshi NGO's permission to work within Myanmar. They could be registered with Myanmar NGO's as is being done by BRAC in Afghanistan. This can help alleviate poverty and empower women among Arakanese Muslim population, through micro credit and non formal education.

5. Both the countries can develop a mechanism to address the immediate resolution of the remaining Rohingya refugees. This is not an intractable problem.

6. The Chinese and Indians can be brought on board in the efforts to address the Rohingya problem. This agreement between Sheikh Haseena and Wen Jiabao on the quadrilateral arrangement can be utilized to involve both India and China.

The international community appears to be moving away from its aggressive policy of isolating from Myanmar. The *Nargis* Hurricane created several problems for Myanmar. It resuscitated the idea of humanitarian intervention i.e. R2P or the Responsibility to Protect. In 2005, the United Nations principled a doctrine where every government is the responsible for the protection its own population. If for some reason that government is unable or unwilling to protect their own population then the responsibility devolves on the international community which operating through the UN would discharge this responsibility. The French were particularly keen to begin the process of R2P in Myanmar. However, saner sense prevailed and R2P in Myanamr was based on the idea of creating developmental situation which would prevent the slide from the anarchy in the first place. The idea was based on development rather than the usual regime change military intervention. Myanmar, as mentioned earlier, has a very interesting foreign policy. It has been clever in the sense that there is just about enough engagement to avoid being seen as an international threat, just enough support from China and Russia in order not to have anything adopted against Myanmar at the UNSC, just about enough changes to appear that it is better off than other failed states in the region or elsewhere. Thant Myint-U, the historian in his "River of Lost Footsteps" powerfully argued for engagement as a tool for effecting change. The ethnic conflicts in Myanmar have negative consequences both for the region as well as the world. Hence greater focus is required on the region. The Greek philosopher Heraclitus said we never step into the same river twice. Change therefore is exorable and therefore Myanmar also will change. Our concern must be with calibrating endeavors so that change is for the better both for Myanmar, for region and for the world.

EFFECTS OF THE CONFLICT BETWEEN THE CEASEFIRE GROUPS AND THE MILITARY GOVERNMENT ON CHINA SINCE 2009

LI Chenyang

The Northern States of Shan and Kachin, that form the focus of this paper, comprise a geo-politically important area in Myanmar. Bothe these states lie adjacent to the Yunnan Province in China and Tibet. The Shan State covers an area of 155,801 square kilometers and has a population of 8,461,500, which is the largest and most-populated state among Myanmar's 14 divisions and states. The Kachin State encompasses 89,041 square kilometers which is the third largest state in Myanmar and with the population of 1,553,100. The coverage and the population of the two states accounts for 36.2% and 17.9% of Myanmar's total respectively. Moreover, the two states' boundary line on land accounts for more than 50% of Myanmar's total.

This region is similarly important for China. Sixteen ethnic groups live on the Sino-Myanmar boundary line which covers an area of 2,210 kilometers. Only 250 kilometers are under effective control of the Myanmar military government, the rest is controlled by five ceasefire groups. They are the Kachin Independent Army (KIA), New Kachin Democratic Army (KDA-N), Myanmar National Democratic Alliance Army (MNDAA), United Wa State Army (UWSA) and National Democratic Alliance Army(NDAA) from north to south. Nearly 50,000 square kilometers are controlled by these five ceasefire groups, while their scope of operation exceeds 100,000 square kilometers with the population of about 1,750,000. Ceasefire groups in northern Myanmar have been engaged in drug trafficking, gambling, smuggling and many other illegal activities driven by interests such as the need for long term survival, which makes this area the main source of some criminal activities such as drugs, gambling and pornography in Southwest China. This seriously affects the security and stability of China's border areas. Since the plan to transform the ceasefire groups to Border Guard Force (BGF) was implemented in late April 2009, the relationship between ceasefire groups in northern Myanmar and the Central Government has been tense. Although no new armed conflicts have broken out in the region since September 2009 due to China's positive mediation, the chances for conflicts in northern Myanmar have remained high. Conflicts between ceasefire groups and Myanmar military government in northern Myanmar have adversely affected China especially Yunnan Province.

Transformation of Ceasefire Groups to BGFs: Background and Progress

Many adjustments have been made in the policy towards ethnic groups of Ne Win Government since the State Law and Order Restoration Council (SLORC) (called State Peace and Development Council (SPDC) after November 1997) took over in September 1988 which has led to the accomplishment of many achievements. Seventeen anti-government minority armed forces have reached ceasefire agreements with the military government. The Military Government has strived to solve the situation completely. After Khin Nyunt, the former Premier, stepped down in October 2004 the military government hastened its pace to settle the problems with ceasefire groups. At first, the government tried to make the ceasefire groups surrender completely, but later tried to transform these into Border Guard Forces (BGF).

Regulations Relating to Ethnic Groups in the Constitution of the Republic of the Union of Myanmar (2008)

There is no specific solution listed in the Constitution of the Republic of the Union of Myanmar (2008) approved by referendum. The ideas of the Myanmar's military government about how to solve the problems with the ceasefire groups can be drawn from the following articles of the new Constitution.

- **Article 3**- "The State is where multi-national races collectively reside"

- **Article 10**- "No part of the territory constituted in the Union such as Regions, States, Union Territories and Self-Administered Areas shall ever secede from the Union"

- **Article 56**- "The Self-Administered Division and Self-Administered Zones are delineated as follows: grouping Leshi, Lahe and Namyun townships in Sagaing Division as Naga Self-Administered Zone; grouping Ywangan and Pingdaya townships in Shan State as Danu Self-Administered Zone; grouping HoPong, HsiHseng and Pinlaung townships in Shan State as Pa-O Self-Administered Zone; grouping Namhsan and Manton townships in Shan State as Pa Laung Self-Administered Zone; grouping Konkyan and Laukkai townships in Shan State as Kokang Self-Administered Zone; grouping six townships — — Hopang, Mongma, Panwai, Nahpan, Metman and Pangsang (Pankham) townships in Shan State as two districts which are forged into 'Wa' Self-Administered Division"

- **Article 338**- "All the armed forces in the Union shall be under the command of the Defense Services"

These regulations show that all the areas under the current control of KIA, KDA-N and NDAA will never be designated as Self-Administered Zones separately. The Wa Self-Administered Division will be smaller in the future and at the same time; the armed forces of each ceasefire group will be under the command of the Defense Services.

The Basic Content and Application Program of Transformation Plan of Ceasefire Groups introduced in 2009 by Myanmar Military Government

"Reign but not rule" has been the policy of the military government towards the areas controlled by ceasefire groups for quite some time. The ceasefire groups enjoy their autonomy relying on their own armies; as a result, the authorities always consider them as one of the major threats to national stability and the interests of military group. To ensure the smooth conduct of the 2010 elections the military government suggested and actively pursued the transformation of armed elements of the ceasefire groups into "Border Guard Force" led and administrated by the Defense Services. For the sake of conducting the reorganization smoothly, committees are set up at three different levels. The first level is "Transitional Policy Committee". Senior General Than Shwe, the Chairman of SPDC is the president, while Vice-Senior Maung Aye, the Vice-Chairman of SPDC is the vice president and the members comprise all the committee men of SPDC. The second level is "Transitional Working Committee" whose president is Lieutenant General Ye Myint, the Chief of Military Affairs Security, and other members comprise the commanders of each command area. The third level is made up of commanders of each command area called "Transitional Military Committee". Since late April 2009, the government has negotiated with ceasefire groups several times, publicized the constitutional spirit of "one country one army" and persuaded each ceasefire group to accept reorganization. The specific reorganization scheme is as follows:

- The armed forces of each ceasefire group must be reorganized into battalions, each battalion consists of 326 officers and soldiers.

- The battalion commander and one vice-battalion commander are members of ceasefire groups, and the other vice-battalion commander should be an officer from the Defense Services.

- There should be a certain amount of officers and soldiers from the Defense Services in each BGF battalion and the treatment of all the staff is to be in accordance with the *Tatmadaw*.

- The standard of specified number of personnel in each organization after reorganization is regulated, for example, UWSA is 3,000, MNDAA is 1,000 and NDAA is 500.

The military government intended to finish the original plan by three steps. The first step was to finish registration of armed personnel and equipments by the late of June 2009. The second step was to carry out reorganization between July and October 2009. The third step was to train the reorganized army according to the new regiment. However, huge resistance emerged in the process and among the main ceasefire groups in northern Myanmar, only KDA-N was willing to accept transformation.

The Course of the Kokang Event

During the process of reorganization, about 70 personnel of the Tatmadaw went to a weapon repair factory owned by MNDAA (Kokang Group) without conforming to the former due date on 8th August 2009. The spot check on drugs was resisted by the MNDAA. More than 300 soldiers of MNDAA encircled the Tatmadaw soldiers and after a confrontation for 5 hours', the Tatmadaw soldiers retreated. This event caused immense panic in Kokang area. About 10,000 people fled to Nansan in China between 8th and 10th August. This situation was salvaged due to Chinese mediation but the refusal of the local government of Kokang special region led by Peng Jiasheng to accept reorganization has left a constantly tensed environment. The Myanmar Peace and Democracy Front consisting of MNDAA, UWSA and NDAA held a conference on the Kokang Event on 21st August, and issued a joint statement endorsing the stand and measures taken by the government of Kokang special region, disapproving the military government for striking and suppressing ceasefire groups in the name of drug-control and appealing to the two sides to settle the divergence through talks. On 24th August, Bai Suocheng, the Vice-Commander of MNDAA staged a coup and established a new Central Executive Committee for Kokang area. The military forces of Myanmar government marched into and occupied Laukkai, the capital of Kokang and appointed Bai Suocheng as the new leader of Kokang special region.

On 27th August, intense armed conflict broke out between MNDAA and the Tatmadaw resulting in the migration of thousands of inhabitants of the border area into Chinese territory. Finally, MNDAA gave up resistance on 29th August because the Tatmadaw adopted heavy armaments such as heavy artillery in the fight. According to the report of Myanmar government, 15 policemen and 11 soldiers died, 13 policemen and 34 soldiers were hurt and 8 soldiers from the ethnic group died in this event. Besides 3 shells were thrown into Chinese territory which left two Chinese border residents dead and several injured.

The Situation in Northern Myanmar after Kokang Event

After the Kokang Event, the Tatmadaw continued to deploy a large number of forces in northern Myanmar, aiming directly at ceasefire groups such as UWSA, NDAA and KIA. In order to safeguard its own interests to the largest extent and being on the defensive, the ceasefire groups agreed to accept reorganization conditionally and negotiated with the Myanmar military government several times. The ceasefire groups are said to have introduced conditions in the process in order to postpone and sustain the current situation. At the same time, some ceasefire groups such as UWSA and KIA have quickened the process of carrying arms expansion and war preparations. No large-scale armed conflicts broke out in northern Myanmar after Kokang Event because of the Chinese mediation but the negotiations on reorganization have been difficult and the Myanmar Central Government had to extend the deadline for reorganization to 31st December 2009. However, under the high pressure of the military government, some ceasefire groups such as KDA-N, Karenni Nationalities People Liberation Front and MNDAA led by Bai Suocheng have accepted to the reorganization in November 2009 successively.

The negotiation between the military government and UWSA, KIA and NDAA run into a deadlock. The conditions proposed by these armed forces have led to a situation where no one is compromising. Till 31st December, the main three armed ethnic forces did not submit the list of personnel and armaments required by the government. Influenced by the tough attitude of some armed ethnic forces, Democratic Karen Buddhist Army and Shan State Army which had a tendency to accept reorganization, claimed to maintain status quo, not wanting to be reorganized into the BGF. Subsequently, the deadline for reorganization had to be extended to 28th February and 27th March 2010. No agreement has been achieved despite the Chinese mediation. In late March and early April 2010, the military government informed each ceasefire group again that the deadline for accepting reorganization was 22nd April. If the ceasefire groups would accept the scheme proposed by the government, the reorganization should be finished by 28th April; if they would not accept the scheme, they would be announced as illegal organizations after 28th April. Subsequently, a joint declaration was issued to reject being reorganized by UWSA, KIA, NDAA and SSA-N on 16th April. Although divergences existed in how to deal with these ceasefire groups which have declined reorganization within the military government, they have not been announced as illegal organizations even after 28th April, nor did the government launch any military attack. At present, the military government is still promoting the reorganization of ceasefire groups. The difference is that the unified negotiation has been changed. Now each military area is in charge of its own reorganization within its jurisdiction.

Impact of the Instability in Northern Myanmar on China

The outbreak of the Kokang Event has not only posed a serious threat to the security and stability of southwest China but also caused casualties and property loss for Chinese citizens. The situation in northern Myanmar has been tense since then. Most of China's alternative cultivations in northern Myanmar have been stalled. A number of major cooperative projects between China and Myanmar have been affected as well.

Impact on the Security and Stability of Yunnan-Myanmar border

The Kokang event and the subsequent sustained tension in northern Myanmar seriously affected the security and stability of Yunnan's border region. If another war erupts in northern Myanmar, the impact will be more severe.

1. Impacts on the Security and Stability of Yunnan's border

On August 8th, 2009, the Tatmadaw required to check MNDAA arsenal using the excuse of drugs, which led to a confrontation between the MNDAA and the Tatmadaw across Lincang, Yunnan. On August 30th, Myanmar government forces announced their occupation of the whole Kokang region. The situation was temporarily stabilized. However, this event caused a serious threat to the security and stability of Yunnan's border region. Two Chinese citizens were killed and another 15 injured in the incident. More than 37,000 refugees moved across the border into China. The property of Chinese citizens' has also been damaged. The Chinese government had to use substantial human resources and materials as well as finance to accommodate the refugees and ensure the stability of the Sino-Myanmar border.

2. Illegal Activities of Discontent Chinese Citizens in the border

The Kokang event caused widespread concern for Chinese at home and abroad. Some Chinese citizens thought that the Myanmar military government "bullied Chinese in Myanmar" and that may "set off a new round of anti-China wave". Some Chinese citizens tried to call on people on the internet to go to Myanmar as "volunteers" to "support the resistance of Chinese in Myanmar against the military". This brought about difficulties in the management of the Sino-Myanmar border. Such people also have ulterior and impure motives. They spread in Kokang, Wa and the NDAA controlled areas and cross the Sino-Myanmar border frequently. Together with the ceasefire groups' poor management of guns and ammunition in northern Myanmar, the border area of Yunnan is facing a major security risk.

3. Impact of the Potential Armed Conflict in Northern Myanmar

After outbreak of the Kokang event, the northern Myanmar ceasefire groups and the military government remain in confrontation even though negotiations continued between the two sides. As the Myanmar government has determined to solve the problem of the ceasefire groups before the general election, it's possible that small-scale conflicts or even large-scale ones may outbreak in 2010. If there is an outbreak, it will lead to the following major problems.

First, there is the problem of refugees in the Sino-Myanmar border area. The Kokang event has brought more than 37,000 refugees to China. There are more than 40 million people in the Northern Wa region, once the Myanmar government troops attack the Wa State and other ceasefire groups, the number of refugees will increase ten-fold and so will the pressure on China.

Second, there is the problem of illegal militant immigrants and the management of bullets, drugs and other prohibited goods. Once the war breaks out, foreign militants (including the ceasefire group and government army) will enter China through various channels and will affect the security and stability of China's border. Due to the need of the war, prohibited goods like gun and bullet will be significantly increased, and can give rise to large-scale smuggling of weapons and drugs.

Third, the lives and property of Chinese citizens in northern Myanmar will be seriously threatened. Even those who live on the Sino-Myanmar border of China might be injured. Such things have happened in the Kokang event.

Forth, once the military government attacks the KIA, the UWSA or NDAA, it could hurt the ethnic sentiments of China's Jingpo, Wa, Hani and other cross- border ethnic minorities. Coupled with agitation of people with ulterior motives, Sino-Myanmar relations and the security of the border will be in danger.

Finally, northern Myanmar, particularly the areas along Sino-Myanmar border, may be in turbulence for a long period. As the Myanmar government forces cannot completely eradicate the ceasefire groups. A lot of them would split up and engage in guerrilla activities in the border. Generally speaking, China supports Myanmar's central government to solve the problem of ceasefire groups and achieve national reunification. Thus, a few people from some ceasefire groups perhaps will carry out terrorist attacks against the Chinese and Chinese enterprises in Myanmar, which will damage the security, stability and development of China's border.

If the interests of Chinese alternative cultivation enterprises cannot be effectively protected after Myanmar government's transformation of the ceasefire groups, it is possible that some of them may participate in illegal violence on the Sino-Myanmar border.

Impact on the Overall Sino-Myanmar Relations and Strategic Co-operation

China has vital national interests in Myanmar at present and in the future, particularly in areas of energy security and access into the Indian Ocean. This needs cooperation and support from the Myanmar government. Thus friendly Sino-Myanmar relationship has a crucial role in promoting the strategic cooperation between the two nations. The problem of ceasefire groups in northern Myanmar is a touchstone in these relations.

After the outbreak of the Kokang event, Chinese at home and abroad aired lots opinions on the internet. Some of them attacked China's foreign policies; some accused the Myanmar military government for seizing the opportunity to show anti-China views in order to please the West especially U.S.A.; some claimed that the Chinese government should require the Myanmar government to compensate the damaged Chinese enterprises. These words and feelings have to some extent negatively impacted the Sino-Myanmar bilateral relations. Some people in China still spread irresponsible statements damaging the relations due to their personal interests. In addition, in order to avoid potential losses, some enterprises which have investments in the ceasefire groups controlled areas consciously press government officials and academics, trying to make the ceasefire group continually exist. These deeds may produce some adverse effects on the strategic cooperation between China and Myanmar.

Impacts on the Alternative Cultivation and the Drug Situation in Northern Myanmar

The Kokang event and the sustained tension in northern Myanmar caused serious harms to the alternative cultivation. The drug situation is likely to deteriorate again.

1. Negative Impacts on Alternative Cultivation in Northern Myanmar

According to incomplete statistics, 8 Chinese enterprises engage in alternative cultivation in Kokang region, with a total investment of 72.18 million Chinese Yuan (self-reported figures from the enterprises). The main plants are rubber, sugar cane and tropical crops. The specific impacts on alternative cultivation are in the following areas:

(a) Loss of Crops

The Zhengkang Nanhua Nansan Sugar Co., Ltd., the largest alternative enterprise in Kokang region lost 1,500 Mu (1 Mu=0.0667 hectares) of sugar field, which is about 6,000 tons of sugarcane, due to the trench digging and mining. The tea garden of Kunming Jili Trade Co., Ltd. became the battleground and nearly all the tea trees were destroyed.

(b) Loss of Fixed Assets and Property

The vehicles, machinery, equipment and products of the alternative enterprises were looted by some unidentified people, causing heavy loss. The assets and office of Jili Trade Co. Ltd have been occupied by the New Administrative Committee of Kokang region and couldn't be recovered. Zhengkang Nanhua Nansan Sugar Co., Ltd lost 175 tons urea, 260 tons of fertilizer and 18 tons pesticides.[1]

According to the statistics and verification of business sector, 4 of the 8 alternative cultivation enterprises in Kokang region suffered serious losses from the outbreak of the conflict at the end of 2009. The total direct and indirect losses reached up to 31.23 million Chinese Yuan.

(c) Impact on the Operation of Alternative Cultivation

Social order has not been recovered since the Tatmadaw had occupied Kokang region. Instability and security risks continue to exist. The staff of alternative cultivation enterprises are afraid of entering the area, which also causes huge losses to the enterprises. For example, Zhengkang Nanhua Nansan Sugar Co., Ltd called back its 33 permanent employees, leading to the halt of sugar cane management for four months. As a result, the production reduced from the original plan of 300,000 tons to 265,500 tons. According to the current sugarcane market price, it lost an income of 19.3 million Chinese Yuan[2]. Moreover, the company couldn't complete the assigned quota of products selling back and exporting fertilizer, which affects the company's quota in 2010.

2. Impact of Sustained Tension on Alternative Cultivation

(a) Impact on Alternative Cultivation in Other Ceasefire Group Areas

After the Kokang events, the tense situation in the Wa State, the eastern Shan State and the No. 2 special region of Kachin state

---

[1] Data was provided by the Chinese enterprises in northern Myanmar
[2] Data was provided by the Chinese enterprises in northern My anmar.

persists. To avoid property damage and casualty, most companies withdrew their workers and even shipped valuable equipment back to China. The operation of alternative cultivation in these three special regions has once stalled. For their first three years after planting, the rubber and tea need personnel management to ensure a high survival rate. Thus, the evacuation of Chinese technical personnel will have substantial influence on the growth of rubber and tea.

The Liliang Biological Products Co., Ltd of Yunnan, the largest alternative cultivation enterprise in the No. 4 special region of eastern Shan State, shipped back the materials for 2009 and 2010 in Sele Sugar Refinery. The company also transported 1,400 tons sugar products from Myanmar to China before the tariff quota issued. While the quota has been issued, the company has no sugar to sell back. The company lost hundreds of million Yuan due to this alone and its sugar import quota in 2010 also has been affected.

Meanwhile, the operational costs of alternative enterprises also increased significantly due to the tension in northern Myanmar. Although Ying Yi Firm of Ruili Economic Development Zone is located in Myanmar government controlled area, it is difficult for the company to find workers after the Kokang event. The daily wage doubled from 30 Chinese Yuan to 60 Chinese Yuan, while the transport costs increased from 100 Yuan per ton to 150 Yuan per ton.

(b) Decreasing of Annual Planting Acreage

At present, all the 118 Chinese enterprises in northern Myanmar carry out alternative cultivation according to the No. 22 Document issued by the Sate Council in April 2006, and the "Cooperation Agreement on the Prohibition of Illegal Trafficking, Abuse of Narcotic and Psychotropic Drugs between PRC and the Union of Myanmar". Due to the Kokang event and the persisting tension in northern Myanmar, Chinese companies think the risk is too high to continue operating alternative cultivation. Few companies expanded their investment since the Kokang event while most of them would like to wait until northern Myanmar is back in peace.

(c) Challenge Facing the Legal Status of Alternative Enterprises and Projects

Up until September 2009, 118 companies in the 8 prefectures of Yunnan engaged in alternative cultivation in northern Myanmar. Among them, 89 companies operate cultivation in ceasefire group controlled area, such as the No.1, No. 2, and No. 4 Special Regions in Shan State, and No. 1, No. 2 Special Regions in Kachin State while 30 firms are in the central government controlled zones. The total investment in northern Myanmar is about 583 million Chinese Yuan, forming an asset of nearly 1.2 billion Chinese Yuan. In addition to the investment in the No. 1 Special Region, 50 enterprises invested 264 million Chinese Yuan in Wa (the No. 2 Special Region of Northern Shan State); 18 enterprises invested 57 million Chinese Yuan in the No. 4 Special Region of Eastern Shan State; 49 enterprises invested 194 million Chinese Yuan in Kachin State and the central government controlled areas. Some companies carry out alternative cultivation in two Special Regions at the same time.

The majority of alternative projects are in ceasefire group controlled areas. The contracts were signed with Special Region governments or local enterprises. Due to various reasons, those projects were neither reported to Myanmar central government nor approved by the Foreign Investment Committee of Myanmar. Once the central government controls all the areas of the ceasefire groups, the Chinese enterprises will suffer huge economic losses if their contracts are not accepted by Myanmar's central government. Among all the 118 enterprises, only Jin Chen Investment Co., Ltd has been insured by the Export Credit Insurance Company of China.

If the Myanmar central government transformed all the ceasefire groups successfully, it may recognize the alternative enterprises as legitimate. But it will be a long and complex process for the specific certification. It also cannot rule out that the central government will reduce the land lease area and term, set new barriers and add new taxes on the companies.

3. Impact on Sino-Myanmar Anti-Drug Cooperation and the Drug Situation in Northern Myanmar

(a) Impact on Sino-Myanmar Anti-drug Cooperation

The international anti-drug cooperation of Myanmar has been stalled due to the Kokang event. Myanmar did not send representatives to several recent international conferences on narcotics, such as the 33rd Asian-Pacific Meeting of Heads for anti-Drug Enforcement and the Tripartite Talks on Remote Monitoring of Opium Poppy. Thus the anti-drug cooperation between China and Myanmar was affected. Moreover, Myanmar has not clarified how it deals with the three poppy cultivation area coordinates presented by China.

(b) Worsening of Drug Situation in Northern Myanmar

The result of remote measurements of Chinese department shows that there were 338,900 Mu poppy in northern Myanmar in 2008, 59,900 more than the year before. The opium poppy cultivation area was nearly 40,000 Mu in the No. 1 and No. 2 Special Regions of Kachin State, where the government has announced the implementation of forbidding the planting of opium poppy. There is also a large area of poppy cultivation in Myanmar government controlled areas like Taunggyi, Tangyan, Lashio, Namkham, Mantong. It is much more obvious in the transition area between Myanmar central government and No. 1 and No. 2 Special Regions of Kachin State and the Myanmar side along the Tengchong-Myitkyina road.

In order to respond to possible attacks and enhance bargaining power with the military government, the UWSA, the Kachin Independence Army and other major ceasefire groups are intensifying their military operations, such as recruiting, veterans recall, purchasing weapons, food and other war materials. To meet the huge military spending, the ceasefire groups may return to drug trafficking or even organize poppy cultivation for the necessary special funds. In short, the drugs will be the only choice for the ceasefire groups to get finance as gambling and tourism are not available, the timber and minerals are gradually running out in the Special Regions and the new pillar industries(such as rubber) are not formed yet. In addition, drug traffickers can take advantage of the instability in northern Myanmar. In fact, the poppy cultivation in Myanmar's northern region has increased to 364,500 Mu by the end of 2009, and more than 42,0000 in 2010.

Once the war breaks out again in northern Myanmar, the ceasefire groups will be decentralized in order to survive and those armed men are likely to expand poppy cultivation and drug trafficking. In the absence of government management or under the "weak government" control, new drug cartels may appear and former poppy cultivation farmers will return to poppy cultivation for making a living. In short, a large-scale war in northern Myanmar may destroy China's efforts made for alternative cultivation for the past 20 years and reverse the drug situation in northern Myanmar.

4. Potential Impact on the Construction and Operation of Sino-Myanmar Oil and Gas Pipeline

The construction and operation of Sino-Myanmar oil and gas pipeline might be affected by the instability, although the planning routes of the pipeline don't cross through the controlled areas of the big ceasefire groups. If the Myanmar government uses force to resolve the problem of ceasefire groups, the progress of the alternative cultivation projects will be affected. The defeated ceasefire groups might try to destroy the pipeline to abreact their anger. Moreover, there are a number of opposition voices against Sino-Myanmar pipeline in Myanmar. For instance, Shwe Gas Movement and Burmese Muslim Association attempts to combine with another 115 civil social organizations from 20 countries and present protest letters to Chinese Ambassadors in India, Bangladesh, Thailand, South Korea and Japan, in order to stop the construction of the pipeline. Meanwhile, online signature campaign was organized to invite international NGOs and anti-Myanmar government organizations to take part in the global action of "No Blood for Gas" on October 28th, 2009. This is also known as "people all over the world against the Sino-Myanmar oil and gas pipeline project".

In addition, members of the ceasefire groups are using the opportunity to incite national sentiment. When Peng Dashun, son of Peng Jiasheng, was giving an interview with Phoenix TV, he called on the Chinese government not to sit and see the ceasefire groups bullied by the Myanmar military government, saying that "do not let the black oil overtake the red blood of Chinese descendants". Therefore, once the central government attacks UWSA or the Kachin Independence Army, the construction of the pipeline may be forced to shut down and if the ceasefire groups cannot be eliminated completely, they are likely to shift their anger to China and damage the pipeline.

5. Impacts on Other Aspects

(a) Impact on Chinese Enterprises' Other Investment in Northern Myanmar

Due to the tension in northern Myanmar and the central government's unswerving will to solve the ceasefire groups problem, the legitimate rights and interests of other Chinese enterprises will inevitably be affected. With the tension intensified, the KIA needs more finance. Villagers in Dan Pei, a Kachin village in the upstream of Irrawaddy River at the junction of Mali Hka River and N'mai Hka River, submitted a petition to the northern Myanmar military commander against China's construction of two dams there on October 9th, 2009. On October 28th 2009, "Kachin Development Network Organization" sent an open letter to "Power Investment Corporation of China", asking the company to stop construction of hydropower projects in Kachin and withdraw investments from Myanmar. They said the building of dam causes ecological damage, forces people to relocate, brings about more flood and earthquakes.

(b) Threat to Chinese citizens and overseas Chinese in Myanmar

With the deepening economic and trade cooperation between China and Myanmar, the number of Chinese citizens in Myanmar grows year by year. According to Professor Zhuang Guotu, the most famous expert on overseas Chinese studies, there are as many as 1 to 1.1million immigrants from China to Myanmar since 1988. Most of the immigrants are traders, management and technical personnel, labors for logging, mining and constructions and farmers, of whom a considerable portion has no fixed location and a higher proportion is undocumented immigrants. The statistics from the Chinese Embassy in Myanmar shows the Chinese citizens and overseas Chinese in Myanmar are nearly 2.3 million while some foreign data is up to 3 million. Once another war breaks out in northern Myanmar, the lives and properties of overseas Chinese will be threatened. If this is mishandled, an anti-China ideological trend and movement might appear.

6. Impact on China's Public Health Security[3]

The Sino-Myanmar borders are more than 2200 km. Every year, millions of people cross the border from both sides to engage in trade, services, logging, mining and agriculture among other things. They have made a tremendous contribution to the economic development of Greater Mekong Sub-region (GMS).

The region has subtropical rainforest climate, which is suitable for the breeding of disease vectors. Far away from the central government, the borders areas have limited investment for infectious diseases prevention. The ability of preventing and controlling infectious diseases is very weak in the Sino-Myanmar border areas due to lack of funds and policy supports. For a long period, the border of Yunnan is under the state of passive anti-infectious diseases. In the Myanmar side, most of the border regions have weak health system. There is no professional department responsible for communicable disease prevention. The relevant data is also lacking. Sino-Myanmar border regions have a very high rate outbreak of epidemics such as malaria, tuberculosis, measles, cholera, typhoid, dengue fever, meningitis, encephalitis and diarrhea.

The most serious challenge facing Yunnan, China's southwest gate, is the cross-border spread of infectious diseases. According to the statistics from Disease Control Department of Yunnan, the proportion of foreign imported infectious diseases has increased year by year. In some cases, its proportion is as high as 75%.

---

[3] The materials in this par agraph are provided by Mr. Wang Bangyuan, China/Myanmar Programme Office, Health Unlimited Organization.

Most of Sino-Myanmar borders on the Myanmar side are controlled by ceasefire groups. Those Special Regions are extremely poor ethnic minority areas, most of which are about 50-100 km from the border of Yunnan. Those regions lack health investment due to political instability. The present medical service is very backward. There are five Special Regions and one militia controlled area between Gongshan of Nujiang County and Mengla of Xishuangbanna, with a population of about 700,000. Only four hospitals exist in the six regions. People lack medical treatment as well as food. The local governments are unable to response to these needs while the central government offers little investment. Each region has different infectious disease outbreak rates. Major threats for Yunnan come from dengue fever, diphtheria, cholera, typhoid, meningitis, AIDS, tuberculosis and malaria. This situation has direct impact on the infectious disease prevention targets of Yunnan and China as a whole. In 2009, an outbreak of measles in the second Special Region of Northern Shan State, which is a few kilometers away from Pu'er of Yunnan, caused 64 deaths of children under 7 years old. The No. 2 Special Region of Kachin State is only 10 meters away from Yingjiang, Dehong autonomous Prefecture. An HIV survey was carried out among 10,879 people from July 2007 to June 2009. The result shows that 1,601 people are positive for HIV. The infection rate among those injecting drug users is 68% while 12.7% for general population, 21.9% for pregnant women, 10% for sex workers. Among them, a considerable part is Chinese. Another survey carried out by Health Unlimited (HU) in the No. 1 Special Region of Kachin State in February 2009 showed that among the local military personnel AIDS infection rate is 20% while the infection rate in its three port areas of Kanpaiktee, Panwa and Phimaw is 11%. From June to December 2008, 2,735 people were confirmed with malaria, of who 563 seriously ill and 26 died. Most of those people, including a large number of Chinese, frequently cross the Sino-Myanmar border. That is one reason why the cases of malaria are so many in Tengchong, a county located in the high altitude and cold area across from those three ports of Myanmar.

The annual flow of people the along Sino-Myanmar border is about 1 million. A large number of Chinese technology and engineering staff will live in Myanmar's infectious disease areas for alternative cultivation and hydropower projects. At the same time, lot of Myanmarese will also enter China for making a living. They play an important role in ensuring the development and stability of Sino-Myanmar border. However, the spread of diseases has no border. China's public health security is facing a challenge from the high prevalence of infectious diseases in Myanmar. The Chinese government has to take measures to deal with this problem.

Conclusion

In summation, the confrontation between Myanmar military government and ceasefire groups will be continue for several years. It has threatened the security and stability of China's border, the alternative cultivation and Sino-Myanmar cooperation projects. It may lead to the prevalence of infectious diseases along the Sino-Myanmar border as well. In response the Chinese government has adopted a series of measures to reduce the harm from the conflicts in northern Myanmar.

INDIA'S MYANMAR POLICY: RATIONAL CHANGE

Bibhu Prasad Routray

Myanmar's military ruler Senior General Than Shwe undertook a five day goodwill visit to India in July 2010. The General's itinerary included official business in New Delhi as well as visit to Buddhist shrines of Bodh Gaya and Saranath. Predictably, the visit by the 77 year old military leader came under much criticism from the Myamarese pro-democracy forums who took objection to India welcoming the military ruler and called the Indian move 'shameless'. *Irrawady*, the United States based pro-democracy advocacy forum commented in its August 2010 editorial, "India's red-carpet welcome of Than Shwe strongly indicates that no matter how egregiously his military regime manipulates the process to ensure an outcome and future government in its favor, New Delhi is likely to honor the result of Burma's election."[1] The understandable criticism of this hopelessly marginalized and outnumbered group of pro-democracy activists notwithstanding, Than Swe's visit marked the continuation of India's new Myanmar policy which has come out of the grove of idealism and is rooting itself deep in realpolitik.

The Criticality of Myanmar

Myanmar's criticality for India lies primarily in its geographical location. Both countries share a 1,400 kilometre-long land border. Four of India's north-eastern states, Arunachal Pradesh, Nagaland, Manipur and Mizoram, lie north to south along this border. India also shares the strategic waters of the Bay of Bengal, including in the area of the

---

[1] "New Delhi's Shame", Editorial, *Irrawaddy*, 18, no .8, August 2010, ht tp:// www.irrawaddy.org/article.php? art_id=19194, Accessed 29 A ugust 2010

strategically important Andaman and Nicobar islands where the two closest Indian and Myanmarese islands are barely 30 kilometres apart. Myanmarese ports provide India the shortest approach route to several of India's north-eastern states. Since 1997, when Myanmar became a member of the Association of South East Asian Nations (ASEAN), it also provides India with a welcome geographical contiguity with a politically significant and economically dynamic Asia-Pacific region. Being a close neighbour of China, Myanmar also provides India a transit route from eastern India to southern China.

The Era of Idealism

It would appear strange that in spite of such criticality, Myanmar assumed extremely low priority in Indian foreign policy, even while both India and Burma were close allies in the non-alignment movement in the 1950s and several years preceding that. On the day of Burma's independence on January 4, 1948 Prime Minister Jawaharlal Nehru had said, "As in the past, so in the future, the people of India will stand shoulder to shoulder with the people of Burma, and whether we have to share good fortune or ill fortune, we shall share it together. This is a great and solemn day not only for Burma, but for India, and for the whole of Asia."[2]

The 1962 coup in Burma brought about a complete disruption in this not so thriving bilateral relationship. The military junta fell out with India's favour immediately after the coup which catapulted General Ne Win to power. Ne Win's isolationist 'Burmese Road to Socialism' policy that remained in vogue between 1962 and 1988, included ideals such as the nationalization of industries, repression of minorities, and a police state. These included a severe isolationism, expulsion of foreigners, discouragement of tourists and closing off of the economy. Through out the 1960s and 70s, a large number of ethnic Indians were expelled from Burma. As a result, ethnic Indians who formed the backbone of Burmese government and economy, during the British rule serving as soldiers, civil servants, merchants and moneylenders, were reduced to a negligible minority. According to an estimate, on the

---

[2] Thin Thin Aung & Soe Myint, "India-Burma Relations", http://www.idea.int/asia_pacific/ burma/upload/chap4.pdf

morning of Burmese independence on January 4, 1948 from the British, there were some 300,000 – 400,000 Indians living in independent Burma.[3] According to the spokesman of the Burma Displaced Persons Association, over 12,000 Indian concerns with assets worth Rupees 15 crores were affected. Authors detail the plight of the Indians affected by this nationalistic drive in Burma. "Many Indians were deprived of their means of livelihood. No compensation was paid to them at the time of nationalization. Many of them wanted to go back to India. But even this was not possible for them as they could not pay their passage and the Government of Burma did not provide even passage facilities to them. When allowed to leave Burma, they were not allowed to take anything with them. Such were the conditions of the Indians in Burma that the relations between Burma and India were brought nearly to a breaking point."[4]

By 1964, an estimated 100,000 such refugees had reached India from Burma. This policy of expulsion of Indians was certainly not palatable to India. Moreover, Myanmar's supposed neutral stand in 1962 during the Chinese aggression on India was also seen as a pro-Chinese act by New Delhi. Analysts, however, believe that the Ne Win regime had "kept both India and China at arm's length. The Myanmarese elite have always been suspicious of the motives of the two big neighbours."[5] As a result, stagnancy bordering on the margins of cordiality marked the Indo-Myanmar relations in the next two decades. Occasional visits by heads of government continued between both countries. Indian Prime Minister Lal Bahadur Shastri visited Myanmar in 1965. Both countries signed a boundary agreement in 1967. Prime Minister Indira Gandhi paid a visit to Rangoon in 1969. During her visit, General Ne Win made assurances that Myanmar would not allow any anti-Indian activities on its territory by any state or organization. General Ne Win too paid three visits to India in this period.

During Prime Minister Indira Gandhi's tenure, India was largely neutral and disinterested in Myanmar, because a "commitment to

---

[3] Ibid.

[4] Ibid.

[5] John Cherian, "Coming Closer", *Frontline* (Chennai), 27, no.17, August 24-27, 2010.

democratic values" was prioritized ahead of "security concerns" in the Indian foreign policy agenda towards Myanmar.[6] Rajiv Gandhi continued the same policy of idealism, although he did visit Myanmar in 1987 marking the first visit of Myanmar by an Indian Prime Minister in almost 19 years. However, when the State Law and Order Restoration Council (SLORC) assumed power in Myanmar in 1988, India extended its moral support to the pro-democracy movement.[7] The Indian Embassy in Rangoon was active in helping pro-democracy activists. Embassy officials were in touch with opposition groups like the All Burma Federation of Students' Unions (ABFSU), Aung San Suu Kyi and U Nu during the uprising. When the Burmese student activists fled to the Indo-Burmese border, the Indian Embassy in Rangoon provided them financial assistance to go to India. The Government of India opened refugee camps for these students in Mizoram and Manipur. The then External Affairs Minister (later Prime Minister) Narasimha Rao informed a parliamentary panel in 1989 that "strict instructions" had been given not to turn back any genuine Burmese refugees seeking shelter in India.

There were also reports that India provided financial and material support to the Kachin Independence Army (KIA) and the Karen National Union (KNU) that had joined the opposition to the military regime. The KIA leader appreciating India's stand said, "Appreciate the fact that India has unambiguously supported the cause of democracy in Burma.. any committed democratic government in Rangoon is bound to take the country towards a genuine federation, which is our goal. To that extent, we welcome India's stand."[8]

On November 10, 1990, two Myanmarese students hijacked a Thai plane from Bangkok to Calcutta to draw the international attention to the situation back home. After the nine-hour hijacking drama, the two students gave themselves up to the Indian authorities. After three months in the Calcutta jail, both students were released on bail. At that

[6] Yogendra Singh, "India's Myanmar Policy: A Dilemma between Realism and Idealism", IPCS Special Report, no.37, March 2007, http://www.scribd.com/doc/23192043/India-Burma-Relations-Indias-Mayanmar-Policy

[7] Ibid.

[8] Quoted in S D Muni, *India's Foreign Policy: The Democracy Dimension*, (New Delhi: Foundation Books 2009), p.80.

time, 38 Members of Parliament (MPs) signed the letter requesting the then Prime Minister Chandrasekhar to give them political asylum in India. These student leaders were subsequently released from custody and were allowed to live in India as refugees.

The All India Radio (AIR) carried anti-Myanmar broadcasts in Burmese language, souring relations between the two countries even further.[9] In 1991, India acceded to the requests of the Myanmarese government to stop these broadcasts, after the the Burmese government formally complained that Than Than Nu, the daughter of U Nu, was using 'abusive' language attacking the government of Myanmar. India refused to join US, UK, Germany and Japan to formally present a protest to the military regime against not respecting the result of May 1990 elections.[10]

Former Foreign Secretary Late J N Dixit writes, "Indo-Myanmar relations went into a negative spin in 1990, when the military authorities of Myanmar refused to accept the 1990 electoral verdict of the Burmese people in which Aung San Suu Kyi, the leader of the National League for Democracy, emerged victorious."[11] In 1992, India partnered with the US and the Western countries to sponsor a United Nations resolution condemning the Burmese military junta for its violations of human rights in 1992.

Afterwards, the governments led by V.P. Singh and Chandra Sekhar were so enmeshed in domestic political uncertainties and compulsions of electoral politics that they were not able to structure a cohesive foreign policy with a clear sense of priorities. This time around, India's Myanmar policy remained rooted in idealism, not by a policy of conscious decision, but largely by default.

The era of idealism in actual terms meant that India refused to get into business with the de facto rulers in the country- the military junta.

---

[9] Subhash Kapila, "India - Myanmar Strategic Partnership: Indian Imperatives", South Asian Analysis Gr oup, P aper No. 197 , ht tp://www.southasiaanalysis.org/ \papers2\paper197.htm

[10] S D Muni, *India's Foreign Policy: The Democracy Dimension* , (New Delhi: Foundation Books,2009), p.81

[11] J N Dixit, "R oad to Mandala y", *Telegraph*, March 22, 2006.

It also meant, to the detriment and erosion of India's stakes in that country, that India was seen as a promoter of the cause of democracy in Myanmar. While India was ill placed to actually do much to ensure the restoration of democracy, it actively provided support to a large number of pro-democracy supporters in its own territory. India remained one of launch pads from where the pro-democracy student leaders mounted a mobilization campaign through electronic and print media.

Apart from nurturing a false sense of satisfaction of supporting the 'just cause', this prolonged era of idealism fulfilled none of India's strategic requirements from Myanmar. In fact, it pushed the military junta to ignore several of India's concerns. It was also a time when the northeastern insurgents took maximum advantage of the porous Indo-Myanmar border to set up and operate camps inside that country.

Pragmatism Takes Over

There is no unanimity on the specific year when Indian foreign policy turned pragmatic as far Myanmar is concerned. Authors indicate that it was only in 1992 that New Delhi decided to break the deadlock and start with a policy of 'constructive engagement' with the military regime. Former foreign secretary J N Dixit writes, "Preliminary discussions were held between the government of India and the Myanmar foreign office between February and August, 1992. I was a participant in these discussions, which ultimately led to the visit of the vice-foreign minister of Myanmar, U. Baswa, to India between August 11 and 13, 1992. The Myanmar delegation made three points during this visit. Myanmar respects India's commitment to democracy and hopes India would be patient about the revival of democracy in Myanmar. Second, Myanmar acknowledged that security and political concerns existed which are shared by both countries. Myanmar was therefore willing to cooperate with India in taking joint action to meet the security and strategic interests of both countries. The third point which Baswa made was that Myanmar will be willing to increase economic and technological cooperation with India. Another important anxiety of India was the increasing strategic linkages between Myanmar and China."[12]

---

[12] Ibid.

These meetings appeared to have overhauled India's policy towards greater engagement with Myanmar. India took a decision not to interfere in the internal affairs of that country and engage its military regime. 1994-96 saw enhancement of economic cooperation between the two countries.

Deputy Foreign Minister of Myamar U Nyunt Swe visited India in January 1994. During this six-day visit, Swe held a series of meetings and discussed wide-ranging issues to improve the relationship between the two countries. A Memorandum of Understanding (MoU) was signed on January 21, 1994 to increase cooperation between the civilian border authorities of the two countries and to prevent "illegal and insurgent activities". A bilateral agreement was also signed to regularize and promote border trade to be conducted through Moreh in Manipur and Champhai in Mizoram corresponding to Tamu and Hri on the Myanmar side.

However, the relations between both countries were far from being normal. Former Indian ambassador to Myanmar Shyam Saran says that as he took charge in Yangoon in 1997, the ties were still frigid.[13] Authors point out that it was only with the advent of the BJP led NDA government in 1998 that things really began to change. "Jaswant Singh, the then foreign minister, was the architect of realism in seeing Myanmar as a land and sea bridge towards the Asian region. During this phase (which continues to date), there have been military to military dialogues and political rapprochement. The stakes have also included management of the security situation in the North-east. Initiatives like BIMSTEC also took off during this period."[14]

In July 1999, a meeting was held between the Indian and Myanmarese home ministries in New Delhi to identify means to strengthen cooperation on issues like cross border terrorism and stetting up better communication links. India agreed to organise training for anti-narcotics officials. In November 2000, General Maung Aye, second-

---

[13] Shyam Saran, "The Virtue of Pragmatism", *Times of India*, August 7, 2010.

[14] Marie Lall, "India-Myanmar Relations – Geopolitics and Energy in Light of the New Balance of Power in Asia", ISAS Working Paper, January 2, 2008, http://www.isasnus.org/events/workingpapers/28.pdf

most prominent leader of Myanmar's military junta, brought a delegation to New Delhi. The high-powered delegation included Myanmar's deputy prime minister Lt. Gen. Tin Hla, ministers for foreign affairs, finance, commerce, power science and technology and industry. On that occasion, Union home minister L K Advani said that Myanmar was assisting India by destroying camps of Naga militants in their territory. Advani said that the Myanmarese Army had already destroyed five camps belonging to the insurgents earlier that year.[15]

The first decade of the 21st century has witnessed growing strategic engagement between India and Myanmar. According to the Ministry of External Affairs, relations with Myanmar have become truly multi-faceted, 'with cooperation in a range of developmental and other projects in the areas of roads, power, hydro-carbon, oil refinery, transmission lines, telecommunications and information technology.'[16]

In October 2004, General Than Shwe, leading a delegation of eight cabinet ministers for six days talks, visited Delhi and both sides signed an agreement on security, cultural exchanges and hydro-electric power. In March 2006, President Abdul Kalam visited Myanmar to sign an agreement on cooperation in remote-sensing technology and to sign two MoUs on cooperation in the petroleum sector and in Buddhist studies. Besides these three accords of cooperation, India agreed to extend more than US$37 million in loans to Myanmar. Further visits in the course of 2006 focused largely on the troubled border and defence talks and also discus arms sales. On April 23, 2007, an 18-member Myanmar Army delegation, led by Brigadier-General Tin Maung Ohn visited Kolkata, for the 30th biannual liaison meeting of army officials from both countries. Issues relating to cross-border insurgency, arms smuggling and border management were discussed.

There is a clear realization with the shift in India's Myanmar's foreign policy that India's national interest lies in a strong and stable Myanmar that observes strict neutrality between India and China and

---

[15] "Burma Pledges to destroy Naga Rebel Bases", *The Asian Age*, November 18, 2000.

[16] "Why India needs Myanmar on its Side", July 26, 2010, http://news.rediff.com/column/2010/jul/26/why-india-needs-myanmar-on-its-side.htm

cooperates with India in the common fight against the insurgencies raging in the border areas of both the countries.

How easy has the shift been?

For the policy makers in New Delhi, this has been a reluctant ride back from the era of idealism to the realm of realpolitik. The policy shift has been decried by the Myanmarese pro-democracy activists who accuse India of surrendering its ideals. An editorial in pro-democracy forum Irrawaddy commented, "New Delhi wants to play a prominent role in the international community, even lobbying for a permanent seat on the UN Security Council. But as analysts have noted, India's ability to assume an international leadership role depends—or at least should depend—on its ability to have a positive influence on the world. But ..we believe that India's influence on Burma is far from positive."[17]

In addition, many within India decry the strategic shift as unnecessary. For example, an author writes, "under Suu Kyi, the Myanmar people have been emulating the non-violent methods of Gandhiji. We will be betraying the memories of Gandhi, Jawaharlal Nehru and other freedom-fighters if we fail to support a Gandhi-inspired movement in Myanmar and instead support a military Junta, which rules the country in its interests and not in the interests of the people."[18]

He further adds, "the strategic path need not exclude the ethical and vice versa. A mix of ethical and strategic parameters should govern our policy-making. Presently, the ethical parameters hardly have any influence in the policy-making on Myanmar. This position has to change and ethical parameters should play an important role. Suu Kyi and her supporters are trying to prove that Gandhism has still got relevance and can work in restoring to their people their dignity and freedoms. We should not prove them wrong by continuing with our present policies."[19]

---

[17] "New Delhi's Shame", Editorial, *Irrawaddy*,18, no.8, August 2010, ht tp://www.irrawaddy.org/article.php?art_ id=19194

[18] B Raman, "India Should not Prove Gandhi Wrong & Irrelevant in Myanmar", December 9, 2007, ht tp://dts-presentations.blogspot.com/2009/06/india-should-not-prove-gandhi-wrong.html

[19] Ibid.

The notable opponents to India's policy of pragmatism in Myanmar includes Nobel laureate Amartya Sen who spoke against the India's Myanmar policy in the presence of Prime Minister Dr. Manmohan Singh during a public meeting. "I do not agree with your policy on Burma. In a democratic country like India, I can say this to the Prime Minister," he said.[20]

In addition, there are others who prescribe a middle path. For example, an editorial in *The Hindu* said, "There are strong trade-cum-strategic arguments in favour of engaging the military regime in neighbouring Myanmar, but these should not be allowed to cloud or sideline India's principled policy of supporting the democratic forces in that country. Engagement is not endorsement, apologists for the trade-led policy...Let India engage the junta in Myanmar but let us also simultaneously pile pressure on the regime to return the country to the democratic path. Let us reiterate at every possible forum that a ruthless dictatorship in Myanmar is a major destabilizing force in a region strategically important for this country."[21]

Drivers in India's New Myanmar policy

Essentially four considerations have been instrumental in the redrafting of India's Myanmar policy. Each of these drivers has been so vital to India's national interest that they have forced the country to overlook the concerns of the pro-democracy groups in that country.

Growing Presence of China in Myanmar

Authors like Renaud Egreteau argue that India's rapprochement with Myanmar has to be understood in the light of India's worry of being encircled by China. "The fact that the dragon had filled the diplomatic vacuum by intensifying its relationship with Myanmar since the late 1980s was not lost on India."[22]

A former Indian ambassador to Myanmar argues "Over the years, New Delhi has faced two kinds of criticism on its Myanmar policy. Realists argued that its pro-democracy stance had driven Myanmar into

[20] "Amartya Sen ticks off PM on Myanmar policy", *Times of India*, August 4, 2010.

[21] Quoted in Editorial, *The Hindu*, November 18, 1997

[22] "Realism in India-Myanmar Relations", *Financial Express*, September 15, 2003, http://www.financialexpress.com/news/realism-in-indiamyanmar-relations/89520/

"China's lap." Later, they maintained that the engagement was moving too slowly. They failed to recognise that it was never in Myanmar's interest to choose China over India. Now curiously enough, there is talk of Myanmar playing China against India and India against China."[23]

India fears that the Chinese influence in Myanmar was spreading by the day. Although the Chinese government has always denied that it has any military ambitions in Myanmar, the American and Indian agencies have claimed that the Chinese are building monitoring facilities at Myanmarese ports near the strategic Straits of Malacca as part of their so-called "string of pearls" strategy to encircle India.

In 1949, Burma was one of the first countries to recognise the People's Republic of China. But relations between both countries soured in the 1960s following anti-Chinese riots in Rangoon. The military regime under General Ne Win had maintained a policy of equidistance from both India and China. The Myanmarese elite have always been suspicious of the motives of the two big neighbours. But following a crackdown on pro-democracy protesters in 1988, when the West imposed broad sanctions on Myanmar, China stepped into the void, providing aid and weapons and ramping up trade. Northern Myanmar was opened up to Chinese trade in a big way by the mid-1990s.[24]

China is said to have invested more than $1 billion in Myanmar, primarily in the mining sector, and is the Myanmar's fourth largest foreign investor. Bilateral trade grew by more than one-quarter in 2008 to about $2.63 billion. Chinese firms are heavily involved in logging in Myanmar. Myanmar gives China access to the Indian Ocean, not only for imports of oil and gas and exports from landlocked southwestern Chinese provinces, but also potentially for military bases or listening posts.[25] Additionally, Myanmar has been a major recipient of economic assistance over the past decade, generally provided in the form of grants, interest-free loans, concessional loans or debt relief. "Chinese economic assistance and cooperation programs are usually tied to Chinese state-

---

[23] Rajiv Bhatia, "Crafting a Richer India-Myanmar Partnership", *The Hindu*, August 10, 2010.

[24] John Cherian, "Coming Closer", *Frontline* (Chennai), 27, no.17, August 24-27, 2010.

[25] "Five Facts about China-Myanmar Relations", *Reuters*, June 1, 2010, ht tp:// in.reuters.com/article/idINIndia-48959920100601

owned enterprises, and are therefore often indistinguishable from state commercial investments. This makes it impossible to account for the full extent of China's economic assistance and investments in Myanmar. Nor do official figures reflect the reality of the economic relationship between the two countries: Chinese investments are grossly underestimated by Myanmar's official figures and, to a lesser extent, Chinese official figures."[26]

Beginning November 2009, China National Petroleum Corporation (CNPC) has started construction of a large-scale crude oil port in Kyaukpyu, in western Myanmar. The port is part of a larger, multibillion-dollar project designed to carry oil and natural gas across Myanmar and into southern China. When finished, it will enable China to take deliveries of oil from the Middle East and Africa without sending it through the Strait of Malacca, a congested shipping lane that some Chinese leaders fear could be blocked by pirates or foreign powers. A related pipeline will also allow China to unlock large natural-gas reserves off Myanmar's western coast. The project underscores Myanmar's growing commercial ties with China. It is also expected to generate billions of dollars in revenue for Myanmar's military regime, enhancing its ability to fund operations without heeding pleas by Western governments to implement democratic changes.

The Myanmar government, at the end of the 1980s, turned to China to help fulfill its plan of enlarging and modernizing its armed forces. China obliged. And over the years, this close military cooperation with China has been cemented. Currently the largest supplier of weapons to Myanmar, China also provides the Myanmarese army with training in the technical use of weapons and weapon systems. Goods bought from China over the years have included armoured personnel carriers, tanks, fighter aircraft, radar systems, ammunition, surface-to-air missiles and short-range air to-air missile systems. Much of the weaponry, such as an August 2008 batch of 200 military trucks, were observed crossing into Myanmar through Ruili on the China-Myanmar border.[27] When

---

[26] "China's Myanmar Dilemma", International Crisis Group, *Asia Report* No.177, September 14, 2009, http://www.crisisgroup.org/en/regions/asia/north-east-asia/china/177-chinas-myanmar-dilemma.aspx

opposition and ethnic groups have questioned Chinese officials about arms sales, they replied that China only provides major military equipment, not small arms: "the heavy weapons that cannot kill your people".[28]

In recent times, the Myanmarese Army and Navy have received supply of M-11 rocket components, artillery guns, communication equipments, electric lighting and signal equipment and speedboats from China. In fact, the Myanmar navy resembles PLA navy in many respects. China is assisting the Myanmar Air Force in upgrading of its communication set up and also training and generation of new edition of aviation and border maps. China is also assisting in undertaking a maritime survey of its territory. Media reports in late August 2010 indicated that two Chinese warships arrived at Myanmar's Yangon port on a 'friendly visit', marking the first such port call since 1988. An unnamed Chinese diplomat told, "These two navy destroyers arrived at Yangon's Thilawa port on Sunday to promote relations between the two militaries."[29]

Additionally, China for a number of years has acted as a protective shield for Myanmar in the United Nations Security Council by vetoing resolutions against the military junta. In September 2009, China blocked the inclusion of Myanmar on the agenda of UN Security Council.

India's Quest for Energy in Myanmar

India currently ranks as the world's eleventh greatest energy producer, accounting for about 2.4 per cent of the world's total annual energy production, and also as the world's sixth greatest energy consumer, accounting for about 3.3 per cent of the world's total annual energy consumption. Despite its large annual energy production, India is a net energy importer, mostly due to the large imbalance between oil

---

[27] "200 Military Trucks, were Observed Crossing into Myanmar through Ruili", August 27, 2008, http://myamarnews.blogspot.com/2008/08/200-more-military-trucks-delivered-from.html

[28] "China's Myanmar Dilemma", International Crisis Group, *Asia Report* No.177

[29] "Chinese Warships Pay Visit to Myanmar", August 30, 2010, http://www.earthtimes.org/articles/news/341623,pay-visit-myanmar.html

production and consumption. Myanmar's oil and gas reserves are of critical interest to India's future energy requirement. Myanmar has oil reserves of around 600 million barrels and total gas reserves of 88 trillion cubic feet (TCF). Despite protests from the West, Indian companies like the overseas arm of India's Oil and Natural Gas Commission - ONGC Videsh Ltd - and Gas Authority of India Limited (GAIL) and ESSAR etc have made investments in the oil and energy sector of Myanmar. OVL and GAIL together hold 30 per cent stake along with Daewoo 60 per cent and Korea Gas 10 per cent of offshore Block A-1 gas field.

It was during the 2001 visit of the then external affairs minister Jaswant Singh to Myanmar that India started seriously thinking about bringing gas from Myanmar. The February 2003 visit of Myanmarese General U Win Aung to India further boosted this cooperation in the hydrocarbon, power and energy sectors, particularly in the exploration of Myanmar's onshore oil and gas reserves.

However, in spite of the involvement of OVL and GAIL in exploration activities in the offshore A1 and A3 natural gas fields along the Rakhine coast, India vis-à-vis China has suffered a number of setbacks in getting gas from Myanmar. Myanmar in 2008 withdrew India's status as preferential buyer and in stead declared its intent to sell them to China National Petroleum Corporation (CNPC) for 30 years beginning 2013. Starting October 2009, the CNPC started building a crude oil port in Myanmar to cut out the long detour oil cargoes take through the congested and strategically vulnerable Malacca strait. Earlier, in a similar move in December 2005, Myanmar had declined gas supply to the Myanmar-Bangladesh-India pipeline. Instead, it had signed an agreement with Hong Kong-listed Petrochina, under which Myanmar's Ministry of Energy agreed to sell 6.5 TCF from A-1 block (Rakhine coastline) reserve through an overland pipeline to Kunming (China) for 30 years.[30] This had made the proposed tri-nation Myanmar-Bangladesh-India pipeline project redundant. However, India has little option but to stay engaged in Myanmar.

---

[30] Anand Kumar, "Myanmar-Petrochina Agreement: A Setback to India's Quest for Energy Security', *South Asia Analysis Group* , Paper no. 1681, January 19, 2006, http://www.southasiaanalysis.org/%5Cpapers17%5Cpaper1681.html

Insurgency in the Northeast:

For decades, majority of the seven states in India's northeastern region, have witnessed emergence and growth of insurgency movements, with demands ranging from independence, autonomy, tribal rights etc. Estimates indicate that the number of such groups could be as high as 130. While a number of these insurgencies have ended, many still continue impacting on the security situation of the region. They have constantly challenged India's nation building project in this part of the country and have remained hurdles in the processes of development. The remoteness of the northeastern region and years of neglect and apathy by the central government in New Delhi have led to a feeling of alienation in the psyche of the people of this region. This constantly feeds these armed groups.

In the last two decades, policy of the Indian government has gone through a process of transformation. Huge amount of developmental funds have been made available for the region. However, the insurgency movements continue to act as spoilers resulting in the continuation of the cycle of underdevelopment and alienation.

Myanmar, contiguous to Mizoram, where insurgency ended in the 1980s and also to Nagaland and Manipur where insurgency is still continuing, has served these armed groups in a variety ways. Since the beginning of these armed insurrections, ethnic ties and tribal linkages between the people on either side of the border, has facilitated their movements and finding of safe haven and camps in those areas. Narratives on the insurgency movements, both by Indian as well as foreign scholars, detail such activities.

There are several accounts detailing the journeys undertaken by the Mizo, Naga and Manipuri rebels, starting 1960s to China through Myanmar seeking assistance and arms. Some groups travel through the Nepal-China border as well. There also have been instances when groups like the PLA in Manipur had their cadres trained in China. Between 1966, when the first 'Naga Army' batch reached China for training through Myanmarese territory to 1980, China had trained several batches of Naga and Mizo rebels and a few dozen Manipuri rebel leaders.[31] Such official Chinese support to these rebels is believed to have ended. However, China continues to be a place for procurement of weapons on payment by the many of these rebels.

Majority of these armed groups established their camps in Myanmar in the mid 1970s. These facilities principally served three purposes. (a) as a shelter after East Pakistan (Bangladesh) was lost as a safe base area, (b) a crucial link zone through which rebels could go to China for training and weapons and (c) a safe training and regrouping zone. Much of these purposes still remain valid, even while changes have occurred in the nature and kind of support these groups generate in foreign locations.

At the instance of India, Myanmar has conducted on and off military operations against the northeastern rebels since the 1980s. Writers like Bertil Lintner in his seminal book 'Land of Jade' details first hand experience of a military raid on a Naga rebel camp. However, once the soldiers have gone back from these areas, the rebels have reclaimed their facilities.

There also have been occasions when the Myanmarese have used the rebels as a bargaining chip against India. The Operation Golden Bird conducted jointly by the Myanmarese and Indian army in April-May 1995 had netted more than 200 rebels belonging to several Assam, Nagaland and Manipur groups. But suddenly the Myanmarese pulled out of the joint operation, allowing the trapped rebel column to escape. Analysts link this with India's 1993 decision to award Aung San Syu Kyi with the Jawaharlal Nehru Peace Prize. Again in November 2001, the Myanmarese army raided four Manipuri rebel bases, rounded up 192 rebels and seized more than 1600 weapons. Surprisingly, all these rebels including the chief of UNLF chief Rajkumar Meghen were released.

Indian Army sources believe that currently there are approximately 40 to 50 camps of the Northeast-based insurgent groups in Myanmar. Out of these 25 to 30 are identified as bigger camps or of established

---

[31] Subir Bhaumik, "Guns, Drugs and Rebels", *Seminar* (New Delhi), no. 550, June 2005, http://www.india-seminar.com/2005/550/550%20subir%20bhaumik. htm#top

nature.[32] The long presence of the insurgents in Myanmar has provided them with a vital sense of security. In the event of any long-term military operation in states like Manipur, the insurgents have the option of moving into their safe bases in Myanmar. As the counter-insurgency operations have intensified in Manipur, these bases have served as the training centres for the fresh recruits. Moreover, it is in these camps that the insurgents amass weapons procured from a variety of sources in Southeast Asia and possibly China.

Of late, reports indicating a tactical level of understanding between the insurgents and the lower rung cadres of the Myanmarese military have emerged. These reports, based on intelligence inputs point at the bonhomie between the insurgents and the military personnel, largely sustained by regular gifts and money. In return, the insurgents are warned against impending operations by the forces thereby allowing them to vacate the camps long before the men in uniform arrive. In return for regular protection money, certain army officers are providing logistic support to these insurgents, including medical facilities. They are also assisted to get contract jobs and carry out their business activities.

Reports also indicate that the Myanmarese army is also using the services of the insurgents to keep track and also carry out occasional attacks on Myanmarese rebels some of whom have found refuse on the Indian side.

Southeast Asia has long served as the arms bazaar for the northeastern insurgents. Arms into the northeast have either come through Myanmar or through Bangladesh. However, there are indications that post a series of seizures in Chttagong and other parts of Bangladesh, Myanmar has emerged as the sole route for weapons into the northeast. Camps in Myanmar allow these rebels to stockpile these weapons and transfer them at appropriate time into India. The Naga rebels have traded with the surplus weapons by selling them to the smaller outfits in the northeast.

---

[32] Oken Jeet Sandham, "Myanmar Based Militant Activities on Rise on Indian Side", April 26, 2010, http://www.e-pao.net/GP.asp?src=11..260410.apr10

The northeastern insurgents have also indulged in smuggling of drugs from Myanmar. While outfits like the UNLF in Manipur have an anti-substance abuse policy, groups like the NSCN have freely indulged in such trade. The easy availability of such drugs have made youth in states like Manipur, Mizoram and Nagaland vulnerable to a host of problems including AIDS. It is estimated that Manipur's share in the estimated 3.5 million AIDS/ HIV cases in India is over 11 percent. The Myanmarese drug lords are also encouraging tribal farmers, and in some cases the insurgents to plant poppy. Unless these new plantations are destroyed and gainful agricultural alternatives provided to the farmers, the India-Myanmar border will soon be dotted with poppy fields feeding the processing plants in western Myanmar.

Past instances of Myanmarese decision to loosen the stranglehold on the insurgents notwithstanding, there are also reasons to believe that the Myanmarese authorities lack capacity to carry out sustained operations against these insurgents. Moreover, there seems to be no inherent interest on their part to hold on to these areas once the insurgents are dislodged. This has been articulated to the Indian authorities and New Delhi consequently is initiated measures to enhance the counter-terrorism capacities of the Myanmarese army, just not in terms of equipping them with sophisticated weapons and other communication devices, but also improving infrastructure along the border areas.

In order to secure Myanmarese cooperation and strengthen its control over territories where the northeastern rebels are camping, India has supplied military hardware to that country. On 21 May 2010, responding to the Myanmarese demands for road building machinery, Indian Army handed over heavy machineries and other necessary spare parts to their Myanmarese counterparts at Moreh.[33] India hopes that the building of roads and other constructions in the remote and inaccessible areas would augment the control of the army over those areas. On 5 & 6 May 2010 a joint Indo Myanmar mega medical, dental & veterinary camp was conducted jointly by officials of Myanmar and India along Indo-Myanmar border. Approximately 2000 locals on both

---

[33] Asem Lalit, "Road Equipment given to Myanmar", *Imphal Free Press*, May 22, 2010.

sides of the border benefited from the services of the general physicians, specialist doctors, dentist and veterinary doctors of the Indian Army and Assam Rifles as well as Medical staff from Myanmar.[34]

Look East Policy

Renaud Egreteau reasons that this shift was part of India's Look East Policy (LEP), which in line with the economic reforms hoped for a rapprochement with the economically successful South East Asian states.[35] The LEP, launched under the P V Narasimha Rao-led Congress Government through which the wished to connect its economy with the flourishing economy of the neighbouring Southeast Asia necessitated that India mends its fences with Myanmar. The broad objectives of the LEP during the 1990s were three-fold: to institutionalise linkages with ASEAN and its affiliates; to strengthen bilateral relationships with member states of ASEAN; and to carve a suitable place for itself to prevent Southeast Asia falling under the influence of any one major power.[36]

The LEP continued to receive serious attention during the NDA regime as well. The then Foreign Minister Jaswant Singh made two visits to Myanmar in 2001 and 2002: the first visit to inaugurate the India-Myanmar Friendship Road, and the second to start talks on building the ambitious Trans-Asia highway project. Myanmar was crucial to the Indian government in view of the BIMST-EC (Bangladesh, India, Myanmar, Sri Lanka and Thailand Economic Cooperation) and the Kunming Initiative, an effort involving India, China, Myanmar and Bangladesh.

In addition, bilateral trade between the two countries has expanded considerably in the past few years & is almost at USD 1 billion dollars now. India imports mostly agricultural items (beans, pulses, and forest based products) & exports primary and semi finished steel and

---

[34] "Indo Myanmar Mega Medical And Faternization Dental & Vet. Camp", *Imphal Free Press*, May 7, 2010.

[35] Marie Lal l, "Indo-Myanmar Relations in the Er a of Pipel ine Diplomacy", *Contemporary Southeast Asia*, 28, no.3, (2006):.424-46.

[36] G V C Naidu, *"Wither the Look East Policy: India and Southeast Asia,"* Strategic Analysis, 28, no.2 (Apri l-June 2004), p .332.

pharmaceuticals. There is also marginal trade at the border trading post at Tamu – Moreh & Rhi-Zowkhatar. In fact, the first Border Trade Agreement between India and Myanmar was signed in January 1994. As per the agreement, border trade was to be conducted through Moreh in Manipur and Tamu in Myanmar and Champhai in Mizoram and Hri on the Myanmar side. Trade started officially on April 12, 1995. Several bottlenecks, however, continue to mar any effective border trade at these points till date.

Export of Democracy

Guided by these strategic objectives, India has decided to refrain from the task of working towards establishing democracy in its neighbourhood. While many would interpret this step to be a conscious decision, it is also based on the realisation that public pressure on the military junta is unlikely to yield results. The years' of sanctions by the United States and the European Union is largely perceived to have failed in goading the Myanmarese junta to accommodate the pro-democracy camp. On the other hand, it has made the de facto rulers of that country more rigid and un-amenable to change. As former Foreign Secretary Shyam Saran, who also served as India's ambassador to Myanmar points out, "The enduring hostility that the regime has faced from the US and its western allies has also engendered a sense of siege and sometimes even paranoia among the generals. Suu Kyi has unfortunately become, in their eyes, an instrument in the hands of the West to force a regime change."[37]

In 2006, the then External Affairs Minister Pranab Mukherjee said that India cannot "export democracy" to neighbouring countries and that India had to deal with governments "as they exist".[38] Shyam Saran notes, "As a democracy, India would welcome the establishment of inclusive and broad-based multiparty democracy in Myanmar."[39] However, this desire can not hold India's long term and strategic interests in the country to ransom. As a result, India still urges that Aung Sang

---

[37] Shyam Saran, "The Virtue of Pragmatism", *Times of India*, August 7, 2010.

[38] John Cherian, "Coming Closer".

[39] Shyam Saran, "The Virtue of Pragmatism"

Suu Kyi should be released and allowed to play a constructive political role in the country. But these have taken place only in private parleys with the Myanmarese military rulers.

Current level of Engagement

A certain degree of warmth between India and Myanmar is perceptible. "But over the past decade, India has at least managed to sustain a policy of engagement if not overt friendship with the hardliner military rulers in Myanmar. New Delhi is now moving into a new phase of closer cooperation."[40] Both sides have exchanged high level visits in past few years. These include visits by Vice Senior General Maung Aye, Vice-Chairman of the State Peace and Development Council of the Union of Myanmar, in April 2008 and M. Hamid Ansari, Vice President of India, in February 2009.

In January 2010, both countries held Home Secretary level talks in Nay Pyi Taw. Myanmar assured India of possible support for apprehending insurgent leaders like Paresh Barua and others belonging to a number of northeastern groups like NSCN-IM and separatist groups of Tripura.[41] In April 2010 both countries held joint secretary level talks in Tawang in Arunachal Pradesh. The symbolism of Myanmar attending the Tawang meet was not lost as China disputes the territory as its own.

Senior General Than Shwe's July 2010 India visit, his second visit to the country in six years, resulted in both countries inking five pacts, including one in the field of security and agreed on close cooperation between security forces of the two countries in tackling the pernicious problem of terrorism.[42] The pacts include a treaty on mutual legal assistance in criminal matters, a MoU on Indian grant for small developmental projects, agreement on cooperation in the field of

---

[40] Nitin Gokhale, "India-Myanmar Smoke Peace Pipe in T awang", April 5, 2010, ht tp:// news.rediff.com/column/2010/apr/05/india-takes-myanmar-to-tawang-for-strategic-talks.htm

[41] Rahul Mishra, "Elections in Myanmar", August 19, 2010, http://wwwidsa.in/idsacomments/ ElectionsinMyanmar_rmishra_190810

[42] "India, My anmar Sign on the Dot ted Line, B oost Ties", July 27, 2010, ht tp:// news.rediff.com/report/2010/jul/27/india-myanmar-sign-on-the-dotted-line-boost-ties.htm

science and technology and a MoU on Indian assistance in restoring the Ananda temple in Bagan, a renowned Buddhist shrine and a major tourist site in central Myanmar.

The Ministry of Home Affairs (MHA) sources have indicated that mutual legal assistance agreement will help India "combat transnational organized crimes, trans-border terrorism, drug trafficking, money laundering, counterfeit currency, smuggling of arms and explosives. Under the provisions of the treaty, Indian insurgents caught in Myanmar can be handed over to India."[43] The treaty has enabling provisions that will help both countries expediting criminal investigations, judicial proceedings, gathering evidences and assisting each other during investigations. It would also pave the way for examining witnesses in each other's countries, including in jails. The pact also has a 'cost compensation' clause allowing Myanmar to seek expenses incurred on special investigations carried out by it on India's request.[44]

Both countries also agreed to cooperate in the fields of information, science and technology. India will give $60 million as grant for the construction of a road linking India's north-eastern region to Myanmar and another grant of $10 million to buy agricultural machinery.

India and the Parliamentary Elections in Myanmar

General Than Shwe's India visit in July 2010 coincided with the Obama administration's renewal of sanctions against Myanmar. A day before Than Shwe arrived in India, Philip Crowley, US State Department spokesman urged India "to send a clear message to Burma that it needs to change its course." He said, "Others who have relationships with Burma share a responsibility to communicate directly and forcefully to Burma about its responsibilities, whether they're protecting the region against the risk of proliferation or telling Burma directly that it should

---

[43] Elizabeth Roche, "Myanmar Pact to Help India Contain North-East Militancy", August 1, 2010, http://www.livemint.com/2010/08/01234856/Myanmar-pact-to-help-India-con.html

[44] Jayanth Jacob & Manish Tiw ari, "India, My anmar Pact to Help Curb NE I nsurgents", *Hindustan Times*, July 8, 2010.

more constructively engage its opposition and other ethnic groups within Burma."[45] Subsequently, the Obama administration has decided to support the creation of a UN inquiry into alleged war crimes by Myanmar's military rulers.[46] Such policies of retribution, however, have been challenged by many. David I. Steinberg, a professor of Asian studies at Georgetown University and the author of 'Burma/Myanmar: What Everyone Needs to Know', commented, "imposing additional sanctions on Burma's regime or forming still more commissions will only salve our consciences. Neither will help the Burmese people, persuade the government to loosen its grip on the population, or even assist the United States in meeting its strategic or humanitarian objectives. In fact, such moves would hinder negotiations and relations with a new government that, even if far from a model for governance, would probably give the Burmese more political voice and freedom than they have had in half a century."[47]

The Indian government has, however, stayed away from the US-led condemnation against the military junta for its human rights violations and crackdown on members of the National League for Democracy. At the government level, India, along with China and ASEAN countries, was silent when the rest of the world condemned the Burmese government for blocking Aung San Suu Kyi outside Rangoon and later putting her under house arrest. India was in the minority group of nations that voted against the decision of the International Labour Organisation (ILO) to take action against the regime for failing to curb forced labour in the country. Tint Swe, a member of Myanmar's government-in-exile, subsequently said that such resolutions are ineffective tools against Myanmar's military leadership. "The people

---

[45] Narayan Lakshman, "India should tell Myanmar to change course: U.S.", *Hindu*, July 24, 2010.

[46] "US supports UN Myanmar war crimes inquiry", August 17, 2010, http://www.google.com/hostednews/afp/article/ALeqM5iWDIfK9BB fbaQ99GyO1 mG8 nylbJQ

[47] David I. Steinberg, " Is Burma on the Verge of Transformation? ", *The Washington Post*, August 21, 2010, http://www.washingtonpost.com/wp-dyn/content/article/2010/08/20/AR2010082005021.html

of Burma are not excited by news from the UN. As long as power is in the hands of the military junta, UN bodies will have to go through the annual rituals."[48]

The United States State Department spokesman Philip Crowley on August 13, 2010 said, "Given the oppressive political environment in Burma, there is not a level playing field for these elections. They cannot be inclusive or credible under these circumstances."[49] However, for India the parliamentary elections scheduled to be held on November 7, 2010 in Myanmar are a step forward. The elections, howsoever, imperfect they may be, provide the people of Myanmar an opportunity to elect a new President, two houses of Parliament and 14 regional legislators and governors. The attempt by the military government to establish a "disciplined democracy" under a parliamentary system of government may not herald an ideal situation for pro-democracy activists, but it still is an improvement over the complete absence of democracy in the country. India further feels that through a process of close engagement it can promote leverages with the ruling regime to nudge it gently towards national reconciliation.[50] During the Than Shwe's India visit, New Delhi did not raise the issue of restoration of democracy in Myanmar. As a former Indian ambassador commented, 'Hidden in a 45-para (joint) statement was a small paragraph which reflected India's emphasis on "comprehensively broad-basing the national reconciliation process and democratic changes being introduced in Myanmar."'[51]

A Prudent Policy?

It is early to assess whether India's pragmatic policy in Myanmar would pay off. It is not clear whether India would take a hard stand on

[48] "Useless UN and ILO Rituals bring No Change, Burmese Dissident says", November 24, 2009, http://www.asianews.it/news-en/Useless-UN-and-ILO-rituals-bring-no-change,-Burmese-dissidents-says-16944.html

[49] "Myanmar Polls Cannot be 'Credible': US", August 13, 2010, http://www.google.com/hostednews/afp/article/ALeqM5jUOU0YPTv3 uN1z WKXmYln8sZ7y9Q

[50] Gurmeet Kanwal, "Why India needs Myanmar on its Side", July 26, 2010, http://news.rediff.com/column/2010/jul/26/why-india-needs-myanmar-on-its-side.htm

[51] Rajiv Bhatia, "Crafting a richer India-Myanmar partnership", The Hindu, August 10, 2010.

Myanmar's suspected move to acquire nuclear weapons with the help of North Korea. External Affairs Minister S M Krishna ambiguously stated in the Parliament on August 26, 2010 that "The government is trying to gather information about such peripheral activities. We monitor such activities closely as we are concerned about security of the country (India)."[52] It is also not clear whether India can achieve strategic objectives in Myanmar in terms of fulfilling its energy requirements and pushing that country to act against the northeastern insurgents. However, there seems to be no other choice for India. Being a crusader for democracy and aligning itself with the US camp for pressurizing Myanmar has far less chance of success, than a policy of constructive engagement.

---

[52] "India 'Monitoring' Myanmar", *Straits Times*, August 26, 2010, http://www.straitstimes.com/BreakingNews/Asia/Story/STIStory_571362.html

EXPORTING THREATS, TRANSMITTING INSTABILITY: CONFLICT IN MYANMAR AND ITS EFFECTS ON THAILAND

Pavin Chachavalpongpun

Thailand shares a 2,400 kilometre border with Myanmar, of which only about 61 kilometres have been demarcated.[1] The long strip of unsettled border has over the years led to several undesired consequences, disturbed bilateral relations between Myanmar and Thailand and also affected the security situation on the Thai side.[2] On the surface, it is convenient for Thailand to accuse the Myanmar government of "exporting threats" and "transmitting instability" across the border, simply because of the continued political conflicts between the military junta and the ethnic minorities. At a deeper level however, the nature of Thai policy toward Myanmar and the security imperatives of Thailand seemed to have willingly invited the troubles generated by the political unrest in Myanmar. In other words, Bangkok's long-held buffer policy vis-à-vis Yangon represents one of the main reasons why Thailand has been unable to ward off such negative impacts originating from Myanmar. Thailand has long assisted a number of ethnic minorities living along the Thai-Myanmar border in their rebellion against the central government, and at the same time treated them as a buffer against the perceived Myanmar threat, even though such a threat has never been

---

[1] Supalak Ganjanakhundee, "Government Pushing Burma on Settling Border Issues", *The Nation*, 2 July 2010.

[2] Sai Myo Win, *Shan: The Thai-Burma Border Conflict and Shan Resistance* (Unrepresented Nations and Peoples Organisation, 28 February 2010), <http://www.unpo.org/content/view/255/236/> (accessed 21 May 2010). Sai Myo Win is General Secretary of the Shan Democratic Union (SDU), an umbrella organisation of all Shan exiles.

clearly defined. The buffer policy has brought with it several skirmishes, the inflow of refugees, the smuggling of drugs and arms, as well as the spread of infectious diseases. This study argues that the way Thailand has conducted its relations with Myanmar justifies the existence of transnational effects.

Two contemporary case studies are discussed here in order to support the argument. First, as the next election in Myanmar is approaching, the military regime seems to adopt a strategy that requires ethnic groups to take part in the elections. Their support would substantiate its claim that the whole country is behind the election. Resistant groups will therefore be suppressed if they refuse to participate in the election and this could provoke a rise in refugee numbers into Thailand, especially into the buffer zone. Second, Thailand has continued to depend heavily on Myanmar's energy in order to feed its growing industrialisation. In the process, Thailand has invested in several projects involving the building of pipelines and dams in Myanmar. Most of these projects instigate forced relocation of those who had lived in the planned construction areas, thus sparking conflicts between the government and the local residents. Some have relocated in Thailand as illegal migrants in search of a new livelihood. These two cases reaffirm the inseparable link between Thai policies towards Myanmar and the inevitability of the spill-over effects into Thailand as a result of the implementation of its own policies.

The Infamous Buffer Zone

During the Cold War period, Thailand resorted to a policy of buffer state which supported the anti-Rangoon, anti-communist ethnic minorities along the border with Burma.[3] The Thai authorities perceived that these minorities represented bulwarks for Thailand against any foreseeable foreign threats that might appear from Burma and beyond in the form of physical and ideological intrusions.[4] Painting Burma as a security

---

[3] The chapter uses the names Burma and Rangoon in all pre-1989 events. The names of the country and capital were official ly changed in 1989 to My anmar and Y angon respectively. In 2005, the My anmar gov ernment moved the capital to Naypyida w, approximately 200 miles north of the old capi tal Yangon.

[4] Despite the fact that the ethnic insurgents were de facto allies of the Burmese Communist Party (BCP), the Thai government ensured that the military and financial assistance

threat became one of the tactics employed by successive despotic regimes in Thailand. And Burma was a perfect enemy since it destroyed the old kingdom of Ayutthaya in 1767. Thai military elites like Field Marshal Phibun Songkhram (serving as Prime Minister from 1938-1944 and 1948-1957) were content to perpetuate such image of an inimical Burma in order to justify the existence of their authoritarian regime. Therefore, instead of trying to revive friendly ties with Burma and helping to conclude its persistent civil wars, leaders in the Thai military further exacerbated the situation while assisting ethnic rebels to fight against the Rangoon regime through the provision of financial assistance and arms.[5] Thailand went along with the American plan to supply arms and funds to potential ethnic rebels through its northern territory in an attempt to contain communism in Burma.[6] The Burmese government protested to Thailand about the flow of weapons and complained that these rebel groups were exchanging some valuable natural resources from the areas of their occupancy for weapons from the Thai side.[7]

The buffer zone set in place by the Thai leaders at the end of the 1940s has been in operation, in an on-and-off fashion, up to the present

---

offered to the ethnic groups would keep the BCP "inactive" in the areas under the Thai occupation. For details see, Charles B. Smith Jr., *The Burmese Communist Party in the 1980s* (Singapore: Institute of Southeast Asian Studies, 1984).

[5] Juajan Wongpolganan, "Thai-Burma Border Politics and the Marginal People: the Mons in their Sanctuary in K anchanaburi's Westernmost District of Sangkhlaburi" , unpublished paper. A t <http://www .tu.ac.th/resource/publish/ interview/tu_doc/ 5%5B1%5D%5B1%5D.Thai-Burma.pdf> (accessed 21 May 2010). Also see, Peter Carey,*Burma: The Challenge of Change in a Divided S   ociety*, (Oxf ord: St. Anthon y, 1997), p. 140.

[6] President Truman positioned Thailand as a gateway for activities in Burma. CAT (Civil Air Transportation Company) aircraft ferried to Chiang Mai and Chiang R ai in northwestern Thailand loads of ammunition and small arms from stockpiles of World War II weapons maintained by the CIA on Okinawa. The munitions were then turned over to the Thai border police who arranged deliveries to Li Mi (Kuomintang leader in Burma). US Army engineers were also sent to Monghsat via Thailand to upgrade the tiny airfield into a base capable of handing large cargo airlift. Further discussions on Thailand's aid to the KMT see, John W. Garver, *The Sino-American Alliance* (New York and London: An East Gate Book, 1997), pp.149-150.

[7] Robert H. Taylor, *Foreign and Domestic Consequences of the KMT Intervention in Burma*, (Ithaca: Department of Asian Studies, Cornel l Universi ty, Data P aper No.93, 1973), p.20.

day, except during the governments of Chatichai Choonhavan (1988-1991) and Thaksin Shinawatra (2001-2006), which preferred amicable relations with Myanmar based on their policy of turning battlefield into marketplace. Relations turned particularly frigid during the Chuan Leekpai government (1997-2001) as Thailand resurrected its buffer zone. His Democrat Party adopted a pro-democracy policy toward Myanmar mainly to please its Western allies. Foreign Minister Surin Pitsuwan, now Secretary-General of the Association of Southeast Asian Nations (ASEAN), replaced the policy of constructive engagement vis-à-vis Myanmar with his own initiative, the so-called flexible engagement policy. In contrast with the old policy that aimed primarily at acclimatising Myanmar with the regional reality, the flexible engagement policy opened doors for Thai leaders to voice their concerns over the situation in their neighbouring state that could engender an impact on their country. Myanmar was infuriated and condemned this policy as outright interference in its domestic affairs. Today, as the Democrat Party is leading the government in Thailand, Myanmar has occasionally expressed its suspicion over the continued Thai support for certain activities of the opposition and the ethnic minorities that challenge the power position of the leaders in Naypyidaw. For example, Thailand, as Chair of the ASEAN Standing Committee, in 2009, released a statement criticising the decision of the Myanmar government for the arrest of Aung San Suu Kyi, leader of the opposition National League for Democracy (NLD), following the uninvited visit of the American, John Yettaw, to her lakeside residence. Myanmar furiously responded to Thailand while renouncing the statement as a breach of ASEAN's non-intervention principle. Foreign Minister Nyan Win reportedly said, "Some countries in our region and others have strong interest in the case of John Yettaw and Aung San Suu Kyi. But their interest in the case has been found over-proportionate, overlooking the principles of non-interference in internal affairs and should not have happened."[8]

Along the way, Thailand has consolidated its connection with various ethnic minorities along its border with Myanmar; this has posed as a main obstacle behind the rebuilding of a trusted relationship between the two countries even when they have actively engaged in

---

[8] "Suu Kyi Trial an Internal Matter", *Straits Times*, 29 May 2009.

their usual bilateral economic activities. The remaining buffer zone seems to serve Thailand's psychological and strategic need—the need to nurture ethnic minorities to counterbalance the power of Naypyidaw. Moreover, long years of Thailand's unremitting support for ethnic minorities have made some Thai soldiers sympathetic toward their battle against the military regime. Therefore, with the inexorable link between Thailand and the ethnic minorities, the country has continued to host a myriad of problems associated with the internal conflicts in Myanmar.

The Imminent Election

Myanmar will hold its first parliamentary election in two decades as a symbol of its regime flirting with liberal democracy. After years of being under extreme pressure from the international community, the military government came up with its own roadmap towards democratisation. The State Peace and Development Council (SPDC), the governing body of the current regime, boasted that it has been successful in fulfilling the necessary requirements in order to prepare the nation to be transformed under a new democratic rule. However, sceptics dismissed the upcoming election as a mere plot to prolong the military's influence in politics. After all, this will be a military-led transition. The election date has not yet been set. But political observers anticipate that it may be organised on 10 October 2010, thus the so-called 10-10-10, which is considered auspicious in a country so fanatical about numbers and astrology.[9] In the period leading up to the election, the SPDC has enacted laws and put in place certain rules to ensure the military's grip of power in the post-election period. The Union Election Commission Law was announced in March 2010, stating that the military possesses the ultimate power over the election results. It states that anyone currently serving a jail term will be banned from joining a political party and participating in the election. This law practically bars Suu Kyi and her involvement in the election.[10] It also prevents more than 2,000 anti-junta political prisoners and members of insurgent groups from partaking in the poll.

---

[9] Wai Moe, "Election to be Held in October?" , The Irrawaddy, 8 January 2010, ht tp:// www.irrawaddy.org/article.php?art_id=17548#comment, Accessed 22 May 2010.

[10] "Burma Law Formally Bars Aung San Suu Kyi from Election", BBC News, 10 March 2010 http://news.bbc.co.uk/2/hi/asia-pacific/8559048.stm, Accessed 22 May 2010

As a result, Suu Kyi's NLD, overwhelmingly winning the 1990 election, declared that it would boycott the poll because of the "unjust" electoral law. The NLD's decision has undoubtedly further diminished the legitimacy and credibility of the state-sponsored election.

While the Union Election Commission Law is an "official" tool for the military junta to manipulate the election, some behind-the-scene measures have also been adopted particularly in regards to prescribing the new role of the ethnic minorities. The SPDC has begun to coerce various ethnic minorities, which consist of about 40 percent of the total population, to play a part in the election. In doing so it has had to exercise force upon them. Damir Sagolj argues that the involvement of the ethnic minorities will strengthen the claim of the SPDC that all political players are supporting the election.[11] However, the military government will find its mission increasingly elusive because the ceasefire agreements which it signed with a number of ethnic groups are coming loose at the seams. Over the years, some ethnic minorities, including the Shan, the Karen and the Kachin, have shared their growing resentment against the political domination by the majority Bamar (Burman), without having to look far back into their bitter historical relations. Hence, they have occasionally engaged in intense fighting with the *tatmadaw* (Myanmar's army). More crucially, as Tin Maung Maung Than notes, "Internal tensions within the ceasefire groups continue to threaten peace and security within their own communities."[12] With the imminent election, the SPDC has been trying to forcibly recruit rebel fighters for an army-run Border Guard Force (BGF), a scheme first launched in 2008.[13] Under this scheme, ethnic armies would be downsized into several battalions consisting of 326 men. Each would have a contingent of Myanmar army and non-commissioned officers and operate under the central command of the

---

[11] Damir Sagolj, "Burma Election could Provoke a Rise in Refugees into Thailand and China", *The Telegraph*, 7 January 2010, ht tp://www.telegraph.co.uk/expat/expatnews/6946188/Burma-election-could-provoke-a-rise-in-refugees-into-Thailand-and-China.html, Accessed 22 May 2010.

[12] Tin Maung Maung Than, "Human S ecurity Challenges in Myanmar", in *Myanmar: State, Society and Ethnicity*, edited by N. Ganesan and K yaw Yin Hlaing, (Singapore: Institute of Southeast Asian Studies, 2007), p. 193.

[13] Sagolj, "Burma Election could Provoke a Rise in Refugees into Thailand and China."

Myanmar Army. The junta has said it will provide weapons, equipment, uniforms and even salaries to the proposed units.[14] The military government set a deadline of 28 April 2010 for the armed groups to "merge or disarm" as it has been tightening its position ahead of the election.[15] The majority of the country's 18 ceasefire groups, including the 30,000-strong United Wa State Army (UWSA), Myanmar's largest, have so far rejected the SPDC's demand.[16] Now that the deadline has passed, the military government will be declaring that these ceasefire groups are now illegal organisations. More clashes between the state and the ethnic minorities can therefore be anticipated.

Retrospectively, heavy fighting between the *tatmadaw* and the ethnic Kokang Army in August 2009 forced more than 30,000 refugees to cross into China, an incident that caused frictions between the leaders in Naypyidaw and Beijing. Initially described as part of a drug raid, the attack of the *tatmadaw* appeared to be a violent warning against the Kokang for refusing to disarm and join the national army. Similarly, Thailand has been affected by deadly confrontations between the Myanmar army and the ethnic groups in the areas adjacent to their common border. In June 2009, for example, thousand fled into the buffer zone inside Thailand when the Myanmar army clashed with the Karen National Union (KNU), a group that has sought independence for the past 60 years and still repudiates becoming a part of the BGF. The KNU also had to fight with the Democratic Karen Buddhist Army (DKBA) which aligned with the military. As a result, two Thai soldiers and one civilian were injured and hundreds of villagers were evacuated. From the perspective of the junta, these clashes have not only served to neutralise the KNU, but also to seize rich natural resources for logging and mining in the area occupied by the KNU. In another incident, *The*

---

[14] Brian McCartan, "Drugs, Guns and \War in Myanmar", *Asia Times*, 4 November 2009, http://www.atimes.com/atimes/Southeast_Asia/KK04Ae02.html, Accessed 24 May 2010.

[15] Tini Tran, "Ethnic Groups in Myanmar Gear up for War, Peace", *Burma Digest*, 19 April 2010 http://burmadigest.info/2010/04/19/ethnic-group-in-myanmar-gears-up-for-war-peace/, Accessed 22 May 2010.

[16] Francis Wade, "Kachin Army Holds Mass Public Forum", *Democratic Voice of Burma*, 20 April 2010, http://www.dvb.no/news/kachin-army-holds-mass-public-forum/8655, Accessed 22 May 2010.

Irrawaddy reported that, in late April 2010, hundreds of ethnic Shan, Lahu, Chinese and Thai businesspeople, including some families of UWSA personnel, moved to the Thai-Myanmar border area because they feared a serious flare-up of fighting between the government's troops and UWSA units based in southern Shan State. Several thousand UWSA soldiers and their families live in southern Shan State opposite Fang District of Thailand's Chiang Mai Province. The UWSA has been under immense pressure from the military regime to become a BGF.[17]

Immediately, Thai military authorities warned that thousands of refugees would flee into Thailand if war broke out in southern Shan State. The ongoing conflicts will certainly further complicate the Thai-Myanmar relations built on long-standing mutual distrust and create instability along their border. They will bring other kinds of threats, such as the inflow of drugs, arms and infectious diseases. At present, Thailand houses up to 140,000 refugees from Myanmar in many camps set up along the border, in the buffer zone. Strategically, Thailand could see the benefits of supporting the ethnic rebels and discouraging them from joining the BGF. Thailand could be of the impression that a successful unification between the *tatmadaw* and the ethnic forces could reconstruct Myanmar into an even bigger threat for the country. Thus, a buffer zone could remain tactically useful in the eyes of Bangkok even if the country has to bear the humanitarian and security costs that come with the inflow of refugees. When Thai Foreign Minister Kasit Piromya visited Naypyidaw in March 2010, he urged his Myanmar counterpart to include all parties concerned in the democratisation process. He said, "I am concerned about the national reconciliation and the inclusiveness of the whole new political process."[18] But the Thai sincerity in Myanmar's political stalemate was challenged when the military junta asked Kasit to instead urge the ethnic rebel armies to take part in the country's reconciliation plan. The junta's request seemed to emphasise the political ties between Thailand and the ethnic groups. The chance of Thailand playing the role of a mediator in the peace talks

---

[17] Saw Yan Naing, "Hundreds Flee Threat of War in Shan State", *The Irrawaddy*, 29 April 2010, http://www.irrawaddy.org/article.php?art_id=18348, Accessed 22 May 2010.

[18] "Thailand to Press Burma to Open Elections", *The Irrawaddy*, 2 April 2010, http://www.irrawaddy.org/article.php?art_id=18183, Accessed 22 May 2010

between the junta and the rebels is slim simply because of its implementation of the buffer zone policy. This explains why the Thai efforts in national reconciliation in Myanmar have proven a failure.[19]

The Politics of Energy

Thailand has through the years heavily depended on the energy sources from Myanmar in order to meet its rising domestic demand. The Thai energy need has met with a favourable response from Myanmar leaders who wish to trade their country's energy wealth for cash, seen as one way of sustaining the regime in power. Currently, Myanmar represents two sources of imported energy for Thailand; one is the natural gas exported through the pipeline and the other is the electricity produced by hydropower dams built in Myanmar. The areas chosen for the construction were heavily militarised. Under these projects, human rights have been reportedly abused as thousands were forced to relocate so as to pave the way for the state to construct the pipelines and the dams. Accordingly, some have flooded into the refugee camps in Thailand, triggering political, economic and social crises, including the problem of security along the border, health issues, and the engagement in illegal activities.

Myanmar is blessed with bountiful natural gas mostly found in the Andaman Sea and the Bay of Bengal. In 1995, the 260-kilometre Yadana natural gas pipeline was constructed; it links the Andaman Sea, across Tenasserim Division in southeast Myanmar, with Thailand in the province of Kanchanaburi. Prior to the construction, Thailand's PTT Exploration and Production Company Limited (PTTEP) concluded a 30-year sales agreement with the military junta to purchase the Yadana gas.

---

[19] The Abhisit government has recently made a bold step in the new implementation of its policy toward Myanmar. Departing fr om its pr o-democracy, pro-West and anti-junta standpoint, Prime Minister Abhisit appointed his commerce minister to transform battlefields along the border into marketplaces, even when he previously profoundly criticised his predecessor, the bil lionaire Thaksin, for being obsessed with economic gains at the expense of promoting democracy in Myanmar. Abhisit could argue that Myanmar is now entering into a new political phase (with the incoming election)—one with a greater sense of political openness, and that it would only be logical if the Thai government, at present or in the future, would diversify its options, not only concentrating on preserving its security-centric, pro-democracy position, but also giving prominence to bilateral economic activities

Statistically, Thailand's gas imports from Myanmar exceed US$1.5 billion per annum; and accordingly to Matthew Smith, this has provided the military regime in Myanmar with approximately 30 percent of its hard currency.[20] Meanwhile, EarthRights International, a non-governmental organisation specialising in legal action against perpetrators of human rights abuses, reported, "Since the project's beginnings in the early 1990s, it has been marred by serious and widespread human rights abuses committed by pipeline security forces on behalf of the companies, including forced labour, land confiscation, forced relocation, rape, torture, murder. Many of these abuses continue today."[21] Consequently, thousands of villagers fled into Thailand as refugees.[22]

More recently, the Thai government has sought the other source of energy in Myanmar—the hydropower. The Electricity Generating Authority of Thailand (EGAT) has strongly defended its investment in projects in Myanmar, through the building of a series of hydropower dams on the Salween River, as part of protecting the country's energy security. EGAT has argued that hydropower from the Salween was needed because it was cheap and helped increase the country's fuel diversification. It said, "This is of strategic importance to national security and also to strengthen Thailand's standing as a regional trade hub."[23] Despite protests from human rights groups, EGAT went ahead with the construction of the Hutgyi dam, signing an agreement with a Chinese state-owned enterprise Sinohydro Cooperation and Myanmar's Hydro Department of the Ministry of Electric Power. The plan was to build a 1,360-megawatt hydropower dam on the Salween in the strife-ridden Karen state, 47 kilometres from the Thai-Myanmar border in Sop Moei district, Mae Hong Son province.[24] Testifying before the Senate Committee in early 2006, Nipol Pienpak, the Hydropower Engineering Division manager of EGAT, insisted that the Myanmar military

---

[20] Matthew Smith, "Gas Pipeline Controversy", *Bangkok Post*, 22 May 2007.

[21] http://www.earthrights.org/campaigns/yadana-pipeline, Accessed 23 May 2010

[22] Smith, "Gas Pipeline Controversy".

[23] Supara Janchitfah, "Energy Forecasts are Unrealistic", *Bangkok Post*, 2 April 2006.

[24] "Abhisit Cool to Opponents of Salween River Dam Plan", *Bangkok Post*, 24 November 2009.

government reassured him of the absence of any social and environmental impact caused by the construction of the dam.[25] However, many non-governmental organisations and civil society organisations have confirmed that the project has brought about a large number of displaced ethnic Karen in the Karen state of Myanmar. Reportedly, more than 400 Karen asylum seekers were waiting to be accepted in the refugee camps on the Thai border. They informed the Thai local authorities that they were forced to relocate so that the dam could be constructed and the roads could be built, especially from the location of the dam to the villages on the border.[26]

The quest for energy sources in Myanmar has seemed to cost Thailand more than it had earlier expected. The incoming refugees are the inevitable by-product of Thailand's energy policy vis-à-vis Myanmar. On the Thai side, the important question is how to compromise the need for imported energy and the consequences emerging from that need in the forms of refugees, instability along the border, and even the occasional conflict with Myanmar. The overemphasis on energy security which has driven the Thai authorities to consistently search for energy sources in Myanmar, even to the point of ignoring, consciously or otherwise, human rights abuses in that process, reflects the exploitative aspect of Thailand's policy toward its neighbour.

The Dire Effects

This year's election and the extensive Thai projects in the energy sector in Myanmar have yielded a myriad of harmful effects on Thailand. Internal conflicts in Myanmar have compelled the opposition and the ethnic minorities to flee the state's intimidation, retribution and abuse. Many of them have for decades sought refuge in Thailand, not only because of the close proximity and the porous border it shares with Myanmar, but also because Thailand has been known as a haven for refugees. While the Thai government has explained away the need to

---

[25] Supara, "Energy Forecasts are Unrealistic".

[26] The outcome of the conference on "Thailand's Position, Roles and Policy towards Burma/Myanmar", organised by Faculty of Political Science, Chulalongkorn University, 6 October 2009.http://www.reliefweb.int/rw/rwb.nsf/db900sid/MYAI-7VR7E7?OpenDocument, Accessed 24 May 2010.

shelter the refugees on humanitarian grounds, it has also continued to exploit the border zone to fulfil its security imperatives while dealing with the Naypyidaw regime. However, it is important to note that the Thai government seems to fully recognise that refugees from Myanmar, like those from other neighbouring countries, have also posed threats to the country. It is thus ironic that in an attempt to block any threat from the military regime in Myanmar, it has made itself vulnerable to other kinds of threats brought about by the refugees. This explains why the Thai policy toward refugees could sometime be erratic, just like its policy toward Myanmar. Successive governments in Thailand, while cherishing the political significance of the ethnic insurgents, have deported a large number of refugees back to an uncertainty in Myanmar. It also explains why Thailand has not always played a good host to the refugees. There have been many cases involving abuses against the refugees at the hands of the Thai authorities. More importantly, the unpredictable stance of Thailand vis-à-vis the ethnic insurgents and the refugees has further distanced the country's from Myanmar; it has caused a considerable strain on bilateral relations. As long as the two countries are unable to overcome their decades-old mutual distrust, the Thai buffer state policy will never be dismantled. This buffer zone has served as a sanctuary for ethnic rebels and refugees to fall back to whenever the Myanmar military junta orders a crackdown on them.

The Inflow of Refugees

Most literatures focus on the tormenting experiences of the refugees who flee their homeland and face uncertainty in the host country. For this chapter, it instead aims at highlighting some of the effects caused by the influx of refugees and ethnic insurgents on Thailand. For more than three decades, the military regime of Myanmar has been severely criticised by the international community for human rights abuses against its own people. The power struggle between the military regime and its many opponents has led to persistent internal conflicts which partly elucidate the reason why there is still no end in sight to the refugee situation. Allegedly, the *tatmadaw* has gradually overrun ethnic territories, displacing more than a million people from their home. The Thailand-Burma Border Consortium (TBBC) reports that the military regime has brought terror to the people as villages have been destroyed or relocated, land confiscated, roads driven through, military bases established and the natural resources exploited. The recent battle between the SPDC and the Karen National Liberal Army (KNLA) drove at least 4,000 new refugees into Thailand's Tak province.[27]

Today, there are nine refugee camps along the Thai-Myanmar border; all of which are becoming very crowded. Of 400,000 refugees, there are approximately 140,000 Myanmar refugees in Thailand who escaped from forced relocation or ongoing fighting with the *tatmadaw*, making it the largest group of refugees in the country. Thailand deports up to 1,000 Myanmar citizens a month on ground of illegal entry.[28]

The study of Gil Loescher and James Milner on the refugee situation in Thailand unveils that tensions between refugees and the local population often arise as refugees are perceived to receive preferential treatment, especially as access to local social services such as health and education becomes increasingly difficult while such services may be widely available in the refugee camps. Moreover, competition between refugees and the host population over scarce resources is becoming an increasing source of insecurity. In the same way, reductions in assistance in the camps may lead some refugees to pursue coping strategies such as banditry, prostitution and petty theft, which creates additional local security concerns.[29] For example, for local businesses in Thailand, the overflows of Myanmar refugees may have been a boon. Often in high demand, they are hired as illegal workers because the business owners do not have to abide by labour laws. The Asia Society gives an account that they enter the lowest levels of the Thai labour market which Thai workers have turned their backs on because of the hard work and risks involved; jobs which have been

---

[27] Thailand-Burma Border Consortium,

[28] Buhm Suk Baek and Gauri Subramanium, *Myanmarese Refugees in Thailand: The Need for Effective Protection*, Cornell Law Student Papers, (Ithaca: Cornell Law School J.S.D./ Doctoral Student P apers, 2008), p . 7.

[29] Gil Loescher and James Milner *Protracted Refugee Situation in Thailand: Towards Solutions*, Presentation to the Foreign Correspondents' Club of Thailand, 1 February 2006, http://www.refugees.org/uploadedFiles/Investigate/Anti-Warehousing/Countries/Loescher%20and%20Milner%20060201%20PRS.pdf, Ac cessed 24 May 2010.

nicknamed the 3Ds in Thailand: dirty, difficult and dangerous (fishery, construction, sex work in closed brothels, rice mills and some types of agriculture).[30] At the same time, in more competitive industries, such as manufacturing, the refugees-turned-illegal workers have begun to frustrate local workers who may have lost out to this cheap labour. Tensions occasionally erupt. The affected legal workers have requested the Thai government to adopt tough measures against the Myanmar refugees who have been accused of being mere economic migrants and not real asylum seekers. Furthermore, the presence of refugees from Myanmar has boosted the culture of corruption among Thai officials. In the report of the U.S. Committee for Refugees and Immigrants (USCRI), refugees seeking to leave the camps to work must do so illegally, risking detention or deportation, and must pay bribes to Thai camp administrators, local authorities and others, sometimes as much as 15,000 baht.[31]

Another serious effect on Thailand is the rise of prostitution. Prostitution is closely knitted to the problems faced by refugees from Myanmar who come to Thailand searching for a better life. *CityLife*, a local publication in Chiang Mai, conducted an investigation on the rise of prostitution among refugees in the north of Thailand, and found that "because most are illegal immigrants, they are often exploited. Many start out working in the construction industry and are paid only a portion of their salaries because the companies they work for know that, without identity cards, they can do nothing about it. And to get identity cards they need cash."[32] As more illegal workers from Myanmar entering in the Thai sex industry, this situation has given rise to the spread of sexually transmitted diseases (STDs). While the incidence of AIDS and other STDs is lower in Thailand than in some other parts of Asia, a 2005

---

[30] Nang Lao Liang Won, "No Human Being is Illegal", *Asia Society*, 2 October 1998, http://www.asiasociety.org/policy-politics/human-rights/no-human-being-illegal, Ac cessed 24 May 2010.

[31] The U.S. Committee for Refugees and Immigrants <http://www.refugees.org/article.aspx?id=1438&rid=1179&subm=33&ssm=87&area=Investigate> (accessed 24 May 2010).

[32] "The Other Side of the Coin: Male Pr ostitutes in Chiang Mai" , *CityLife*, October 2006 <http://www.chiangmainews.com/ecmn/viewfa.php?id=1618> (accessed 24 May 2010).

study revealed that approximately 11.4% of sex workers in Chiang Mai, most of whom were refugees from Myanmar, are HIV positive.[33]

Guns and Ganjas

The Thai-Myanmar border has remained one of the world's most active battlegrounds for ethnic insurgents. Their mission to search for independence or some sorts of autonomy has become an increasingly uphill task now that the military regime in Myanmar is in the final phase of consolidating its power through the electoral process. David Steinberg calls this process "a civilisation of the military regime".[34] Being forced to disarm and join the BGF in the pre-election period, ethnic insurgents have crossed the border into the Thai buffer zone to continue their anti-government campaign. Some have been offered assistance by the Thai military which has favoured the existence of a buffer state.[35] In a number of hot pursuits against the ethnic insurgents, the *tatmadaw* intruded into Thai territories and engaged in fatal gunfire with the Thai army. The shootings might not have been an accident since Naypyidaw firmly believes that Thailand still protects the ethnic minorities, thus sheltering them whenever wars break out inside Myanmar. This mentality has put Thai-Myanmar relations in serious jeopardy. It legitimised the military junta's retaliation against the Thai buffer state with its own offensive strategy; the strategy that has been used to control border relations with Thailand. The *tatmadaw* has indeed implemented the offensive strategy so as to create instability and extreme disorder at the border zone to confuse Thai policy-makers and to remind them of Myanmar's prevailing bargaining power.[36]

The arrival of the ethnic insurgents is not without security troubles. Cross-border arms smuggling has enabled insurgent groups to obtain

[33] Ibid.

[34] Quoted in Larry Jagan, "NLD Considers a Future without The Lady" , *Bangkok Post*, 28 March 2010.

[35] My interview with a high-ranking Thai general stationing in Pitsanulok, 23 February 2010.

[36] Pavin Chachavalpongpun, "Dealing with Burma's Gordian Knot: Thailand, ASEAN, China and the Burmese Conundrum", in *Myanmar: Prospect for Change*, edited by Li Chenyang and Wilhelm Hofmeister (Singapore: Select Publishing, 2010), p. 274.

weapons, such as AK-47s, B-40 rocket launchers, and other small arms, and to use them against the enemies.[37] The prevalence of military hardware in the border areas has further intensified the scale of conflicts between the ethnic minorities and the Myanmar military regime. While Thailand was known to have provided arms and ammunition to the ethnic insurgents during the Cold War, the country has maintained its reputation as both a source of weapons and a transit point for arms smugglings. And the business is becoming more lucrative. On the Thai-Myanmar border, AK-47s and M-16s now cost 10,000-15,000 baht (US$295-440), according to arms buyers in Three Pagodas Pass. A decade ago, AK-47 and M-16 automatic rifles cost about 4,000 baht and bullets were 3 baht a piece.[38] Already, Thailand has become the favourite destination for transnational crime organisations. For example, in March 2008, Russian arms dealer Viktor Bout who made millions of dollars delivering weapons and ammunition to warlords and militants around the world was arrested in Thailand. More recently, in December 2009, five foreigners who crewed an aircraft carrying tons of weapons originating in North Korea were charged with arms smuggling in Thailand. The easy access to illegal weapons has without doubt prolonged the internal conflicts in Myanmar; and in this process, Thailand's security along the border continues to be dominated by concerns of the outbreak of violence and its impact on the lives of Thais who live on the borderland.

Aside from the proliferation of arms sale in the border areas, the drugs trade has long been a destabilising factor and a primary threat to Thailand's national security. In the past few decades, many ethnic rebels relied on the profits from the trade and production of narcotics to fund their combat against the military government. In fact, Myanmar has remained the world's second-largest producer of illicit opium, behind Afghanistan. The U.S. Drug Enforcement Administration (DEA) reports that Myanmar accounts for 80 percent of all heroin produced in

---

[37] Liana Sun Wyler, "Burma and Transnational Crime", *CRS Report for Congress*, 21 August 2008, p. 12.ht tp://www.fas.org/sgp/crs/row/RL34225.pdf, Accessed 24 May 2010.

[38] "Armed Insurgents in Burma Face Shortage of Ammunition", *Burma's Bloggers Network*, http://www.burmabloggers.net/?p=1898, Accessed 24 May 2010

Southeast Asia and is a source of heroin for the United States.[39] But the production has recently declined due partly to successful crop substitution programmes supported by various international organisations. Ethnic minorities now turn to other kinds of drug, such as methamphetamines, known in Thai as *yaa baa* (crazy pills), since the manufacturing can be mobile, thus highly evasive, and yet colossally profitable. This profit has been utilised to support the ethnic insurgents' paramilitary forces. The key market for the *yaa baa* is Thailand. The narcotic situation in Thailand was so severe that former Prime Minister Thaksin Shanawatra had to declare the "war on drug" campaign in 2003 which resulted in the extra-judicial killings of more than 2,500 drug suspects. The second war on drug campaign was announced by the Samak Sundaravej government in the middle of 2008, purportedly because of the new surge in *yaa baa* consumption in the country. The Thai government has blamed both the ethnic insurgents who have made their living and financed their crusade on the narcotic production as well as the Myanmar government for its lack of seriousness in tackling the issue. Assigning blame also suited the Thai position for externalising the source of drugs even when in reality there are many Thais who are involved in the narcotic network.

Guns and ganjas (a general Thai term for drugs and a specific term for marijuana) represent yet another derivative of the internal conflicts in Myanmar. They have been vital for the ethnic insurgents both as a source of funds and a deadly tool in eliminating their political opponents in Naypyidaw. Unfortunately, both have created undesired effects on Thailand too. Some Thai "middle men" may have gained considerable benefits from the drug and arms trade. But at the national level, they are hurting their own country which has indisputably become the black market for world's arms and Thai youths who have fallen prey to narcotics.

Conclusion

Internal conflicts in Myanmar have created a security crisis along its frontier with Thailand. This chapter explored two contemporary cases,

---

[39] U.S. Drug Enforcement Administration, *Drugs of Abuse*, 2005, http://www.usdoj.gov/dea/pubs/abuse/doa-p.pdf, Accessed 24 May 2010.

the looming election and the Thai dependency on energy sources in Myanmar, in order to demonstrate the connection between such internal conflicts and the inevitable side-effects on Thailand. For Thailand's own strategic reason, a series of Thai governments has approved, and still nurtures, the buffer zone in order to contain the so-called Myanmar threats. In doing so, Thailand has piggybacked both ethnic insurgents and refugees from Myanmar who have run away from conflicts at home in order to rebuild their lives in Thailand. This Thai policy has put a grave strain on the country's relations with the military government of Myanmar. It has also acted as a foundation of mistrust between the two countries' governments. The Thai security forces are anxious about Myanmar's scheme to construct a unified BGF as this will directly pose as a security challenge to Thailand. But piggybacking the victims of internal conflicts in Myanmar has proven to be an expensive decision. Thailand has had to bear the hefty cost of sheltering refugees. The security, economic and social costs range from the proliferation of military weapons, the nefarious drugs trade, the conflicts between the refugees and the locals, the spread of infectious diseases, and the encouragement of a corruption culture in Thailand. Ironically, and perhaps perplexingly, Thailand has seemingly imported these threats and instability from across the border as part of strengthening its own security immunity against such threats and instability from Myanmar.

TRANS-BORDER EFFECTS ON NORTHEAST INDIA

K. Yhome

India-Myanmar border region shares deep historical and cultural affinities, allowing regular movement of people, ideas and goods in and out the border without any natural barrier. The linkages through the porous border allow developments on one side affecting the other. In many ways, the socio-political and economic life of the Northeast, particularly those states [Arunachal Pradesh, Nagaland, Manipur, and Mizoram] having direct border with Myanmar, have been influenced by the way of life on the other side. The political boundary remains an imaginary line and all sorts of interactions thrive along the border, though considered 'illegal' because of the restrictive border policies. To a large extent, the 'closed door' policies had nurtured negative trans-border consequences of Myanmar's internal conflicts on Northeast India.

For a long time, understanding of trans-border consequences of Myanmar's internal conflicts on Northeast India has been largely from the security perspective. However, this perspective has failed to explain the larger societal consequences and tends to see trans-border issues from a narrow perspective. In the recent years, there have been changes taking place on both sides of the border and there are emerging opportunities, notwithstanding the potential pitfalls. Understanding some of the trans-border consequences of conflict, which have had serious impact on the region, may help find ways to avoid the pitfalls.

This paper attempts to examine the trends of trans-border consequences of internal conflicts in Myanmar on Northeast India and analyzes the factors that shape and motivate negative transnational ties and their consequences. An analysis of the factors that obstruct 'legal' trans-border activities will allow us to develop a framework of governance in the borderlands that ensures civilian control over the border space.

The paper is structured in five sub-sections. The first section provides an understanding of Myanmar's internal conflicts – nature and consequences. The second section deals with the changing approaches and dynamics of Indo-Myanmar borderlands. The third section provides an understanding of the nature of trans-border relations and trans-border consequences of conflicts in Myanmar. The fourth section examines the emerging discourses on borderlands and ways of developing alternative borderland governance. The fifth section looks at the key factors that shape the nature and consequences of trans-border ties.

Borderland: From Frontier to Gateway

There are significant transformations taking place in the borderlands of India and Myanmar in the past two decades – changing the way the region sees itself and the way others sees it. The paradigm shift in the way nation-states look at their borders from "frontiers" to concepts such as "land bridges" has been a major driver of change in the borderlands. India's former Minister of State for External Affairs, Shashi Tharoor described the Northeast as the "doorway" to Southeast and East Asia and vice versa.[1]

The memories of shared history and culture between Northeast India and Myanmar weakened soon after their independence in the 1940s. In the 1960s, Myanmar adopted an inward-looking policy and closed itself to the outside world. The official ties between India and Myanmar became minimal up till the 1990s. The Indo-Myanmar border region has been neglected for decades by the central governments in both countries. The end of Cold War in the late 1980s saw new realignments of relations driven less by ideological factors and in the era of globalization, "connectivity" become the buzzword. In the changed environment, the border regions have been seen as "gateways"

---

[1] "Meet Highlights Potential of North-East", *The Hindu*, 12 April, 2010

in the efforts to boost economic and commercial activities. The geographical proximity of Northeast India with Yangon, Bangkok or Kunming than with New Delhi or Mumbai has now become a fashionable thing to say.[2]

In the recent years, borderlands have regained their importance in foreign policy analyses, not only from the security/military perspective but also from economic and connectivity dimensions based largely on the notion that in the era of globalization, political boundaries will gradually become irrelevant. New Delhi launched its "Look East Policy" in the early 1990s, to boost its trade and commerce with Southeast Asia. The Northeast region is now being projected as the "arrowhead" of India's "Look East" policy.[3] This is a major change from a complete absence of the region in the policy when it was first conceptualized.[4]

The Northeast's geographical "isolation" from "mainland" India has been identified as one of the main reasons for underdevelopment and which in turn fuel resentments that gets accumulated in tension and over a period of time gets channelized into violent armed struggles. While recognizing the geographical factor as a reason for the region's instability, there has been not much effort in exploring alternatives options. One of the reasons why government and scholars have not look towards Myanmar as an option to develop the Northeast was because of the consequences of Myanmar's internal conflicts. Until recently, there has been a strong mental block among elites who had perceived Myanmar in a poor light. For many decades, people in the Northeast tend to look towards the west than to the east and very little attention have been paid on opening up the border with Myanmar.

---

[2] For instance, Kunming in China is only 1,726 km from Ledo in Assam, where the Stilwell Road begins. Located as i t were geogr aphically, the Northeast is most susceptible to external influences.

[3] NER Vision 2020, "The Vision Statement " at ht tp://mdoner.gov.in/writereaddata/newsimages/vision%20statement%2020205117088053.pdf

[4] Rajiv Sikri, "India's Look East Policy: A Critical Assessment", October 2009, Institute of Peace and Conflict Studies at http://www.ipcs.org/pdf_file/issue/SR85-SEARPInterview-Sikri1.pdf

Changing Dynamics of the Indo-Myanmar Borderlands

The landscape of Indo-Myanmar's borderlands has undergone dramatic transformation since the late 1980s when initiatives were taken to transform the political economy of Indo-Myanmar borderlands. Since the late 1980s, the Myanmar military government entered into ceasefire agreements with several ethnic armed groups. The government also adopted market-oriented economy. This has had a major impact on the borderlands. Martin Smith argues that "the post-1988 government has targeted the economy for control and market oriented reform and, through an admixture of ceasefire agreements and rapprochement with neighbouring countries, gained greater access to more areas of Burma than any previous administration."[5]

It is interesting to note that the governments in New Delhi and Naypyidaw adopted similar approaches towards development of their respective borderlands at about the same time with the hope that development would help support peace in the border areas. In 1987, the central government of India initiated the Border Area Development Programme (BADP) "to provide adequate social and economic infrastructure, promotion of participation in development, eliminate sense of alienation, and instilling a sense of security among the border people."[6] In September 2001, a new ministry called Ministry of Development of North Eastern Region (DONER) was set up to act as the nodal Department of the Central Government to deal with matters pertaining to socio-economic development of the eight States of North East (the eighth state includes Sikkim). Over the years, the central government has increased the expenditure for development of the northeast region and the budget was raised to Rs.1,760 crore for 2010-11, up 19 percent from the previous fiscal.[7]

---

[5] Martin Smith, "State of Strife: The Dynamics of Ethnic Conflicts in Burma", Policy Studies 36, East-West Centre, W ashington, 2007.

[6] Pushpita Das, *India's Border Management: Selected Documents*, (New Delhi:Institute of Defence and Studies and Analyses, 2010), p. 23.

[7] The revised budgetary allocation for the fiscal 2009-10 was Rs.1,475.21 crore and for this year it has been hiked to Rs.1,759.33 crore. Out of which about Rs.623 crore have been earmarked for the "schemes to ensure integrated socio-economic development of the eight states of north eastern r egion", at least Rs.5 cr ore for construction and

In 1989, the Myanmar government also established a similar programme called the Border Areas Development Programme (BADP) which was upgraded into a ministry in 1992 called the Ministry for Progress of Border Areas and National Races and Development Affairs (PBANRDA).[8] The Ministry has two departments – Progress of Border Areas and National Races Department that is responsible for the development of border areas and national races and the Department of Development Affairs which is responsible for urban development. The PBANRDA has been implementing development of border areas.[9]

Another similar approach that New Delhi and Naypyidaw adopted towards the ethnic insurgencies was the idea of entering into ceasefire agreement with the ethnic armed groups since the late 1980s. The government of India initiated what is known as "innovative methods" in dealing with insurgencies in the Northeast. This method has been defined as a shift "from merely arming the state machineries to a strategy of agreements and negotiations alongside improved counter-insurgency measures"[10] with the aim "to restore normalcy in the region". The first ceasefire agreement was signed with the National Socialist Council of Nagaland (Isak-Muivah)/ NSCN (IM) on August 1, 1997 and subsequently, with the National Socialist Council of Nagaland (Khaplang)/ NSCN (K) on April 28, 2001.

The government also initiated armed suspension agreement framework known as the Suspension of Operation (SoO). By 2008, the

---

improvement of roads of economic importance to be carried out through the Border Roads Organisation (BRO)IANS, 26 F ebruary, 2010.

[8] See Myanmar's official website of the Ministry for progress of Border Areas and National Races and Dev elopment Af fairs (PBANRDA) at ht tp://www.myanmar.gov.mm/PBNRDA/index.htm

[9] The regions where the development measures are being taken are as follows: 1. Kachin Special Region (1); 2. Kachin Special Region (2); 3. Kokang Region; 4. Wa Region; 5. Shan R egion; 6. K achin North East R egion; 7. P alaung R egion; 8. K yaingtong East Region; 9. Homein/ Mong Htaw/ Mong Hta Region; 10. Maw-pha Region; 11. Pa-O Region; 12. Kayah/ Kayan Region; 13. Rakhine Region; 14. Chin Region; 15. Naga Region; 16. K abaw R egion; 17. Kayin Region; 18. T anintharyi R egion; and 19. Mon Region.

[10] See Innovative Methods in Fighting Insurgency in North-East India, Ministry of Home Affairs, Go vernment of India at http://indiago vernance.gov.in/fbestpractice/attachments/innovative_methods_in_fightinginsurgency_in_ north_east_india.pdf

government has signed SoOs with four northeast insurgent groups.[11] This has created relative peace in the borderlands. However, both India and Myanmar are yet to take the ceasefire agreements to their logical conclusions – i.e. to find permanent political settlements. While there are no easy solutions, efforts need to continue to reach permanent political solutions in the near future.

Another aspect of the changing landscape of borderland is the border trade between India and Myanmar that was opened in April 1995. Currently, the border trade with Myanmar is functional only at Moreh-Tamu and Zokhawthar-Rhi. While Indo-Myanmar bilateral trade has been showing an upward trend, border trade has not grown as desired. Besides the two points for border trade with Myanmar, India has identified further points to be developed for border trade namely, Lungwa/Ledo, Pongru and Pokhungri in Nagaland and Nampong, Vijayanagar and Khimiyang in Arunachal Pradesh. But so far, the Government of Myanmar has not been enthusiastic to the proposal of opening further trading posts and has indicated that the existing trade point in Moreh should be strengthened first and full potential before any new trading point is opened.[12]

These initiatives have expanded civilian activities in the borderlands. The long neglect of the border region has allowed criminal and anti-social elements to use it at their will and though there has been a gradual expansion of the civilian space in the border region, all efforts needs to focus on how civilians can recapture the border region for productive and constructive purposes, beneficial to people on both sides of the border. One of the main factors in facilitating the process of achieving these goals is connectivity.

---

[11] These groups includes the Kuki National Organization (KNO), Manipur in August 2008; Tripartite agreements between the Government of India, the Government of Assam with the National Democratic Front of Bodoland (NDFB) on April 24, 2005; Achik National Volunteer Council (ANVC) Meghalaya on July 23, 2004;\ Dima Halam Dagoah (DHD) in the North Cachar Hills area, Assam since January 1,2003; and United Peoples Democratic Solidarity (UPDS – in the Karbi Anglong Area of Assam) on August 1, 2002.

[12] In this regard, a trade centre building with modern communication facilities has been constructed at Moreh. Further, a sum of Rs. 95 lakh has also been appr oved under the critical infrastructure scheme for the development of roads and street lighting at Moreh.

Myanmar's Internal Conflicts

Before dealing with trans-border issues it may be useful to understand Myanmar's internal conflicts. The nature of Myanmar's internal conflicts is historical, ideological, and ethno-political. The origin of much of contemporary conflicts in the country can be traced back to the colonial policies and subsequent policies of the central government.[13] Myanmar's internal conflicts are of two fold. At one level is the conflict between the pro-democracy forces and the military (or the *Tatmadaw*) and at another level are the numerous ethno-political conflicts between the State dominated by ethnic Burman-Buddhist majority and the various ethnic 'minority' nationalities.[14] For the purpose of this paper, the focus has been on the ethno-political conflicts because these conflicts are directly related to the present study. However, consequences of the conflict between Myanmar's military and the pro-democracy forces have been examined where and when relevant.

Underlying the roots of conflicts in present-day Myanmar, Burmese historian Thant Myint-U argues that two colonial legacies, namely, "a legacy of institutional weakness" which has been taken advantage by the *Tatmadaw* to consolidate its power over the years and the emergence of an exclusivist "Burmese ethnic nationalism... based on older Ava-based memories has never allowed the development of a newer identity which would incorporate the diverse peoples inhabiting the modern state." These two colonial legacies combined have, to a large extent, created what has come to be known as the "Burma Problem".

Myanmar has seen some of the longest ethnic insurgencies in the world.[15] Since its inception, the country's political landscape has been characterized by violent conflicts. Examining the factors behind the

---

[13] There are a plethora of studies done of the origin of conflicts in Myanmar. See Myint –U Thant, *The Making of Modern Burma*, (Cambridge: Cambridge University Press, 2001); Myint-U Thant, *River of Lost Footsteps: A Personal History of Burma,* (New York: Faber and Faber, 2007).

[14] For a detail discussion on the "poltics of ethnicity", see Martin Smith, *Burma: Insurgency and the Politics of Ethnicity,* (London: Zed Books, 1991).

[15] Smith, "State of Strife: The Dynamics of Ethnic Conflicts in Burma".

long-standing structures of conflict and the drivers of socio-political change in the country, Martin Smith argues that "a historic inter-mix of cultural, military, socio-economic and international causes has been integral to sustaining Burma's conflict environment at different times."[16] The 'militarization' of the country had devastating consequences, affecting almost every aspect of the society. As Martin Smith argues that "militarized politics have had a deeply divisive impact on nation-state formation in a country where non-Burman peoples feel excluded from a government and national armed forces that have become increasingly Burman-centric as the years gone by."[17]

The conflicts have had serious socio-political and economic consequences on the country. Modern Myanmar's "political and social climate [has] too often [been] characterized by disunity"[18] – a consequence was the emergence of "multiple nationalisms."[19]

The idea of ethnic differences combined with nationalistic ideology took a violent turn soon after independence leaving a legacy of conflicts having direct impact on nation-state building. Martin Smith's study on the consequences of Myanmar's internal conflicts on state-building illustrates that protracted conflicts and violence has had "a profound effect on political culture and the formation of institutions" in Myanmar.[20]

According to Martin Smith, Myanmar's "state has often been administered on the basis of crisis-management with different actors struggling to maintain their dominant positions... As a result, reforms in Burma have been introduced only in *ad hoc* form; democratic

---

[16] Smith, "State of Strife: The Dynamics of Ethnic Conflicts in Burma", p. ix.

[17] Smith, "State of Strife: The Dynamics of Ethnic Conflicts in Burma", p. 20.

[18] A product of the colonial "r eified ethnicit y" of the My anmar society. See Rachel M. Safman, "Minorities and State-building in Mainland S outheast Asia", in N. Ganesan and Kyaw Yin Hlaing, eds. *Myanmar: State, Societ y and Ethnicit y,* (Singapor e: Institute of Southeast Asian Studies and Hiroshima Peace Institute, 2007), p. 51.

[19] Robert H. Taylor, "British Policy towards Myanmar and the Creation of the Burma Problem", in N. Ganesan and K yaw Yin Hlaing, eds. *Myanmar: State, Societ y and Ethnici ty,* (Singapore: Institute of Southeast Asian Studies and Hiroshima Peace Institute, 2007), p. 75-6.

[20] Smith, "State of Strife", p. 25.

governance has never become established; and unregulated economies and insurgent movements have all flourished...."[21] Smith argues that Myanmar is "trapped in a spiral of such long-standing malaise" and the country faces "formidable challenges in reconciliation and nation-state formation if sustainable peace and democratic reforms are ever to be achieved."[22]

Importantly, as Martin Smith rightly observed, in "conflict zones, the line between 'legality' and 'illegality' is frequently blurred"[23] having adverse socio-economic consequences, particularly in the border regions. Martin Smith argues that "illegality" and "insurgency became a way of life" and "ethnic conflict and illicit narcotics remain intertwined".[24] All these had a catastrophic impact on the country's economy leading to failure of the government economy on the one hand, and the booming of the black market on the other.[25] In December 1987 Myanmar was classified in the category of the World's Least Developed Countries (LDC) by the United Nations and the country continues to remain in that category even today.[26] The prolong conflicts have had grave humanitarian consequences. There are about 540000 internally-displaced persons and over 155,000 refugees in official camps along Myanmar-Thailand border alone.

---

[21] Ibid.

[22] Ibid., Smith further argues that in such an environment "political culture and the very system of government can evolve around the conditions of conflicts" where "rulers prefers 'weak and formal institutions' to prevent the emergence of organizations that can challenge their authority" and "conflicts are fostered in the community by rulers since this is likely to encourage local leaders to seek the patronage of the state ruler rather than resolve disputes, as the formerly would have, among themselves". Power has been "personalized in both government and opposition" to prevent "local populations from participation in decision-making" and hence "the politics of inclusion" remains elusive.

[23] Martin Smith, "The Paradox of Burma: Conflict and Illegality as a Way of Life", IIAS No.42, Autumn 2006, p. 20.

[24] Ibid.

[25] Ibid.

[26] Ibid. All sorts of items crossed border – from cattle, timber, jade, to opium going out of Myanmar and manufactured goods coming in to the country. In 1987 the annual black market accounted for US$ 3 billion or 40 per cent of the gross national product.

Transnational Consequences of Conflicts in Myanmar on India's Northeast:

India's Northeast is ringed by China to the North, Bhutan to the west, Myanmar to the east and Bangladesh to the south and is connected to "mainland" India by a narrow-strip of land, strategically, called the "Siliguri Corridor". The region is inhabited by over 200 ethnic groups and many have been fighting against the Indian State demanding autonomy to self-determination for over six decades. Over the years, the Northeast has come to be known as a region plagued by violent conflicts. The nature of conflicts in Northeast India is largely ethno-political and much of the conditions and consequences of conflicts in Myanmar are shared by the Northeast. The dominant feature of the political landscape of Northeast has been described as a 'culture of violence', a result of 'securitization' of the Northeast society for decades.[27] Consequently, violence and 'militarization' has become 'a way of life' in many parts of the region.[28]

Not all the attributes of the Northeast have been a result of transnational consequences of conflicts, but the fact that similar conflict conditions exist in the Northeast makes it easy of trans-border influences and thereby facilitating linkages and networks which reinforces the "culture of violence" in the region. The foremost trans-border consequence of internal conflicts in Myanmar on Northeast India is the idea of armed struggle itself. As noted earlier, insurgency in the border hills of Myanmar and Northeast India began almost during the same period. From early on India's northeast insurgent groups have got support and assistance from the insurgent groups in Myanmar's northern region.[29] Many insurgent groups in the Northeast region have been

---

[27] Mandy Turner and Binalakshmi Nepram, *The Impact of Armed Violence in Northeast India: A Mini Case Study of the Armed Violence and Poverty Initiative,*   (Bradford:Centre for International Cooperation and Security, University of Bradford, November 2004)

[28] Sanjib Baruah, "Post-frontier Blues: Deficits of Democracy, Development and Peace in Northeast India", Policy Studies 33, East West Centre, Washington, 2007

[29] For instance, in the 1966 the Kachin Independence Army (KIA) helped Naga insurgent groups to go to China and later the KIA also trained and armed the NSCN, ULFA, and Manipuri insurgent groups. See Subir Bhaumik, *Troubled Periphery: Crisis of India's North East*, (New Delhi: Sage Publications, 2009), pp. 174-77.

able to sustained there movements because of the sanctuary and support they received from the other side of the border.

The decades of armed violence in the Northeast have had serious societal consequences. A study has noted that there is an "underground economy" or black economy that has been thriving in the region largely through illicit drugs and guns trade.[30] One of the results of the prolong conflicts has been the displacement of thousands of people in the region.[31]

The fact that for a long time the Myanmar central government had very little control over the borderlands, the ethnic armed groups were *de facto* rulers of the border regions. In fact, whenever there have been talks about coordinated operations between the armies of the two countries against Northeast insurgent groups based in Myanmar, there has been apprehension raised on whether such operations would be successful given the limited control of the Myanmar government over the border areas. The existence of many insurgent groups in the region because of the easy accessibility of guns and the heavy armed forces presence has militarized the society.

The long trans-border conflict relations have also impacted upon the very functioning of the state machinery. One often hears the "unholy nexus" between political leaders and underground groups. The complex situations in conflict zones in which this relationship have emerged. There is a tendency to look at the issue from the legal point of view. One of the main reasons for the protracted conflicts in the border region has been because of the excessive use of force by the government.

India shares 1,643 km land border with Myanmar running through 16 districts in 4 States namely Anjaw, Lohit, Changlang, Tirap districts in Arunachal Pradesh; Mon, Tuensang, Phek and Kiphiri districts in Nagaland; Ukhrul, Chandel, Churachandpur districts in Manipur and

---

[30] Turner and Nepram, "The Impact of Armed Violence in Northeast India", p. 21.

[31] It may be mentioned here that not all internal displacements are induced by ethnic conflicts, there are development-induced displacement largely as a result of construction of mega dams in the region. See Monirul Hussain, *Interrogating Development: State, Displacement and Popular Resistance in Northeast India, SAGE Studies of India's North East,* (New Delhi: Sage Publications, 2008).

Champai, Serchip, Lunglei, Chhimttuipui, Lawngtlai districts in Mizoram. On the Myanmar side, the Northeast borders Kachin State, Sagaing Division, and Chin State. The Naga, Chin, Mizo, Kuki, etc. inhabit the hilly borderlands with their presence on both sides of the border. Cultural and historical ties had never lost and interactions have always existed with people and goods moving from both sides.

For a very long time, the nature of trans-border relations between India and Myanmar has been characterized as 'illegal'. In the absence of any legal mechanism for trans-border ties, 'illegal' activities became the dominant feature. It is not surprising that trans-border consequences of Myanmar's internal conflicts on Northeast India have been negative in nature. It is well known that border lines tend to get more blur as one gets closer on the ground. India-Myanmar land boundary is no exception and in fact the border is highly porous. For the past several decades, restrictive policies adopted by the governments of both countries which have failed to encourage positive trans-border ties.

The existence of similar 'conditions of conflict' in Myanmar and the Northeast are glaring. In fact, the conflict conditions are so similar and if names are interchanged, it would still seem real. In this context, the depth of trans-border influences had been further strengthened. Trans-border consequences of Myanmar's internal conflict on Northeast India have provided uninterrupted supply of both idea and tool for India's Northeast insurgents and criminal networks to operate and sustain their activities of violence with adverse consequences.

The conflict conditions of the border and the nature of border management provided a fertile ground for 'illegal' activities to flourish. While conflicts of any kind could have little positive effects, the negative impacts of conflicts may vary according to the conditions of the place and people on which they impact upon. As Myanmar turned into the "regional epicenter of many international crime and smuggling networks,"[32] the consequences was felt directly on the border regions. The long porous and rugged forested terrains between India and Myanmar provided the best hiding places to carry out 'illegal' activities.

---

[32] Smith, "The Paradox of Burma", p. 20.

Guns, drugs and conflicts became inseparable with devastating consequences and the combination has created a political economy of violence.

It is known that small arms and light weapons are in large number in the Northeast region, though actual statistics are not available on guns possession.[33] Many studies have established that easy availability and accessibility of small arms has a direct correlation with the growth of armed groups. According to a study, the 1990s saw a proliferation of insurgents groups in the Northeast.[34] Although there is not evidence to suggest that arms came from the Myanmar's ethnic ceasefire-groups which had entered into ceasefire agreements with the Myanmar government in the late 1980s and the 1990s because Myanmar's ethnic insurgent groups and arms bazaar are not the only sources of arms.[35] However, the rise of insurgent groups in the Northeast with the decline of violence in Myanmar in the 1990s, it may not be wrong to suggest that the proliferation of Northeast insurgent groups have been impacted as a result the changed conflict situation in Myanmar. In the recent months there has been report citing intelligence sources that the United Wa State Army (UWSA) has become a major supplier of 'Chinese-made' arms to rebel groups in South Asia including the Northeast insurgents.[36]

There are more then 19 narcotic trafficking routes from Myanmar to the Northeast.[37] Illicit narcotic trade has long become a transnational phenomenon. Northeast ethnic insurgent groups have been affected by what is infamously known as the "Burma Syndrome". Some ethnic armed groups such as the Wa in the Shan State of Myanmar are known for their drug lords. Some insurgent groups in the Northeast have been taxing drug mafias to finance their operations.[38] United National

[33] Turner and Nepram, "The Impact of Armed Violence", p.17

[34] Ibid. p.4.

[35] A study has identified 13 sources of small arms and light weapons. Turner and Nepram, "The Impact of Armed Violence", p.18

[36] Subir Bhaumik, "Where do 'Chinese' guns arming rebels really come from?", BBC News, 3 August 2010.

[37] Binalakshmi Nepram, "Armed Conflict and Small Arms Proliferation in India's Northeast East – Part II", The WIP, June 15, 2007.

[38] Bhaumik, "Troubled Periphery", p. 196.

Liberation Front (UNLF) and the People's Liberation Army (PLA) are reported to have provided protection to drug mafias.[39] Narcotics and conflict have become closely inter-linked. Black market economies have thrived and have played a pivotal role in financing insurgencies. The gun-running and the narcotic trade are only symptoms of a large malice – the rampant illegality and corruption, hurting the region's economy.

Like the borderlands of Myanmar, where the Myanmar army indulge in all sorts of illegal activities, some authorities in bordering states of India's Northeast have been indulging in various illegal activities. For instance, in June 2010, the Police Headquarters of Nagaland issued a statement against information about collection of illegal taxes by various agencies including police, excise, forest etc. at various check gates in highways and directed all district police to sternly deal with any police personnel involved in such activities.[40] Another instance is the gun licence racket in Nagaland.[41] Cases of fake arms licences have been busted continues to be reported from different parts of the country.[42]

Another consequence is the issue of refugees and migration. India has also been at the receiving end of Myanmar's conflicts that have pushed thousands of people in to the Northeast region. Though the crisis of refugee and migrant workers from Myanmar into the Northeast is relatively small compared to the scale of Myanmar refugees and migrants in Thailand and other neighbouring countries, they have created social tensions between local population and the migrants. A largest number of Burmese (both refugees and economic migrants) has been concentrated in the state of Mizoram. According to some estimates, there 50,000 to 1,00,000 Burmese in Mizoram. As the number of Burmese in Mizoram grows, there have been tensions between local people and refugees at in the past. Local Mizos feel that the refugees will settle permanently in their land. The growing number of Burmese population

---

[39] Ibid.

[40] "Police have no authori ty to col lect tax es: State DGP", *The Nagaland P ost*, 23 June, 2010.

[41] Samrat Choudhury, "Small Arms, Large Casualties", *The Hindustan Times*, April 23, 2003

[42] See *The Hyderabad Deccan*, 30 June, 2010 and *The Times of India,* 8 June, 2010.

in Mizoram has been causing concern among Mizo people in the small state with a population of about eight lakhs. The possibility of social tensions may not be ruled out in future.[43]

Nagaland, Manipur, and Mizoram bordering Myanmar, have been recorded as HIV high prevalence States in India. In the early 1980s drug use became popular in northeast India and it wasn't long before HIV was reported among injecting drug users in the region. In all the three states, injecting drugs use has been identified as one of the driving force behind the spread of HIV.

Most of the state governments have taken up the issue of HIV/AIDS and drugs in their respective states. Mizoram has on certain occasion launched anti-foreigners campaigns to drive them out of the state.[44] India has been fencing its border with Myanmar at the request of the Manipur government as a policy response to tackling smuggling of narcotics and guns.[45] However, there has been no coordinated approach among the Northeast state, for instance, states like Mizoram, Nagaland, and Arunachal Pradesh have not raise the question of fencing. One of the worst affected states of the Northeast as a result of illegal arms and narcotic trade is Manipur. The state government has been taking measures to tackle trans-border issues. The Manipur government has begun construction of fencing the border where smuggling of arms and drugs has been highly prevalent.

Borderland Governance

There are alternative discourses on the Northeast and its ties with Myanmar emerging in the recent past. Jairam Ramesh has argued that "the future of the Northeast lies in political integration with India and economic integration with Southeast Asia".[46] Some have talked about

---

[43] "We are Lik e Forgotten People" Human Rights W atch, 27 January , 2009, at http://www.hrw.org/en/reports/2009/01/27/we-are-forgotten-people-0?print

[44] Julien Levesque and Mirza Zul fiqur Rahman, "T ension in the *Rolling Hil ls*: B urmese Population and B order Trade", IPCS R esearch Papers, I nstitute of P eace and Confl ict Studies, April 2008.

[45] Reuters, 22 October 2008.

[46] Jairam Ramesh, "Northeast India in a New Asia," *Seminar,* (550) June, 2005.

"re-imagining" borderlands[47] and making the "periphery as hub" or "turning the periphery into the centre of growth". Others have questioned the use of the term "periphery" because such term tends to see the Northeast region as "being periphery of a periphery".[48] Some see the Northeast not so much "landlocked" but "interlocked". These new theoretical discourses have been deconstructing the way the "Northeast" has been seen as a *region* and providing new ways in shaping perceptions in re-imagining the region. These ideas have been welcomed both at the governmental level and by the people of the region. Trans-border issues cannot be tackled by focusing only on one side of the border. India should not only end responsibilities at its border. In fact, the borderland between India and Myanmar cannot be seen as separate entities given the nature of ties that exist between the two sides of the border. This will serve two objectives – strategic and borderland development.

This paper attempts to strengthen the new discourses in understanding borderland governance. In so doing, the paper identifies the important factors and examines their role in shaping trans-border ties between India and Myanmar. An understanding of these factors will allow us to formulate necessary actions and policy guidelines for governments of both countries. Some may counter-argue that opening up of border may further attract more negative consequences. This paper contends, on the contrary, that the result of the negative consequences has been primarily because of the restrictive or 'closed-door' border policies. Also, negative trans-border consequences could be better prevented and monitored if more attention is given to the border areas.

---

[47] For instance see Nimmi Kurian, "T ransnational Neighbourhoods, Subnational Futur es: Reimagining North East I ndia" and R afiq Dossani and Srinidhi Vija ykumar, "I ndian Federalism and the Conduct of Foreign Policy in Border States: State Participation and Central Ac commodation since 1990", in Ami tabh Mat to and Happ ymon Jacob , eds., *Shaping India's Foreign Policy: People, Politics, and Places* , (New Delhi: Har-Anand, 2010).

[48] Ibid.

Some observers have warned the negative implications of the government initiatives such as border trade.[49] There are negative implications of border trade, however, these issues have been there even in the absence of border trade and the problems are largely a result of ineffective government monitoring. In fact, the same study also points out that efforts need to be on how to strengthen the monitoring mechanism rather the shooting down the idea of opening up the border. As India and Myanmar further expand their interactions through their land border, they are in an advantageous position to take a clue from the negative consequences of Myanmar's experiences of opening up its border with China and Thailand.

Cross-border exchanges and interactions in the field of culture, trade and commerce needs to be encouraged. There are sub-regional institutions such as the Bay of Bengal Initiative for Multi-Sectoral Technical and Economic Cooperation (BIMSTEC), the Ganga-Mekong Cooperation Programme (GMC), and the Bangladesh-China-India-Myanmar (BCIM) that provide the border region to take advantage of the opportunities. Although at multi-lateral institutions such as BIMSTEC or the GMC there are various sub-regional economic cooperation schemes for the development in the sub-region with economic objectives, bilateral initiatives for the development of border areas are largely to serve political and military objectives and less social and economic objectives. It may be argued that infrastructural development in the border area can all be considered as strategic assets. The new paradigm of borderland governance needs to be firmly rested on two notions that 'illegal' trans-border activities grow because 'legal' activities are prohibited and civilian control over the border weakens where borderlands are militarized. Hence, the objective should be to expand civilian space over military and 'legal' space over 'illegal'.

Factors Shaping Trans-Border Ties

There are many factors that shape the nature and consequences of trans-border ties between India and Myanmar's borderlands. Three key factors that could promote or hinder trans-border ties are – the

---

[49] Levesque and Rahman, "Tension in the Rolling Hills: Burmese Population and Border Trade", IPCS Research Papers, Institute of Peace and Conflict Studies, April 200

pace of infrastructural development in the borderlands; bilateral ties between India and Myanmar; and Myanmar's political future.

Infrastructural Development

Connectivity is one of the critical tools to promote interactions between people living along the border and hence development of infrastructure remains the priority. In the past decade or so, the government of India has laid great emphasis on border infrastructure such as connecting towns and villages along the border. India has also been assisting Myanmar in developing it border infrastructure. The Tamu-Kalemyu-Kalewa road is one such example. The two countries have also agreed to develop inland water navigation from the Bay of Bengal via the Kaladan River to Mizoram. The Kaladan Multi-model Transit and Transport Project, when developed, will provide the Northeast access to the sea. Under the sub-regional organization BIMSTEC, India, Myanmar and Thailand are building the Tri-lateral Highway that will connect India's Northeast with Thailand via Myanmar.[50] There are also other rail and road projects and plans that are currently being developed for more linkages between India and Myanmar. One such plan is to re-open the historic Stilwell Road which links India to China via Myanmar.[51] For a long time, the security establishments of the two countries have been averse to the idea of opening up the Stilwell Road. In January 2010, Myanmar assured India of reopening the Stilwell Road. According to reports, Myanmar's Minister Foreign Minister has requested the India government to help build the section of the Stilwell Road in Myanmar during the 5th North East Business Summit held in Kolkata.[52]

---

[50] BIMSTEC: Cooperation Report 2008, a report of Centre for Studies of International Relations and Indian Chamber of Commerce, (New Delhi: Bookwell, 2008).

[51] The 1,726 km Stilwell Road connects India's northeastern state of Assam to Kunming in southwest China's Yunnan province, after cutting through the Pangsau pass in Myanmar. Named after American General Joseph Stilwell, who led its construction, Stilwell Road was a vital lifeline for the movement of Allied Forces during World War II as they battled to free China from Japanese occupation. Chinese labourers, Indian soldiers and American engineers took three years to build the road. The Stilwell Road on the Indian side is about 61 km long. The major stretch of 1,033 km lies within Myanmar, while the stretch in China is 632 km.

[52] "Myanmar Okays Reopening of Stilwell Road", *The Assam Tribune*, 11 January, 2010.

The above projects will go a long way in facilitating greater connectivity between people in the borderland of India and Myanmar. At the same time, there is need for India and Myanmar to explore ways to collaborate in developing the region between the Brahmaputra River and the Irrawaddy River. The region forms a compact region. To begin with, the focus can be on the development of the fertile Hukawng Valley and Moguang Valley in the Chinwin River. Today, most of the agricultural products from these Valleys go to China. The aim of infrastructural initiative needs to focus on how to facilitate people-to-people contacts across the border. Better connectivity will in effect help promote tourism industry in the borderlands which could provide a major source of revenue for the people of the region.

The Bilateral Factor

The current government policies of both countries encourage more interactions in border region. This will, in turn, push for more legal activities in the border areas. Trans-border consequences cannot be prevented and in fact with the rapid changes taking place in terms of improving infrastructural sector, it will be even more difficult to curb movement of people and goods across the border. Hence, the way forward is not to curb people movement across the border but to institute appropriate identification and monitoring mechanisms. The existing bilateral institutional mechanisms are created largely with security objectives of maintaining peace and tranquility along the border. There is need to expand bilateral institutions focusing on socio-cultural and economic aspects of the border relations. The governments of both countries need to develop mechanisms for other aspects similar to the bilateral mechanisms on security issues.[53]

It could be naive to assume that military-bases in the region would be fully removed. However, the military presence can be reduced.

---

[53] Bilateral institutional mechanisms at various levels with the objective to facilitate dialogue in managing and monitoring illegal activities such as movement of insurgents, narco-trafficking, etc. There is Foreign Office Consultations (FOC) at the level of Foreign Secretary; National Level Meeting (NLMs) and Sectoral Level Meetings (SLMs) at the Home Secretary and Joint Secretary of the Ministry of Home Affairs; and Border Liaison Meetings (BLMs) between local Area Army Commanders at designated places very six months.

Hence, a realistic approach could be to enhance military capabilities rather than militarizing the region. Today, New Delhi and Naypyidaw seems ready to take forward the hard earned relationship. In the current geo-political context, it appears that New Delhi and Naypyidaw will strengthen their relationship in the foreseeable future and with no serious bilateral issue that could potentially reverse the relationship, means that the borderlands will continue to remain a major area of bilateral initiatives between the two countries.

Myanmar's Political Future

Perhaps, the most important factor that will continue to shape the nature of trans-border ties is the political future of Myanmar. The political future of Myanmar remains uncertain. Any major political turmoil in Myanmar will adversely affect trans-border ties. There is little sign the conflict-ridden political atmosphere will disappear in the near future. However, the political situation in the country will not remain static and as it gradually evolves, it will have its impact on the borderlands.

Parallel with the protracted-conflicts and political divisions, there have been changing taking place over the years. Myanmar has adopted a new constitution in 2008 and under the auspices of this constitution the country plans to conduct its first national elections in two decades later in 2010. The seeming political transition will certainly have its impact on the political landscape of the country and particularly on the ethnic nationalities. Although the outcome of the political transition process remains fragile, there is a process that has been set rolling and which may bring some structural changes in the polity. This will not be without its implications on the internal conflicts the country has been embroiled in for decades.

Conclusion

The current policies are in favour of greater interactions and linkages. From geo-economic perspective, many have argued that the Northeast can develop if only it is opened to the economies of the neighbouring countries in the age of globalization. In this context, it is impractical to keep the border closed and militarized. Experience shows that prohibiting the use of border for social and economic activities has been counter-productive as such approaches have only facilitated criminal and anti-social activities to grow in the border. A practical approach would be to allow social activities by creating necessary legal mechanisms to regulate and monitor movements of people and goods across the border. These initiatives will help achieve both de-militarization and encourage civilian activities along to the border. The rapidly changing dynamics of borderlands and their implications on the prospects of transnational relations between India and Myanmar will continue to grow in the coming years and there is an urgent need to recognize the changes and institute necessary mechanisms to deal with them so that they could be channelized for interests of the greater number in the region.

Conflicts in Myanmar: Regional Integration and Responses

REGIONAL INTEGRATION AND INTRA-STATE CONFLICT: INVESTMENT FOR PEACE IN MYANMAR

Anna Louise Strachan

The Union of Myanmar occupies a strategic position in Southeast Asia, surrounded by China, India, Bangladesh, Thailand and Laos. It has the potential to serve as a gateway between Southeast Asia and the countries of the Indian subcontinent. Myanmar's immediate neighbours have sought to gain influence in the country despite the fact that it is often seen as a pariah state, not only by the West, but by most of the world. They have sought to improve connectivity using Myanmar as a transit point. While many factors have rendered progress on this front slow and ineffectual, Myanmar's continuing instability, in particular the ongoing ethnic conflicts which have plagued the country for decades, is frequently seen as the main impediment. Other regions have nonetheless succeeded in making significant progress towards integration despite ongoing conflicts. This paper will therefore argue that while intra-state conflict is one of the factors behind slow progress on regional economic integration, many other factors, some of which are arguably more important, have hindered progress on this front. This will be done by looking at the impact of intra-state conflict in Myanmar on regional integration in a general sense and then considering the same issue in the context of Bangladesh and India and the member countries of ASEAN (Association of Southeast Asian Nations). This will illustrate the extent to which regional integration is affected by intra-state conflict in all contexts.

The definition of conflict is broad and in the case of Myanmar what constitutes a conflict remains unclear. According to the Uppsala Conflict

Data Programme (UCDP) there were just two active armed conflicts in Myanmar in 2008. These were between the government and the Karen National Union (KNU) and the government and the Shan State Army – South Command (SSA-S). The UCDP places both conflicts in the "minor" category.[1] According to the Institute of International and Strategic Studies (IISS), six active intra-state conflicts beleaguer Myanmar. These are between the Karen National Liberation Army (KNLA), the Karenni National Progressive Party (KNPP), the SSA-S, the Chin National Front (CNF), the Shan United Revolutionary Army (SURA) and the Arakan Liberation Party (ALP) and the government.[2] The 2009 Heidelberg Conflict Barometer, however, lists a plethora of conflicts.[3] Many of the groups mentioned by the Heidelberg Institute for International Conflict Research (HIIK) signed ceasefire agreements with the military junta in the 1980s and 90s. HIIK also classifies the situation between Myanmar's opposition parties and the ruling military junta as a conflict. While Myanmar's military junta and the country's ceasefire groups undoubtedly have an impact on progress towards integration and greater connectivity, it is not possible to discuss all these issues at sufficient length in this paper. 'Intra-state conflict in Myanmar' in this paper therefore refers to those conflicts which are current and which involve the actual use of violent force.

Violent force frequently involves damage to infrastructure and the disruption of transport as well as human suffering. Violent incidents therefore have the potential to hinder trade, a key element of regional integration. Karen[4] and Shan states, are important transit points in terms of linking South Asia with Thailand. Shan state also has the potential to serve as a gateway to Laos and Vietnam. There is therefore reason to believe that the severe conflict situations in these areas can act as an impediment to regional integration as they cause instability and

---

[1] Uppsala Confl ict Data Pr ogram. *UCDP Database 2010* , Uppsala Univ ersity, www.ucdp.uu.se/database.

[2] International Institute for Strategic Studies,   *Armed Conflict Database Myanmar 2010,* http://acd.iiss.org/armedconflict/MainPages/dsp_ConflictSummary .asp?ConflictID=209

[3] Heidelber g Insti tute f or I nternational Confl ict R esearch. 2009. *Conflict Barometer.* pp. 51-61

[4] Also known as Kayin State.

uncertainty in an area with great economic potential. Improved connectivity and economic integration could, however, provide the stability that is lacking in these areas and therefore greater commitment to these goals is required. This paper argues that the benefits of such a policy outweigh the costs as there is a possibility that rather than intra-state conflict hindering progress towards integration, greater integration may actually serve to resolve some of the tensions in Myanmar.

Acts of violence such as the bomb explosions in Yangon in April 2010 arguably serve as justification for slow progress towards economic integration and improvements in connectivity. While it is unclear who was responsible for the attacks, the junta have blamed previous attacks on minority ethnic groups. Regardless of who was responsible for the attacks, such acts of violence can reduce confidence in Myanmar's ability to be a significant player in any efforts to foster regional economic integration. They also make Myanmar appear to be an unattractive target for foreign investment. It is nevertheless worth noting that a number of countries have played a significant role in regional organisations, despite ongoing conflicts and acts of terrorism within their borders. This paper will therefore argue that undue significance should not be attached to such incidents.

It is in the interests of both India and Bangladesh to foster greater economic integration with Myanmar. Transport links through Myanmar would open up Southeast Asia to the subcontinent and significantly increase trade and interaction between the two regions. It would seem sensible, therefore, that Bangladesh and India seek to develop a joint policy in order to facilitate the resolution of Myanmar's ethnic conflicts. This paper will consider the policy options available to these countries in order to establish the means of intervention most likely to bring stability to Myanmar's conflict stricken provinces. It will be argued that policy options for both countries are limited. Both countries must tread carefully in their dealings with Myanmar's ruling junta in order to prevent Myanmar isolating itself completely. It will further be argued that the danger of pushing Myanmar towards China has been overplayed, notwithstanding China's significant influence there and evidence will be provided in support of this view. This paper will go on to present the argument that fostering economic prosperity in conflict stricken areas is the only realistic policy option available to India and Bangladesh in terms of conflict mitigation. While this is a strategy that carries with it a lot of risk, it enables India and Bangladesh to meet their requirements in terms of connectivity while also facilitating progress towards regional economic integration by creating a more prosperous environment for Myanmar's marginalised minorities and thus resolving some of the issues which have led to the continuation of armed conflict.

It is proposed that ASEAN would also benefit from the resolution of Myanmar's internal conflicts. Progress towards economic integration in the region has been slow, hindered by instability and political infighting. Myanmar has been a particularly controversial issue as ASEAN's longstanding policy of non-interference in the internal affairs of member nations has meant that they have failed to address the many Myanmar related issues that face the organisation. This paper also argues that closer ties between ASEAN and India are the perfect platform for cooperation between India and ASEAN on the resolution of Myanmar's intra-state conflicts. ASEAN also stands to benefit from prosperity in Myanmar's minority areas and must join Bangladesh and India in investing in infrastructural projects. The importance of bringing expertise to Myanmar in order to enable the creation of soft infrastructure and to facilitate trade will also be discussed.

Regional Integration

Attempts at regional integration have been made in both the developed and the developing world. Their recent financial problem notwithstanding, the EU (European Union) is arguably the most notable example of a regional integration success story. Regional integration efforts which include countries from the developing world include the Arab League, the AU (African Union), ECOWAS (Economic Community of West African States) and ASEAN, which will be discussed later in this paper. The initiatives mentioned involve various degrees of regional integration. ECOWAS, for example, has made significant progress on integration. To date, "a free trade area has been established, intra-regional passenger transport has been facilitated, infrastructural measures have been realised, a mechanism for conflict resolution has been initiated, the question of the community's income has been solved, and a functional court of justice has become a reality."[5]

Considerable progress on integration has thus been made, despite the conflicts afflicting a number of its member states. This suggests that regional integration in Asia should also be able to proceed, unhindered by the intra-state conflicts in Myanmar and in other parts of the continent.

At this stage it is important to note that there are numerous levels of economic integration. Schiff and Winters argue that RIAs (Regional Integration Agreements) do not generally aim for economic union but rather seek an increase in competition by eliminating policy interventions and reducing market segmentation.[6] They go on to state that a number of recent RIAs, including APEC (Asia-Pacific Economic Cooperation), are considering an intermediate level of integration, which involves "close governmental cooperation to harmonize domestic regulations and policies, but no supranational authority."[7] It must be noted that plans for an ASEAN Economic Community (AEC) to be created by 2015 go far beyond this. According to the blueprint for the AEC, "the AEC will establish ASEAN as a single market and production base making ASEAN more dynamic and competitive with new mechanisms and measures to strengthen the implementation of its existing economic initiatives; accelerating regional integration in the priority sectors; facilitating movement of business persons, skilled labour and talents; and strengthening the institutional mechanisms of ASEAN."[8]

The question is; are such goals attainable in the foreseeable future?

---

[5] J. Cernicky, "Auslandsinformationen, Sankt A ugustin." Konrad Adenauer Stiftung e.V , 2007, ht tp://www.kas.de/wf/en/33.11781/

[6] M. Schiff and L.A. Winters, *Regional Integration and Development* , (Washington: The International Bank for Reconstruction and Development/ The World Bank: 2003), p.20.

[7] M.Schiff and L.A. Winters, *Regional Integration and Development* . (Washington: The International Bank for Reconstruction and Development/ The World Bank: 2003). p.20.

[8] ASEAN. A SEAN Economic Communit y Blueprint., 2007, p.2.http://www.aseansec.org/ 21083.pdf

Bhattacharyay states that "greater regional integration through enhanced physical connectivity supports trade and investment (including FDI) expansion, and financial market development."[9] This is especially important for developing countries. The members of BIMSTEC (Bay of Bengal Iniative for Multi-Sectoral Technical and Economic Cooperation) are all categorised by the World Bank as falling into the low-income and lower-middle income categories. Moreover, there is great inequality in terms of the GDP of ASEAN members. SAARC (South Asian Association for Regional Cooperation) members also fall into the low-income and middle-income categories.[10] Increasing investment and financial market development are therefore clear incentives for the countries of South and Southeast Asia to pursue greater regional integration.

Brooks and Stone, however, argue that "while regional integration can help less developed countries and regions to access new markets, suppliers, technologies and opportunities, and can help to internalize negative spillover effects and capitalize on economies of scale, progress has not been even across subregions."[11] They go on to say that East Asia and Southeast Asia are ahead of other sub-regions and in particular of South Asia.[12] This can be taken to mean that progress in Southeast Asia has not been as slow as is generally believed. Alternatively, it could mean that progress towards integration in South Asia has been particularly slow. Regardless of the intended meaning, it is clear that there is much room for improvement in terms of progress towards regional integration and in terms of facilitating connectivity. The key task with regard to regional integration and connectivity in South and Southeast Asia is to "revive, renovate, and re-establish Asia's transportation networks, which played a pivotal role in integrating the region in ancient times and to establish Asia-wide intermodal transport

[9] B. N. B hattacharyay, "Inf rastructure Development f or ASEAN Economic I ntegration." *ADBI Working Paper 138*. (Tokyo: Asian Dev elopment Bank I nstitute, 2009), p .3.

[10] World Bank. *Table of Country and Lending Gr oups*, ht tp://data.worldbank.org/about/country-classifications/country-and-lending-groups#Low_income

[11] D.H. Brooks. and S.F. Stone, "Accelerating Regional Integration: Issues at the Border."*ADBI Working Paper 200,* (Tokyo: Asian Dev elopment Bank I nstitute, 2010), p .10.

[12] Ibid.

and transit in order to reduce the trade transportation costs across borders."[13] A regional transit agreement is also required, failing which all Asian countries should accede to existing international conventions.[14]

Brooks and Stone argue that soft infrastructure is as important as physical infrastructure when it comes to accelerating progress towards regional integration. They state that factors like the availability of credit, foreign exchange at reasonable rates, a reliable system of legal recourse and an effective competition policy play a significant role in achieving regional integration.[15] Soft infrastructure is an area in which there is much room for improvement in South and Southeast Asia. Brooks and Stone also argue that once basic physical infrastructure is in place, investment in soft infrastructure and enhancing trade facilitation is more effective than building more physical infrastructure.[16] This must be considered when looking at ways for India, Bangladesh and ASEAN to foster regional integration through investment in Myanmar. A multi-faceted investment and development programme, involving investment in physical infrastructure and the provision of expertise on issues relating to soft infrastructure and trade facilitation is likely to be the most successful approach to regional integration programmes which envisage Myanmar fulfilling the role of a major transport hub.

Economic Integration and Connectivity around the Bay of Bengal: Obstacles and Opportunities

There are numerous opportunities for improving connectivity and for increasing economic integration around the Bay of Bengal. For the purposes of this section Bangladesh and India will be considered as the key players with regard to regional integration. This section will outline the commitments made by the countries in question to promoting

---

[13] B. Bhattacharyay and P. De."Restoring Asian Silk Route: Towards an Integrated Asia."ADBI Working Paper 140. Tokyo: Asia Development Bank Institute, 2009, p. 7.

[14] Ibid., p.7.

[15] D. H. Brooks and S.F. Stone, "Accelerating Regional Integration: Issues at the Border." ADBI Working Paper 200. (Tokyo: Asian Development Bank I nstitute, 2010), p.10.

[16] Ibid., p- 27

connectivity and economic integration before assessing the progress made and the obstacles that continue to exist. Ways, in which the countries in question can move forward, in terms of using Myanmar as a gateway between South and Southeast Asia, will then be considered.

Myanmar is already a member of a number of regional organisations. It has been a member of ASEAN since 1997 and as a consequence is also a member of the ARF (ASEAN Regional Forum) and of the ACD (Asia Cooperation Dialogue). Myanmar is also a member of BIMSTEC and of the MGC (Mekong-Ganga Cooperation). Myanmar also applied for membership of SAARC in 2008, however the application is still under consideration and Myanmar currently holds observer status. Myanmar is a member of the Kunming Initiative (BCIM) alongside, Bangladesh, China and India. It is also a signatory to the Asian Highway Network (AH). This indicates a certain level of commitment to improved transport links and greater regional economic integration on Myanmar's part. Thein lists a large number of infrastructural projects which the Government of Myanmar has recently completely or is currently undertaking.[17] His paper is of interest as it looks at the issue of regional integration from what he terms the "Myanmar perspective." Most writing on this issue pays very little attention to this angle so it provides a means of obtaining information which shows the situation from a different angle. It is, however, worth noting that it is difficult to verifyithe extent of the progress that has been made on these projects and that the list should therefore be viewed with some caution.

In recent years efforts to improve connectivity and to foster economic regional integration have increased. Chaturvedy and Malone argue that while "the Indian government has spoken a great deal about the importance, indeed the primacy, of greater economic cooperation with its neighbours ...results are meagre and unconvincing, as are the achievements of the SAARC."[18] This is a valid argument, however one has to look at the larger picture before judging India's progress on this front. South Asia is a region fraught with instability and almost all of

---

[17] C.C. Thein, "Regional Cooper ation in T ransport: My anmar perspective on BIMSTEC."*CSRID Discussion P aper.* No . 42.2008 pp .14-20.

[18] R. Chaturv edy and D . Malone, "I ndia and i ts S outh Asian neighbours. " *ISAS Working Paper.* No. 100, 2009 p .3.

India's neighbours are embroiled in some form of intra-state conflict. While intra-state conflict is just one of many factors hindering integration, it certainly plays a major part, especially as the issue is not one conflict but dozens of them. According to the HIIK, India alone has 11 conflicts categorised at severity level 3 or above.[19] Referring to linkages between India, Bangladesh and Southeast Asia, Pattanayak states that "problems of connectivity can largely be attributed to the mistrust and suspicion that has been characteristic of Indo-Bangladesh relations since 1977."[20] Like intra-state conflict in the region, this is one of many factors hindering progress on connectivity and regional integration. Other factors include a lack of integrated and harmonised railway networks and a dearth of active overland official trade outlets as well as the absence of trade facilitation policy measures and transit trade.[21]

Bilateral trade between India and Myanmar stood at US$995 million in the period 2007-2008. At present Myanmar's exports to India far outweigh its imports from India.[22] Swaminathan states that border trade between Myanmar and India is negligible. He cites sub-standard roads on the Indian side, a small list of tradable goods and excessive regulations and restrictions as the causes for this. He does state, however, that India and Myanmar are considering plans to upgrade border trade carried out at the Reedkhoda - Tamu-Moye border crossing to 'normal trade.'[23] The reasoning behind India's relative neglect of its border areas in terms of infrastructure is often cited as being the instability in those areas caused by insurgencies and cross-border tensions. It is possible that Myanmar has neglected its border areas for

---

[19] Heidelberg Institute for International Conflict Research, 2009. *Conflict Barometer,* p. 52-53.

[20] Pattanayak, S.S. 2009. "India, Bangladesh and Southeast Asia: Connecting the Neighborhood." *Institute of Peace and Conflict Studies Issue Brief.* No. 113. p.1.

[21] Bhattacharyay, and P. De.. "Restoring Asian Silk Route: Towards an Integrated Asia." ADBI Working Paper 140. Tokyo: Asia Development Bank Institute, 2009, http:// www.adbi.org/files/2009.06.17.wp140. restoring.asian. silk.route.pdf

[22] Saurabh, "Dynamics of Indo-Myanmar Ties." Institute for Defence and Security Analyses. *IDSA Comment*, 2010, Available at www.idsa.in/idsacomments

[23] R. Swaminathan, "India-Myanmar Relations: A Review."*South Asia Analysis Group.* Paper 3480, 2009, www.southasiaanalysis.org/\papers35\ paper3480.html

similar reasons. Such neglect could conceivably have exacerbated instability in these areas. In view of the fact that the current approach has been a failure, it is time to look at this issue from a new perspective. Increased trade and investment will significantly improve the economic conditions in both the conflict afflicted provinces of India's North East and in the neighbouring provinces in Myanmar. Such an approach has the potential to stabilise these areas by bringing much needed development to marginalised communities.

Sikri argues for the benefits of greater connectivity with Myanmar, stating that there is a domestic dimension to India's policy towards Myanmar. He argues that improved economic and communication ties with Myanmar would reduce India's dependence on Bangladesh and could ultimately lead to greater development in India's North-eastern states.[24] While it is possible for India to focus on linkages with Southeast Asia using only its North-eastern corridor as a point of transit, it is advisable for India and Bangladesh to cooperate in order to bring about economic integration. Regional integration requires cooperation amongst all the countries of the region and Bangladesh can play an important role in facilitating connectivity between South and Southeast Asia.

To date Bangladesh's attempts to improve connectivity with its neighbours have been limited. Nevertheless, it did sign a bilateral agreement with Myanmar in 2007 for a Bangladesh-Myanmar Friendship Highway. Bangladesh proposed to bear the full costs of this project.[25] In June 2009, Bangladesh – Myanmar trade stood at US$140 million. The two countries aim for this figure to reach US$500 million by the end of 2010.[26] This is a step in the right direction but does not go far enough. Numerous suggestions have been made by high-ranking officials in Bangladesh, including the Foreign Minister[27], regarding ways in which

---

[24] Rajiv Sikri, "India's Look East Policy: Challenges Ahead." *India Foreign Affairs Journal.* 2 no. 2, (2007), p. 3.

[25] S.S. Pattanayak, "India, Bangladesh and Southeast Asia: Connecting the Neighborhood."*Insitute of Peace and Conflict Studies Issue Brief.* No. 113, 2009, p .3.

[26] BIISS, Statement by Foreign Minister of Bangladesh on Bangladesh-Myanmar Bilateral Relations, 2009, ht tp://www.mofa.gov.bd/Statement/PRDetails.php?PRid=14

[27] Ibid.

the two countries can cooperate to further connectivity and to boost trade. However, these projects largely remain pipe dreams, regularly discussed but rarely reaching fruition. This may be due to the fact that relations between Myanmar and Bangladesh have not always been amiable, becoming increasingly strained in 2009 over a maritime dispute between the two nations. A major military build up by Myanmar ensued in October of that year, and while there has been no question of an outbreak of a major conflict between the two countries, occasional border clashes do occur.[28] Despite these disputes there is still room for cooperation between the two countries on other issues. In the short-term it is essential that the Myanmar question is addressed issue by issue as in totality it is otherwise too complex and too controversial for any headway to be made. In the long-run the resolution of all disputes between the two countries is desirable as greater stability would be beneficial to the entire region.

China is also an issue that is frequently raised when considering Myanmar's potential role as a gateway between South and Southeast Asia. China is believed to exert significant influence in Myanmar. It is also perceived to be in competition with India for this influence. Nevertheless, it is worth noting that the insular nature of Myanmar's military junta does not provide foreign powers, including China, with as much scope for involvement in its internal affairs as is generally believed. Evidence of this is provided by the International Crisis Group (ICG), which details attempts by China in 2007 to improve Myanmar's military government's relationship with minority ethnic groups in an attempt to ease tensions and improve the domestic situation.[29] These efforts did not bring about significant change in Myanmar, suggesting that China's influence and Myanmar's dependence on China are frequently overplayed.

Referring to Myanmar's potential role as a connecting point between China and India and China and Bangladesh, Chaturvedy and

---

[28] S. Roughneen, "Burma, Bangladesh Border Build-up." *ISN Security Watch*. 2009, http://www.isn.ethz.ch/isn/Current-Affairs/Security-Watch/Detail/?fecvnodeid=118633&groupot593=4888caa0-b3db-1461-98b9-e20e7b9c13d4&dom=1& fecvid=33&ots591=4888caa0-b3db-1461-98b9-e20e7b9c13d4&lng=en&v33=118633 &id= 108738

[29] International Crisis Group, "China's Myanmar Dilemma."*Asia Report* No. 177, 2009, p. 5.

Malone argue that Myanmar is "the pivot of many forms of actual and potential transit that India could find highly threatening in a part of the country far from its critical mass."[30] It remains necessary for India to maintain its focus on what can be gained from its own involvement in Myanmar, rather than becoming too preoccupied with China's intentions. If the danger posed by China is real then India's only option of combating it is by stepping up its own involvement in Myanmar. This must be done in such a way as to not threaten the military junta, as should it feel that India is trying to encroach upon its sovereignty it is likely to take steps to terminate India's involvement in the country.

It is also worth noting Frost's assertion that India's influence is still far less than that of China[31] as this too could serve as a hindrance where Indian efforts to resolve India's internal conflicts are concerned. Lall, however, argues that the administration in Myanmar is open to greater Indian involvement as it hopes that India will balance China.[32] Both arguments suggest that there is room for India to increase its influence in Myanmar. Doing so by improving connectivity through infrastructural investment is likely to improve India's position in Myanmar, rather than damaging it in the way that condemning the current human rights situation and other aspects of the junta's rule would do.

In terms of connectivity, the Research and Information System for Developing Countries (RIS) argues that the restoration of the Afghanistan-Pakistan-India-Bangladesh-Myanmar (APIBM) Corridor will go a long way in enabling South Asia to become a connection hub between Central and Southeast Asia. The RIS claims that such a move would benefit Bangladesh as it would become a transit hub for India's trade with Myanmar and Myanmar itself would benefit as it would serve as a transit hub for India's trade with other ASEAN countries.[33] This is

---

[30] R. Chaturvedy and D. Malone, "India and its South Asian neighbours." *ISAS Working Paper.* No. 100.2009, 26.

[31] Frank Frost, "Burma/Myanmar: internal issues and regional and international responses."Parliament *of Australia Background Note*, 2009, pp. 7-8.

[32] Marie Lall, "India-Myanmar Relations – Geopolitics and Energy in the Light of the New Balance of Power in Asia. *Institute of South Asian Studies Working Paper.* No. 29, 2008, p. 3.

[33] Research and Information System for Developing Countries, "Restoring Afghanistan-Pakistan-India-Bangladesh-Myanmar (APIBM) Corridor: Towards a New Silk R oad in Asia."*RIS Policy Brief.* No. 30, 2007, p. 2.

undoubtedly true but, given the security situation in the countries through which such a transport corridor would pass, it is not currently feasible. Afghanistan is currently beleaguered by war and the other countries involved are plagued by significant intra-state conflicts. While intra-state conflict does not have a major impact on regional integration, the level of severity is undoubtedly a factor, which requires careful consideration. Violent conflict frequently involves damage to infrastructure and the disruption of transport as well as human suffering. There is therefore a serious risk that the costs would outweigh the benefits of such an initiative unless these conflicts are resolved. Although some roads have been built in Afghanistan investing in the Afghanistan-Pakistan sector of this transport corridor carries with it a lot of risk and significant progress is unlikely to be made until the conflicts in these countries are resolved. The India-Bangladesh-Myanmar section, however, is viable due to the fact that the conflicts in the these countries are less severe than those in Afghanistan and Pakistan.

In recent years India has become increasingly involved in neighbouring countries, contributing to peacekeeping efforts in Nepal and Afghanistan. In an address at IISS in London, India's Foreign Secretary Nirupama Rao, argued that the international community must work together to realise Afghanistan's potential as a trade, transportation and energy hub. She stated that in the case of Aghanistan "growing economic interdependence would complement efforts to promote peace and prosperity in the region."[34] The same holds true for Myanmar. India has pledged US$1.2 billion to help rebuild Afghanistan's infrastructure and has been involved in numerous projects from running medical missions to erecting power transmission lines and building roads. This has had the effect of bringing about significant increases in bilateral trade and has reportedly aimed at reaching every sector of Afghan society.[35] However, India's involvement in Afghanistan has not come without a price. Indian consulates have been the targets of

---

[34] Foreign Secretary, "Perspectives on Foreign Policy for a 21 st Century India." MEA-IISS Seminar. February 22, 2010, P .7.

[35] "India: Afghanistan's Influential Ally". BBC News, October 8, 2009, http://news.bbc.co.uk/ 2/hi/7492982.stm

explosions and grenade attacks and Indian nationals have been attacked.[36] India also has significant commitments with regard to aid for countries in Africa. As mentioned earlier in this paper, India has already played a proactive role in Myanmar with the focus to date being on providing funding for infrastructural projects. Increasing its funding of infrastructural development in conflict afflicted areas is therefore just a step up from its current level of involvement. Furthermore, India has not shied away from financial investment in Myanmar to date, despite the continuing conflicts in many parts of the country. According to Lall the factors behind this are "the economic development of India's North East, India's increased interest in trade with ASEAN, India's search for energy security and increased Chinese involvement in Myanmar."[37] India should increase its engagement in Myanmar in much the same way it has proceeded in Afghanistan. The risk of investing in conflict afflicted areas should not be a deterrent for India if it is serious about conflict mitigation and about increasing its influence in the region.

Currie argues that India's benefits from its cooperation with the junta have been small on both the economic and security fronts. She claims that Myanmar plays India and China off each other, protecting its own interests above all. She adds that when forced to choose between its two neighbours, Myanmar invariably chooses China.[38] Currie goes on to argue that India should "be more clever about using its own values and role within Asia to change the regional calculus on Burma." She states further that this should be achieved by India collaborating with other democracies in the region to press for political reform and improvements in other areas, such as internal security, which have an effect on the entire region.[39] Such a situation would be highly desirable but Currie fails to go into detail on this subject. While the principle is excellent, it is likely to prove difficult to achieve in reality. Pressure has been put on Myanmar in the past and it has failed to bring about

---

[36] Ibid.

[37] Lall, "India-Myanmar Relations"

[38] K. Currie, "India can mo ve the Needle on Burma. "*Wall Street Journal*, 2010, http://online.wsj.com/article/SB10001424052748703569004575009900765241246.html

[39] Ibid.

significant change. The idea that India, even in collaboration with other democracies in the region, will succeed in bringing about change in Myanmar where others have failed is idealistic. Realistically, India has a better chance of increasing its influence through investment than via political pressure.

Prosperity and stability are inextricably linked and perhaps Myanmar's neighbours need to make some risky investments in order to facilitate conflict resolution within the country. Tentative moves towards improving connectivity have already been made by India. Improved infrastructure and transport links may well have the effect of bringing about change in an indirect manner. Greater prosperity for Myanmar's marginalised minorities could be an indirect way of bringing about peace. Such a policy would, however, depend on the junta's acceptance of foreign resources being allocated in this way. To date it has been reluctant to afford these groups any form of assistance. It may be more amenable to supporting improved infrastructure in minority areas if funding for such projects is coming from external sources. Among key infrastructural projects would be improved transport facilities. It is, however, worth noting that assistance in terms of medical and educational facilities is unlikely to prove a viable option as the junta is not likely to take kindly to what could be viewed as the empowerment of minority groups, especially when this empowerment comes from the world's largest democracy. Notwithstanding this, India must not confine itself to infrastructural projects in Myanmar's conflict afflicted provinces alone. India must continue to invest in manufacturing and pharmaceuticals in Myanmar in a bid to create employment opportunities for those living in border areas. To date such projects have been limited. India must also use its increasing importance on the global stage to advocate a change of policy towards Myanmar in Europe and the United States. India must seek to persuade the world that empowering India's ethnic minorities by providing them with the means to achieve prosperity is the optimal way of improving the situation in Myanmar. This policy is far from ideal as it is long-term and the changes brought about may not succeed in completely ending the bloodshed in Myanmar. However, it does provide a means of meeting India, Bangladesh and ASEAN's needs in terms of connectivity and facilitating greater economic integration while having the potential to mitigate the circumstances which have led to intra-state conflict in Myanmar.

Progress Towards an ASEAN Economic Community

While the member states of ASEAN have professed a desire to further economic integration in Southeast Asia to the extent of creating an ASEAN Economic Community by 2015, progress on this front has been slow. Instability in the region is partly to blame for this lack of progress. Myanmar is not the only country in the region to be suffering from intra-state conflict. Thailand is afflicted both by severe political unrest and by a long-running insurgency in its predominantly Muslim southern provinces. In the Philippines the New People's Army (NPA) and rebel groups like the Moro Islamic Liberation Front (MILF) and the Abu Sayyaf Group have long been responsible for internal strife and in Indonesia separatists in Papua and ethnic clashes in other parts of the country have also contributed to regional instability. Increasing instability in Thailand could act as the most serious obstacle to greater regional integration. Should the situation escalate to conflict level, instability in Thailand is likely to outweigh intra-state conflict in Myanmar in terms of preventing progress on regional economic integration both ASEAN and BIMSTEC. Territorial disputes and non-traditional security threats such as natural disasters also have the potential to hinder progress on integration.

Bhattacharyay argues that "an improved and integrated transport and logistics system in ASEAN is an integral part of the regional integration initiative."[40] He goes on to outline a two track approach to infrastructure and development for ASEAN. He argues that ASEAN must cooperate in building and operating Cross-border Infrastructure (CBI) and in financing infrastructure development as enhancing ASEAN connectivity through CBI requires strong commitment and partnership among ASEAN governments.[41] This is one of the key factors behind ASEAN's slow progress towards regional integration. Strong commitment and partnership among ASEAN governments have not

---

[40] Bhattarcharyay, "Infrastructure Development for ASEAN Economic I ntegration.", p.1.

[41] Ibid., p 4.

reached required levels to date. The reason behind this is not intra-state conflict, but rather disagreement between governments. The military junta's policies are thus a much greater hindrance in terms of regional integration than internal conflict.

At this stage it is worth noting that an assessment of the economic impact of intra-state conflict in Southeast Asia highlights the fact that conflict has had little impact on growth in the region.[42] It seems likely therefore that the same should hold true for regional integration. Conflict does not appear to have served as a significant deterrent for investors and thus should not prevent progress on the infrastructural improvements required to make greater economic integration possible. The resolution of intra-state conflicts in Myanmar and in other Southeast Asian countries is however of great importance as greater stability would have significant social and economic benefits for the region.

The India-ASEAN relationship has developed in recent years. The 2009 ASEAN-Free Trade Agreement (FTA) is just one example of closer ties between India and the nations of Southeast Asia. There has also been increased military cooperation between India and ASEAN. This is a step in the right direction in terms of regional integration yet the full potential of the relationship has yet to be fulfilled. Cooperation on the Myanmar issue would certainly represent progress. Both parties stand to benefit from improved connectivity through Myanmar and from increased stability in the region. In particular, ASEAN must seek to improve infrastructure in the areas bordering with Thailand in a bid to improve trade between Myanmar's war-torn Karen State and Thailand's northeastern provinces. It has recently been announced that a new border trade zone will be opened on the Thai-Myanmar border in Mae Hong Song Province. The aim of the zone is to facilitate land and air freight based trade between the two countries. The project will also involve the building of a new highway.[43] While there has been some scepticism regarding the viability and the usefulness of the project, it

---

[42] A.L.Strachan, "Gr owth despi te bloodshed? Intr a-state conflict in Southeast Asia. " *Mainstream* XLVII no. 46, (2009): 32-35.

[43] Sai Zuan Sai, "New Thai-B urma bor der tr ade z one on an vil.", 2010, ht tp:// www.mizzima.com/business/3594-new-thai-burma-border-trade-zone-on-anvil.html

seems clear that this is precisely the kind of investment required to bring stability to Myanmar's conflict stricken areas.

Discussing US policy in Myanmar, Kurlantzick advocates the prevention of what he terms "the looming humanitarian disaster" arguing that such a move is both altruistically and strategically important as it would prevent the destabilisation of the entire region.[44] He states that a new humanitarian assistance programme would build the institutional infrastructure required for the US to respond should the situation in Myanmar deteriorate. Significantly, Kurlantzick believes that such a programme should be carried out in collaboration with Myanmar's neighbours.[45] If ASEAN, India, Bangladesh and the U.S. could implement 'investment for peace' together then significant change could occur. The lives of those living in Myanmar's border areas would improve significantly. ASEAN arguably stands to benefit the most from such a programme as the consequences of the situation in Myanmar are felt throughout its member nations. These consequences are serious and include large numbers of refugees, a flourishing trade in narcotics and the rapid spread of HIV.

Conclusions and Policy Recommendations

Intra-state conflict in Myanmar is not the key factor preventing progress on regional integration. A whole range of factors impede progress. Resolving the ongoing conflicts in Myanmar would, however, serve to smooth the path to increased connectivity and integration between South and Southeast Asia. It is therefore necessary for Myanmar's neighbours to play a proactive role in resolving these conflicts without alienating the ruling military junta. It seems clear that international approaches to the Myanmar issue have to date been unsuccessful. Recently, there have been many scholars and professionals advocating an end to sanctions, which they argue should be replaced by financial aid. There is however a fear that such funds could be misused. Investment for peace is an option open to all of Myanmar's neighbours and the larger international community and could bring about a

[44] J. K urlantzick, "F ailing State" *The W ashington Monthly*, 2010, http://www.washingtonmonthly.com/features/2010/1005.kurlantzick.html

[45] Ibid.

significant improvement in the living conditions of the country's ethnic minorities. That is because investment would take place in the border areas and where possible the funds would not be made available to the junta but rather to the communities in need of assistance. The logistics of providing aid and investing in this way would have to be looked into very carefully but the idea of transferring funds to communities along the Thai border via Thailand has already been put forward by several scholars. It must be noted that in view of the nature of the military junta in Myanmar, one should not be overly optimistic about what can be achieved. A realistic approach is essential. Even attempts to bring about an end to intra-state conflict in Myanmar through investment must be undertaken with care. Subtle infrastructural development and assistance is required in order to ensure that the junta does not become suspicious of its neighbours' motivations.

To date Bangladesh has had little experience of facilitating conflict resolution as a third party. However, as discussed earlier in this paper, it is in Bangladesh's interests to actively pursue a timely resolution of Myanmar's internal conflicts, in particular those which are being played out on Bangladesh's borders. It is therefore vital that India and Bangladesh cooperate on this matter. Both will reap the benefits of stability in Myanmar and have much to gain from greater economic integration and connectivity. Instability in Central Asia renders efforts to improve connectivity with Europe fraught with difficulty. Moreover, resolving the conflict situations in Pakistan and Afghanistan is likely to prove even more difficult than resolving the intra-state conflicts in Myanmar. Both Bangladesh and India must therefore devote their energies to increasing their involvement in Myanmar and presenting a unified front rather than acting in competition with each other. Bangladesh must also seek to heal rifts with Myanmar to facilitate greater cooperation with regard to improving conditions in the areas along the border between the two countries.

India's stance on Myanmar has earned it a great deal of criticism from the international community. Increased investment is likely to provoke strong reactions from some quarters. It is however important to remind those opposed to a more conciliatory approach to Myanmar, particularly one involving increased foreign investment, that a tough stance has to all intents and purposes been fruitless. Sanctions have failed to bring about change and have only increased the suffering of the people of Myanmar. India has stood apart from the international community on the Myanmar issue thus far and there is therefore no reason why it should be concerned about any additional adverse reaction to its policy decisions in the future. Moreover, India's increasing prominence in global politics could even serve to provide it with an opportunity to alter international opinion on the appropriate policy towards Myanmar. India should seek to convince the international community that economic empowerment is the way to improve the lot of Myanmar's ethnic minorities rather than adding to their woes by punishing them for their government's actions with sanctions. This will however require increased investment in India's North East as well. The ongoing conflicts in the region must be resolved and the Indian government must increase spending on infrastructure so that improvements are being made on both sides of the India-Myanmar border.

ASEAN also stands to benefit from increased investment in Myanmar's conflict stricken border areas. Thailand is particularly affected by the ongoing conflict in Karen state and as a result steps must be taken by the organisation to improve conditions along the border between the two countries. Cooperation on the Myanmar issue also presents an opportunity for ASEAN to strengthen its ties with India and Bangladesh. Improved ties are essential if greater regional integration is to be achieved.

References

ASEAN. 2007. ASEAN Economic Community Blueprint. Available at http://www.aseansec.org/21083.pdf

BBC News. 08/10/2009. "India: Afghanistan's influential ally." Available at http://news.bbc.co.uk/2/hi/7492982.stm

Bhattacharyay, B. and P. De. 2009. "Restoring Asian Silk Route: Towards an Integrated Asia." ADBI Working Paper 140. Tokyo: Asia Development

Bank Institute. Available at http://www.adbi.org/files/ 2009.06.17.wp140. restoring. asian. silk. route.pdf

Bhattacharyay, B.N. 2009. "Infrastructure Development for ASEAN Economic Integration." *ADBI Working Paper.* No. 138. Tokyo: Asian Development Bank Institute.

Bangladesh Institute of International & Strategic Studies. 2009. Statement by Foreign Minister of Bangladesh on Bangladesh-Myanmar bilateral relations. Available at http://www.mofa.gov.bd/Statement/ PRDetails.php?PRid=14

Brooks, D.H. and S.F. Stone. 2010. "Accelerating Regional Integration: Issues at the Border." *ADBI Working Paper.* No. 200. Tokyo: Asian Development Bank Institute.

Cernicky, J. 2007. "Auslandsinformationen, Sankt Augustin." Konrad Adenauer Stiftung e.V. Available at http://www.kas.de/wf/en/33.11781/

Chandra, A.C. 2009. "The Pursuit of Sustainable Development through Regional Economic Integration: ASEAN and its Potential as a Development-oriented Organization." International Institute for Sustainable Development.

Chaturvedy, R and D. Malone. 2009. "India and its South Asian neighbours." *ISAS Working Paper.* No. 100.

Currie, Kelly. 2010. "India can move the Needle on Burma." *Wall Street Journal.* Available at http://online.wsj.com/article/SB1000142405 2748 703569004575009900765241246.html

Foreign secretary. 22/02/2010. "Perspectives on Foreign Policy for a 21st Century India." MEA-IISS Seminar. P.7.

Frost, Frank. 2009. "Burma/Myanmar: internal issues and regional and international responses." *Parliament of Australia Background Note.*

Gaibulloev, Khusrav and Todd Sandler. 2008. "The Impact of Terrorism and Conflicts on Growth in Asia, 1970-2004." *ADBI Discussion Paper.* No. 113. Tokyo: Asian Development Bank Institute.

Heidelberg Institute for International Conflict Research. 2009. *Conflict Barometer.*

Heidelberg Institute for International Conflict Research. 2008. *Conflict Barometer.*

Hlaing, Kyaw Yin. 2009. "ASEAN's pariah: Insecurity and autocracy in Myanmar (Burma)." In Hard Choices: Security, Democracy and Regionalism in Southeast Asia edited by Donald K. Emmerson. ISEAS.

Hussain, W. 2009. "India's Northeast: The Super-highway to Southeast Asia?" *Institute of Peace and Conflict Studies Issue Brief.*

International Crisis Group. 2009. "China's Myanmar dilemma." *Asia Report.* No. 177.

International Institute for Strategic Studies. 2010. *Armed Conflict Database Myanmar.* Available at

Kaplan, Robert. 2000. "Center Stage for the Twenty-first Century: Power Plays in the Indian Ocean." *Foreign Affairs.* Vol. 88(2).

Kennes, W. 1997. "Developing countries and regional integration." *The Courier ACP-EU.* No. 165.

Kurlantzick, J. 2010. "Failing State." Washington Monthly. Available at http://www.washingtonmonthly.com/features/2010/1005.kurlantzick.html

Lall, Marie. 2009. "Ethnic Conflicts and the 2010 Elections in Burma." *Chatham House Asia Programme Paper.* ASP PP 2009/04.

Lall, Marie. 2008. "India-Myanmar Relations – Geopolitics and Energy in the Light of the New Balance of Power in Asia. *Institute of South Asian Studies Working Paper.* No. 29.

Lorch, J and G. Will. 2009. "Burma's Forgotten Conflicts: A Risk for the Region's Security." *SWP Comments.* No. 10.

Minority Rights Group, 2010. "Peoples under threat 2010 – online briefing."

Pattanayak, S.S. 2009. "India, Bangladesh and Southeast Asia: Connecting the Neighborhood." *Institute of Peace and Conflict Studies Issue Brief.* No. 113.

Research and Information System for Developing Countries. 2007. "Restoring Afghanistan-Pakistan-India-Bangladesh-Myanmar (APIBM) Corridor: Towards a New Silk Road in Asia." *RIS Policy Brief.* No. 30.

Roughneen, S. 2009. "Burma, Bangladesh Border Build-up." *ISN Security Watch.* Available at http://www.isn.ethz.ch/isn/Current-Affairs/Security-Watch/Detail/?fecvnodeid=118633&groupot593=4888caa0-b3db-1461-98b9-e20e7b9c13d4&dom=1&fecvid=33&ots591=4888caa0-b3db-1461-98b9-e20e7b9c13d4&lng=en&v33=118633&id=108738

Sai, Sai Zuan. 2010. "New Thai-Burma border trade zone on anvil." Available at http://www.mizzima.com/business/3594-new-thai-burma-border-trade-zone-on-anvil.html

Saurabh.2010. "Dynamics of Indo-Myanmar Ties." Institute for Defence and Security Analyses. *IDSA Comment.* Available at www.idsa.in/idsacomments

Schiff, M. and L.A. Winters. 2003. *Regional Integration and Development.* Washington: The International Bank for Reconstruction and Development/ The World Bank.

Sikri, Rajiv. 2007. "India's Look East Policy: Challenges Ahead." *India Foreign Affairs Journal.* Vol. 2(2).

Strachan, A.L. 2009. "Growth despite bloodshed? Intra-state conflict in Southeast Asia." *Mainstream* Vol XLVII (46).

Swaminathan, R. 2009. "India-Myanmar Relations: A Review." *South Asia Analysis Group* .Paper 3480. Available at www.southasiaanalysis.org/\papers35\paper3480.html

Thein, C.C. 2008. "Regional Cooperation in Transport: Myanmar perspective on BIMSTEC." *CSRID Discussion Paper.* No. 42.

Uppsala Conflict Data Program. 2010. *UCDP Database,* Uppsala University. Available at www.ucdp.uu.se /database.

World Bank. *Table of Country and Lending Groups.* Available at http://
data.worldbank.org/about/country-classifications/country-and-
lending-groups#Low_income

MYANMAR'S MILITARY MINDSET INTENSIFIES INTERNAL CONFLICTS[1]

Larry Jagan

Myanmar is facing a crucial time at present with elections coming up and a move to a civilianised form of government. The future may well be in the balance. The military, who have ruled Myanmar since the coup on the 18 September 1988[2], are planning to introduce a constitutional system that effectively guarantees them political control for the foreseeable future[3]. But there will be differences – the relationship between the top army brass, especially the regional commanders, and the civilian authorities has yet to be worked out[4]. This is bound to lead to friction, especially over the control of resources.

This could also be a watershed in Myanmar's relations with the rest of the world. At least that is what the junta Supremo, General Than Shwe may be thinking – or at least hoping. The elections, the first in 20 years, are also meant to bring an end to the ethnic rebel resistance that has plagued the county for the past five decades or so. Unfortunately the new constitution, adopted in a referendum in May 2009, gives the ethnic groups very little of what they want and essentially dooms the

---

[1] This paper is based on the author's presentation at the Conference on "Internal Conflicts in Myanmar and Trans- Border Consequences" held on 26-27 Ma y 2010 at Singapor e.

[2] In fact the military have ruled Myanmar since 1962 when General Ne Win overthrew the democratic government of U Nu.

[3] Under the Consti tution, 25% of the seats are reserved for members of the military .

[4] There will be a national parliament, and 14 provincial or regional assemblies with Chief Ministers in each state being the 'nominal' authorit y.

whole process. It is a repeat of 1974 which also failed and ended in the mass pro-democracy movement of 1987-88[5].

The biggest stumbling block to stability and development remains the disarming of the rebel ethnic armies that have been fighting for greater autonomy of independence from the centre for several decades, but have ceasefire arrangements with the Myanmar army[6]. The regime wants the ceasefire groups to surrender their weapons and become part of the new Border Guard Force under the command of the Myanmar army. While some smaller groups have already accepted this, several of the main ethnic organisations – especially the Kachin, Mon and Wa – have repeatedly defied the junta's ultimatums.

These ethnic tensions also have a significant international dimension, especially affecting the country's neighbours. There are fears in the region that this ethnic nervousness as a result of instability in the border regions could lead to a mass exodus of people. "If the political situation in Myanmar deteriorates further and fighting erupts we can expect more than 200,000 new refugees, mainly Shan and Wa, this year," said the head of Thailand's National Security Council, Bhornchart Bunnag[7].

China is also acutely aware of the need to make sure that the border area with Myanmar remains secure and stable, and are anxious to make certain that above all else peace is maintained. Many Chinese leaders remember the Great Leap Forward, when almost overnight 200,000 Chinese crossed the border into Myanmar, many of who never returned[8]. What they fear most is a "great leap backwards" with thousands of ethnic Chinese flooding across the border into China for safety and increasing unemployment and tension in the already sensitive southern border region. The mass exodus of some 40,000

[5] When Ne Win realised that 'naked' military power was not the answer to Myanmar's political problems he introduced a new constitution and help elections – albeit for a one-party state — in 1974.i

[6] See Appendix A on the ceasefire armies and those still fighting.

[7] Interview with Bhornchart Bunnagat Chulalongkorn University in February 2010.

[8] Confidential conversations with Chinese government officials in Beijing and Bangkok, in 2007 and 2009.

Kokang, who are all ethnic Chinese, across the border into Yunnan 2009 to escape from the Myanmar army's military offensive, was a major wake-up call for Beijing.

Since August 2009 there has been a flurry of diplomatic activity between the countries, culminating in the official visit of the Chinese premier Wen Jiabao in June 2010. The border situation featured prominently in their bilateral discussions and assurances were given by Than Shwe that there would be no repeat of the border problems of 2010. To make sure that their other main ally was also placated, Than Shwe visited India between 25 and 29 July 2010, and briefed the Indian prime minister, Narasimha Rao on Myanmar's progress towards political change. This was in stark contrast to the regime's attitude to it regional partners in the Association of South East Nations (ASEAN)[9].

The regime's roadmap to democracy, which the elections and the formation of a civilianised government are the penultimate step, was originated by the outward-looking former intelligence chief and prime minister General Khin Nyunt — and then adopted and carried out by the inward-looking junta chief Than Shwe. Many analysts argue that is not only an exit-strategy for the senior general but a means of changing their relations with the outside world[10].

But it will also increase existing tensions and cleavages within the country and create new problems for social cohesion and social control that may yet subvert the gains the junta leaders hope to achieve from this strategy.

Military Mindset

At the root of the dilemmas posed by Myanmar's political conundrum is Myanmar's military mindset which determines the way in which they treat their civilian population, the ethnic minorities and view the international community. The military may not be part of the solution, but they are certainly a key part of the problem. "There will be no

---

[9] Larry Jagan, "Myanmar and Asean, Agree to Disagree", *Asia Times Online*, 26th July 2010.

[10] The hope is that these elections will give the regime legitimacy and as a result may lead to the end of the West-led economic and travel sanctions. Interview with ASEAN Secretary General Surin Pitsuwan, Bangkok, November 2009.

change or real progress in Myanmar until the Generals have gone," said the then Singapore Goh Chok Tong confidentially several years ago. "I regret recommending to our businessmen to invest in Myanmar – none are running at a profit and they cannot repatriate their capital."[11]

More than a decade earlier Bangladesh's foreign minister, Mustifizur Rahman's assessment was chillingly similar. He was concerned about the return of more than 300,000 Muslims from Myanmar – known as Rohingyas – who had fled from persecution and severe human rights abuses and had taken shelter in makeshift camps around Cox's Bazaar in eastern Bangladesh across the border from Myanmar in 1991. After a trip to Yangon to negotiate their repatriation, he said privately: "There will be no solution to the Rohingya problem until the Generals are no longer in power."[12]

The problem is that the Myanmar military leaders' approach to the outside world – and their internal strategic priorities – is introverted and battle oriented. From the Burmese Kings, through Ne Win to the State Law and Order Restoration Council (which later became the State Peace and Development Council in 1997) there has been an over-riding attitude: any engagement with the outside world was something they shunned and only did when it fitted into their own strategic needs. Myanmar's leaders have always been introverted – looking inwards rather than outwards.

Moving the capital inland to Naypyidaw, some 400 kilometres north of the former capital Yangon in 2005, is only the latest clear example of this outlook. It was a strategic tactic as well as being completely in line with their "protective" isolationist ideology. They moved away from the sea[13] – from where the traumatic colonisers came – to the inland hills, the heartland of the Myanmaran ethnic majority, which also gave them greater effective control over the rebellious border regions

---

[11] Interview with Goh Chok Tong in Singapore in November 2002.

[12] Interview with Mustifizur Rahman in London, December 1991.

[13] Moving from the sea (and outward looking) into the hinterland (inward looking and isolationist) is in stark contrast to neighbouring Thailand – which moved its capital from inland to the coast as it opened up to the world.

dominated by the ethnic minorities and insulated government and the top military command from the subversive influence of the civilians in Yangon in particular.

Part of the Myanmar military's outlook stems from their *Myanmaran* approach to the country and the world. It is xenophobic in nature – fear of anything foreign, which is seen as a threat to their racial purity and national security, dominates their attitude to everything and largely pre-determines their position on any matter whether it is the political opposition, the ethnic minorities or the outside world.

For example the junta's hatred of the detained pro-democracy leader, Aung San Suu Kyi is in part because of her marriage to a foreigner, though a Buddhist – the renowned British Tibetan scholar, Dr Michael Aris — who died in 1997. The mixing of blood – through marriage and off-spring – is openly despised by the *Myanmaran* psyche, although centuries of migration have already destroyed the racial purity to some extent.

As a result Aung San Suu Kyi Aris is loathed by many because of her marriage, and since her return to the country in 1987 has been harshly reviled in hundreds of vitriolic articles, cartoons and public speeches because of her indulgence with a *"kala"*[14]. She has been frequently accused of having soiled her iconic blood heritage – she is above all General Aung San's daughter. She is now regarded by many in Myanmar, especially the ruling military as a "traitor" to the traditional *bama lumyo*.

Throughout the 1990s many sarcastic pamphlets and articles were published by the official press. For example this spiteful editorial in the official English-language newspaper: *"Mrs Michael Aris, alias Daw Aung San Suu Kyi … has breached the discipline of the race and its culture and customs. How can there be patriotism when she had not, with patriotic spirit, upheld the principles of preserving one's own race and lineage?*[15]*"

Myanmar history is inundated with examples of this kind of racial prejudice. But it was broader than the white colonialists. It also referred

---

[14] "Kala Phyu" means literally "white foreigner".

[15] *The New Light of Myanmar*, 8 June 1996.

to those who came from the sea (*kula* – to come from the sea) to the west — whether Arabs merchants, Armenian traders, Tamil sailors or Portuguese mercenaries. The invaders from the east were equally feared and degraded. The need to keep Myanmar blood-line pure also motivated then the military intelligence chief to publicly disown his son Ye Naing in 1998 because he had married a Singaporean — though a Burmese citizen herself[16].

But Myanmar's military leaders are xenophobic, chauvinist and isolationist by inclination and strategic vision. While their psyche is derived from centuries of Myanmarn elitist views, it is compounded by their military mindset – hardened by the origins of the Myanmar army form the Thirty Comrades who trained in Japan under a feudalist and imperial Japanese tutelage. The fusion of these two approaches has hardened the overall outlook – xenophobic (including a paranoid fear of foreigners), chauvinist, racist, and self-reliant. This coupled with an unwillingness to negotiate and a total mistrust of civilians.

The junta's leaders believe that only the army represents the country as a whole and can protect the nation (both from its enemies abroad and within). They see themselves as the only unifying force in the country that represents the national interest. "We truly represent the nation, the political parties can only represent a segment of society," said the former deputy head of military intelligence, Major General Kyaw Win[17].

The army's top brass also suffers from a "siege mentality". This was further emphasised by the 2005 move of the whole government apparatus and the war office to the Pyinmana area 400 kilometres north of the former capital, Yangon. This was an important strategic move on the part of the top military ruler, General Than Shwe. But it was not as some have suggested for fear of a foreign invasion, namely the US, but to put the military command closer to the ethnic minority areas in order to better control them, centralise power and keep a closer grip on the

---

[16] Larry Jagan, "View on Khin Nyunt's Disowning of Son", *BBC Asia-Pacific News online*, 26 February 1998.

[17] Interview with MG Kyaw Win in Shan State, March 2003.

regional commanders, and to insulate the military from the civilian population.

Myanmar's top generals do not trust civilians and prefer to deal with other soldiers. It is quite clear that other Asia military leaders have a better relationship with the junta than their foreign ministers. The Thai military were informed within 12 hours after the arrest of the prime minister, Khin Nyunt, and told that he faced possible trial for corruption, while the foreign ministry – and other diplomats in Yangon – had no idea what was happening. The Prime Minister Thaksin Shinawatra was informed and this information was inadvertently revealed at the time by the government spokesman Jakrapob Penkair.

And for those who may hope that the rivalries and personal animosities within the military could be exploited, the Myanmar army has never had a mutiny within its ranks. The esprit des corps within the army is stronger than in any other military – certainly within Asia – and it is a function of the strict internal discipline and rigidly hierarchical approach to authority within the officer corps and ranks. Orders from superiors are instinctively carried out without question.

"Officers and soldiers in the Tatmadaw [Myanmar Army] obey orders and never question their superiors," Major General Kyaw Win said. "That is why we have never been defeated," he added. Myanmar's fighting force is also feared by their Thai neighbours.

When Myanmar soldiers were given orders they carried them out with hesitation, according to Thai military intelligence officers. "If they were ordered to take a hill-side border check-point, occupied by ethnic rebels or Thai soldiers, they would advance until they had secured their objective, no matter how many died in the battle, or their superior officers ordered them to retreat.

More crucially Myanmar's military leaders cannot compromise and do not understand the notion of a win-win situation. For them, any concession means some-one else gains and they lose. In their minds, there are only winners and losers not matter what the case is. Everything is seen in terms of a military battle or campaign. So they are less likely to respond to overt pressure. "The Tatmadaw never negotiates,"

General Khin Nyunt once wrote to Aung San Suu Kyi, according to senior military intelligence officers.[18]

What makes this even harder is that dialogue and discussion are anathema to Myanmar's soldiers and commanders alike. "We never discuss anything, we only obey orders or give them," said a senior Myanmar intelligence officer, Colonel San Pwint[19]. But nonetheless, in the past decade or so there have been signs that the military were prepared to enter talks with Aung San Suu Kyi and the National League for Democracy, while at the same the regime tentatively opened up to the international community. These periodic moments of opportunity were largely the result of the initiatives taken by the intelligence chief and one of the country's top three generals at the time Khin Nyunt.

General Khin Nyunt recognised that progress and prosperity in Myanmar could not be achieved without wider exposure to the outside world. He understood that, in order for the regime to increase trade and attract foreign investment, certain concessions had to be made to the international community's concern about the lack of a political transition to democracy. This was also a way in which the strongest international pressure could be effectively deflected by getting support – usually within the region – to delay sanctions or dodge their impact.

But it is internal considerations, which underlies all the junta's policy-making – and to be effective they need to be in complete control of the country. "We have never ceded any territory to an external enemy," said Colonel San Pwint, making an exception of course for the ethnic rebel groups that have from time to time controlled border areas. From the days of Ne Win – and a lesson learned from their British colonial masters – the military has worked on a "divide and rule" approach towards their perceived enemies – the pro-democracy movement – that they see as standing for anarchy and the end of law and order – the ethnic groups, who they see as not pure, and the international and regional powers, who they fear wants to plunder the country for its

---

[18] Beijing's policy towards Myanmar is based on this assumption. "We know that if we push to hard on the door it will slam shut and we will lose everything," said a Chinese diplomat in a discussion with the author in Bangkok in 2007.

[19] Interview with Col San Pwint in March 2003.

resources, tear it apart and weaken it or overthrow them – regime change.

"Peace talks are detours to our final gaol," one of the leaders of the Khmer Rouge, Kieu Samphan – now facing trial for genocide – one said during the Paris peace talks, which ironically did lead to the end of the civil war, the introduction of a new regime, and comparative peace, stability and development two decades later. But for Myanmar's top military leaders, these peace talks or dialogue is an effective delaying tactic that can be shut down at any moment.

This was the case early 2004, when talks between Aung San Suu Kyi and the military seemed on the verge of a break-through – the NLD would participate in the National Convention that was to be reconvened and complete a draft constitution and the detained opposition leader eventually released from house arrest. At the last minute, Than Shwe simply reneged on all the agreements that had been made at a more junior level when the NLD refused to accept the order of events – participate in the National Convention and then Aung San Suu Kyi would be released.

This approach – whereby discussion and concessions are not part of the political process that may lead to a new civilianise government – has also dogged the junta leaders problems with the ethnic minorities. This is in fact a far more intractable problem that is likely destabilise Myanmar in the near future, even after the elections.

The 2010 elections are something of a leap in the dark for Myanmar's normally overcautious military rulers. The routinely precise and strategic approach of the top military brass is absent[20] No matter what the junta does, Myanmar's ethnic groups are likely to shape the country's political future after the polls. Not only will they have a crucial say in who dominates the national parliament and the provincial legislatures, but the future of the ceasefire armies will determine overall border stability and bilateral relations with key regional neighbours,

---

[20] The army only precedes with proposed plans that hve been thoroughly thought through and all contingencies and eventualities anticipated and contingencies indetified: interview with senior MI officer Brig Gen Kyaw Thein, Rangoon Feb 1994

especially China and Thailand. More crucially the role of the Myanmar's regional military commands – in a post-civilianized government, after the elections – will depend on the ethnic ceasefire groups' attitude and approach.

For their part, the ethnic groups understand the significance of the 2010 elections and are planning to contest them, while maintaining their armed wings. "We know it is essential to keep our arms until we see what sort of government emerges after the elections, and whether we can trust them," said a spokesman for the Kachin Independent Organisation (KIO), Col James Lum Dau[21].

The ethnic groups – both ceasefire groups and those still fighting – understand that they must be unified as never before and that their future existence may depend on it. This has galvanised them, and after a series of secret meetings, many of the groups (including the Karen National Union[22]) have now agreed alliances, including a military pact[23] in the face of a possible junta attack on them. "Never in our history have the ethnic groups been so united," said a senior KIO leader. "Self-preservation has united us all."

In a series of secret meeting, both inside and outside Myanmar some ten ethnic rebel groups, including all the major ethnic armies – both ceasefire and armed groups — have agreed to stand together and adopted a common military strategy. "We are prepared to fight to the bitter end and will never accept the control of the Tatmadaw," said a senior Kachin leader recently.

After a critical meeting in Chiang Mai earlier this year the new alliance unanimously agreed that if the SPDC breaks the ceasefire pacts, all the groups are prepared to engage in a protracted guerrilla war targeting key installations. These will be military targets in Naypyidaw

---

[21] Interview with KIO spokesman, Col James Lum Dau in Bangkok, in an interview in April 2010.

[22] The KNU is sti ll fighting the My anmar army, and despi te splits and def ections, has no entered a ceasefire arrangement with the authorities.

[23] Interview with Zipporah Sein, Karen National Union General Secretary, Bangkok, March 2010.

and throughout the country. It would be a concerted and coordinated campaign, said some of those at the meeting[24]. All the groups agreed to carry out their plan individually, but both the ceasefire groups and the non-ceasefire groups agreed to link up, and synchronise their activities in order to tie down the SPDC troops, according to the final informal agreement.

The ceasefire groups in this alliance include the Wa, Kachin, Kokang, Mon, Mongla group and SSA-north and the others the Karen, Karenni and the SSA-south. While the numbers of guerrillas these armies command may be insignificant compared to the 400,000 strong Myanmar army, but using guerrilla tactics, and targetting military installations in urban areas like Rangoon and even Naypyidaw they could wreak untold havoc, according to western and Asian intelligence officers. Although it may not have been any ethnic group behind the recent bombing in Rangoon during Thingyan, it shows how ill-prepared the junta is for this type of warfare, a retired Indian military intelligence officer, formerly based in Rangoon said.

The ceasefire groups have also grown in confidence in recent months as the junta seems to have been forced onto the back-foot by their refusal to accept the Myanmar military's demand that they disarm and become part of the Border Guard Force (BGF). Some six deadlines for the ceasefire groups to accept this have come and gone, with the final deadline at the end of April[25]. The regime's regional commanders in touch with the recalcitrant ceasefire armies have been persistently threatening them with all-out-war if they continue to resist. But instead of complying with the Than Shwe's orders, the groups are resisting the junta's calls at every conceivable turn.

The Wa have continually postponed planned meeeings with the regional commander, the Kachin have followed suit and now the Mon have refused a meeting with the regional commander[26]. This is unprecedented resistance on the part of the ceasefire groups – and is

---

[24] Private interviews with several participants, Chiang Mai, March 2010.

[25] Now the junta seems to have postponed the final disarming of the key ethnic groups until after the elections.

[26] *Irrawaddy*

part of an overall strategy to postpone the need to openly confront the junta as long as possible. "It's all a delaying tactic," said a KIO spokesman. "Or aim is to postpone a decision as long as possible, we want to keep our arms for at least six months after the new administration" he said. "All new agreements should be negotiated with the new government," he added[27]. In the meantime the groups are preparing to launch a new country-wide ethnic guerrilla war if necessary.

The junta has always believed in the past that by dealing separately with each group they could successfully get their way, with least resistance[28] – the typical "divide and rule" approach of the Myanmar Army – and an effective tactic they adopted from the British colonialists. While it may have worked in the past – it seems to no longer effective, for very few, and only small ethnic groups like the Kokang have agreed to the government's terms.

The ethnic rebel groups have known for years that they would have to surrender their arms in the long run after a political settlement was agreed with the military authorities or a new civilian government[29]– it was part of the ceasefire agreements, although the KIO are the only ones to have a formal, written pact[30]. After the intelligence chief Gen Khin Nyunt announced the 7-step roadmap in August 2003 – shortly after becoming prime minister – the disarming of the ceasefire groups was an important component of the creation of "democratic space", although it was never formally part of the official plan[31]. But Khin Nyunt made it clear that the ethnic ceasefire groups were to surrender their weapons after the constitution was drawn up and before the

---

[27] Interview with Col James Lum Dau, Bangkok, April 2010.

[28] Interview with Col San Pwint, an MI officer heavily involved with the junta's ceasefire negotiations with most ethnic rebel groups, from the Wa and Kokang in 1988-89, in Shan State in March 2002.

[29] Interview with KIO leader Bran Seng in June 1992, Bangkok.

[30] All the ceasefire agreements were verbal and the pacts agreed with the local regional commander, except the Kachin – which was a formal document and signed by General Khin Nyunt and Bran Seng.

[31] It was always understood according to the UN's special envoy on Myanmar, Dato Razali Ismail. Various interviews with Razali in Rangoon and Kuala Lumpur 2003-2005

referendum. He constantly told diplomats and other international visitors that this was the case[32].

The idea of a border militia had also been muted by Khin Nyunt and his military intelligence team some months before his fall in 2004. In fact the MIs were convinced that this was only a matter of time and that the details had been ironed out. Only a few months before the purge of the MIs, the military spokesman, Col Hla Min said an agreement had been reach in principle[33].

Of course as soon as Khin Nyunt was vanquished from the scene, the ceasefire groups suddenly (and perhaps understandably) got an acute case of amnesia. The purge of the MIs, especially the spymaster, unsettled the ceasefire groups, particularly the Wa. None of the major ethnic groups along the border with China – Kachin, Kokang and Wa — trusted the top army commanders, especially Than Shwe and Maung Aye, and felt that Khin Nyunt alone of the top brass at least understood their concerns and priorities[34]. "If Khin Nyunt goes we may have to tear up the ceasefire agreement," said the Wa leader Bao Yuxiang[35]. The apparent Chinese approval of Khin Nyunt may also have been a factor in the ethnic groups' confidence in him[36].

So his exit certainly unsettled the ethnic ceasefire leaders, and there were many in Pangsan (the capital of the Wa autonomous region) that pushed for a break with the junta. But Chinese officials – at the very top level – intervened privately to convince the Wa and the Kokang at least not to push the issue too hard and to trust the regime's intentions, which they reluctantly did. The first sign though that

---

[32] Interviews with EU Ambassador Hamburger, Razali and the Thai Foreign Minister Surakiart Sathinathai

[33] Interview with Col Hla Min; Wa leaders a few months earlier said that they would disarm and become a local armed militia – part of a police force with some 8,000 armed with pistols and 12,000 unarmed 'soldiers': interview with Bao Yuxiang in Pangsan Feb 2004.

[34] Interview with the Kio leaders the late T u Jai and Dr T u Ja in Rangoon Dec 2003. Interview with Kokang leader March 2002.

[35] Interview with Bao Yuxiang in Pangsan, March 2002.

[36] See the forthcoming book by Egreteau and Jagan for a detailed discussion of Khin Nyunt's Chinese connection.

relations between the ethnic groups and regime were not going to be as cosy as under Khin Nyunt was their sudden insistence that they had never heard of a deadline for disarming and were definitely not given one – let alone the BGF. In the post-Khin Nyunt era, there were legitimate grounds for them to be uneasy about any plans for surrendering their arms. The key concern was that under the BGF the ethnic police force would come under the control of the Burmese Army. Under the MI vision, the ethnic militia would be commanded by their own officers, and only nominally part of the Tatmadaw[37].

Their suspicions of the junta's real intentions – eliminating them as a military and political threat in the future Myanmar were reinforced by the cavalier way the National Convention dealt with their objections and concerns over the constitution were summarily dealt with. It became increasingly clear that there was no room for negotiations with the Burmese Army leaders – in the way that it was possible with the MIs. After all this is the way the Tatmadaw operates. Khin Nyunt wrote to Aung San Suu Kyi in the midst of their rapproachment before her release in May 2002, saying she should understand that in the Burmese Army never negotiates[38]. So for the junta there is no such thing as a win-win situation; if some-one wins and the other looses.

The war-experienced ethnic leaders understand the Myanmar military mind better than most[39]. So they are prepared to walk the tight-rope – balancing resistance and without directly provoking the junta. But since their failure to influence the constitutional process there has been an unannounced campaign of quiet but forceful disobedience on the part of the ethnic groups. "The crucial thing is to keep hold of our weapons, that's the only bargaining chip we still have," said a KIO spokesman. "And we haven't fought for our rights for more than three decades to give up now."[40]

---

[37] Discussions with Kachin, Kokang and Wa leaders between Dec 2003 and March 2004 in Rangoon and Pangsan. MI spokesman also seem to suggest that, interview in March 2004.

[38] Discussions with deputy intelligence chief Maj Gen Kyaw Win, Shan State March 2002

[39] Interview with KIO leader, Bran Seng in Bangkok in June 1992.

[40] Interview with KIO spokesman, Col James in Mae Sot, July 2009.

Myanmar's territorial integrity is one of the junta's key priorities. "We must keep our borders intact and prevent any invaders occupying Myanmar territory," said a senior military intelligence officer, who spent much of his army career along in the sensitive border areas, Col San Pwint[41]. And that will remain the army's main mission, while Senior General Than Shwe is in control or even if in the future there is a form of democracy and the Lady is in power, he added. So this going to be one of the military's key concerns after the elections. And already Myanmar's neighbours are beginning to get anxious.

Thousands of ethnic refugees from Myanmar continue to flee across the country's borders into Bangladesh, China, India and Thailand. The numbers are growing as the country's political situation remains uncertain in the run-up to the elections and military offensives against the non-ceasefire rebel groups like the Karen National Union (KNU), according to analysts and aid workers. "The political instability in Myanmar – with the elections due sometime later this year – and pressure on the ethnic armies to disarm, will drive more refugees to seek safety across the border, especially in Thailand," according to a Myanmar academic based in Chiang Mai, Win Min[42].

In recent months there have been increased fears of renewed fighting between several ethnic guerrilla groups and Burmese soldiers as the government tries to force the ethnic rebel armies to surrender their weapons and form a special Border Guard Force under the control of the Myanmar military before next year's elections. The KNU has issued fresh warnings to their supporters of a pending assault against them[43].

Both Thailand and India are nervous about the consequences of more tension in the border regions, though it will be the eastern and northern borders which will be most acutely affected[44]. But China is also seriously concerned about the need to make sure that the border area with Myanmar remains secure and stable, and are anxious to make

---

[41] Days of discussions with Col San Pwint in Shan State, March 2002.

[42] Discussions with Win Min in Chiang Mai in March 2010

[43] Email from KNU leader, Zipporah Sein, July 2010.

[44] See comments of the Thai National Security chief XXX already quoted.

sure that above all else, peace is maintained. Many Chinese leaders remember the Great Leap Forward, when almost overnight 200,000 Chinese crossed the border into Myanmar, many of who never returned[45]. What they fear most is a "great leap backwards" with thousands of ethnic Chinese flooding across the border into China for safety and increasing unemployment and tension in the already sensitive southern border region[46]. Most of the thousands of Chinese who fled across the border to Yunnan last August have not returned despite the return of relative calm[47].

So concerned are the Chinese, that the prime minister earlier postponed visit was hastily rescheduled. Wen Jiabao visited Myanmar at the beginning of June for two-days, meeting Than Shwe amongst other top Myanmar officials. Both sides have been quiet about the details of the trip, but the border issue certainly appears to have been high on the agenda. This was transparently obvious from the Myanmar press coverage of the visit – the border affairs minister was prominent in all the ceremonial photographs published and the footage shown on television.

The Chinese Premier Wen Jiabao and his Myanmar counterpart Then Sein had "reached a broad understanding on protecting the peace and stability of the (Myanmar) border regions" and signed agreements that "signified another step forward in bilateral relations", China's official *Xinhua news agency* reported.

"We are willing to deepen our friendship with Myanmar and expand cooperation, always acting as a good neighbour, good friend and good

---

[45] Confidential conversations with Chinese government officials in Beijing and Bangkok, in 2007 and 2009.

[46] The numbers of Chinese living in Myanmar is difficult to quantify as much of the migration in the last decade or so has been unofficial. Estimates range from 500,000 to over 2 million. Both Chinese and Burmese officials (in interviews in Rangoon between 2002-2004, put the number at over a million.

[47] More than 40,000 refugees fled across the border, from Kokang and some from the Wa areas. Very few have returned as y et – probably w aiting until after the election to decide, ac cording to Chris K aye (WFP head in Y angon), interview in B angkok A ugust 2010.

partner," Wen reportedly told Myanmar's prime minister[48].

Fresh Burmese army offensives are also expected against the KNU in Eastern Myanmar, who have been fighting for autonomy from the central Burmese authorities for more than 60 years, and so far have not negotiated a truce. Fierce fighting in Karen state near the border with Thailand in June and July last year forced more than three thousand refugees to flee across the border for safety, according to the regional office of the United Nations High Commission for Refugees (UNHCR) based in Bangkok[49]. Nearly all of these refugees are still in Thailand, according to the UNHCR spokeswoman, Kitty McKinsey. "Right now, UNHCR does not feel conditions exist for the Karen or any other refugees in the nine camps along the Thai-Myanmar border to return to their homes in safety and dignity," she said.

"I have talked with many refugees in the camps and a number of them do dream of returning home to a Myanmar that is free and peaceful, but most of them also feel that the time is not right for them to return home now," she said.

A further influx of Karen and Mon refugees is expected if fighting resumes. This could also top more than 100,000, according to Jack Dunford, who heads the Thai Burma Border Consortium which helps refugees and displaced people in Eastern Myanmar[50].

The Democratic Karen Buddhist Army (DKBA) — which broke away from the KNU more than a decade ago and formed a ceasefire pact with the Burmese army — has been conducting a massive violent compulsory conscripting of civilians into their militia in preparation for the new border police force, according to KNU leaders. "The press-ganging of Karen villagers started early this year [2009] and is continuing now the wet season is over," said the KNU general secretary Zipporah Sein. "Every

---

[48] For a more detailed account of the visit, see Mitch Moxley, "China-Myanmar Talks a Step Forward in Thawing Relations", *Inter Press Service*, 4 June 2010, Beijing.

[49] Frequent interviews with UNHCR's regional spokeswoman, Kitty McKinsey, from June to October 2009.

[50] Discussions with Jack Dunford in Feb and March 2010 in Bangkok.

village has to provide two soldiers and money for equipment like walky-talky radios," she said[51].

In August 2009 the Burmese army also attacked the Kokang, who call themselves the Myanmar National Democratic Alliance Army (MNDAA), near the Chinese border which resulted in more than 40,000 ethnic Chinese Kokang fleeing into southern Yunnan province[52], most of whom have still not returned even though the fighting has stopped.

For decades Myanmar's ethnic minorities have fled from fighting and persecution inside Myanmar's border areas. "Successive military regimes have tried to eliminate all the ethnic minorities inside Myanmar in an effort to purify the population," said a Karen spokesman, David Thakerbaw[53].

"Decades of persecution, religious intolerance and cultural repression left the country's ethnic groups, including the Kachin, with no option but to fight the Burmese army for their own self-preservation," said the top Kachin leader, Bran Seng, more than fifteen years ago, shortly before he died. "But when the situation did not improve, and years of fighting inflicted even more suffering on our Kachin people, it was time to try another strategy and sign a ceasefire agreement," he said.

In the past 20 years more than a dozen ethnic rebel groups have entered truce agreements with the Myanmar army, but the regime's current plans to have all the ethnic rebel soldiers give up their weapons and form police-style militia is putting those arrangements in jeopardy. Many of the cease-fire groups have resisted this move including the largest organisations the Kachin, Mon and Wa, although some smaller groups have accepted it.

"At a time when we are trying to accomplish everything through politics, the SPDC [State Peace and Development Council] wants to do

---

[51] Interview with Zipporah Sein in Mae Sot in July 2009.

[52] Official Chinese and Burmese figures are lower, 37,000 – but NGOs on the ground put the figure at over 40,000

[53] Interview with KNU spokesman, David Thakerbaw, in Mae Sot in June 2009.

something else," said Col James Lum Dau, a spokesman for the Kachin Independent Organisation (KIO)[54].

"The SPDC wants to dissolve the KIO and its armed wing, the Kachin Independence Army, and force it to come under the SPDC's control," he added. The Kachin National S Party that some members of the KIO formed after leaving the organisation has been consistently refused registration as a political party. This is mainly because the party is an amalgam of Kachin organisations – including a smaller ceasefire and the Kachin Baptist Convention – not just the KIO, which would certainly top the polls if allowed to contest the elections..

Most ethnic minorities have suffered severe persecution, had their land confiscated and forced to work as porters for the Myanmar army. International human rights groups, like the UK-based Amnesty International and the US-based Human Rights Watch, continually draw attention to the plight of these ethnic people.

The situation in the west of the country is even worse, where the Muslims, many of them known as Rohingya, have been continually victimised. "Myanmar's Rohingya minority is subject to systematic persecution; they are effectively denied citizenship, they have their land confiscated, and many are regularly forced to work on government projects," said Benjamin Zawacki the Myanmar researcher for Amnesty International[55].

"The regime creates conditions and circumstances that make it clear to the Rohingyas that they are not wanted or welcome in the country; so it's no surprise that they try to flee the country by the thousands," he added. In the last decade, according to aid workers involved with the refugees in Bangladesh, where most of the Muslims flee to first, more than a hundred thousand have sought safety across the border. "There are some two hundred Rohingyas still living in Bangladesh who have fled from Myanmar in the past fifteen years," said Chris Lewa of the Arakan project who has monitored the situation

---

[54] Interview with Col James, in Bangkok, Dec 2009.

[55] Interview with Benjamin Zawacki, in Bangkok, May 2010.

for nearly two decades[56]. Half of them had fled Myanmar before but were repatriated in the mid-nineties, she added.

In the early 1990s more than three hundred thousand Rohingya fled to Bangladesh to escape persecution and death at the hands of the Burmese authorities, said Nural Islam a Rohingya leader based in London, and a human rights lawyer[57]. Although many of them returned to Myanmar under a UN-sponsored repatriation programme, this has not stemmed the continuous flow of Rohingay refugees. The local Burmese authorities are still building an enormous fence to prevent Burmese Muslim refugees fleeing into Bangladesh. And progress is being made on the possible repatriation of the remaining Rohingyas in Bangladesh, according to the country's foreign minister, Dr Dipu Moni[58]. And there are signs that the Myanmar government has realised the voting potential of this group – many are being granted citizenship (and given national identity cards) after decades of being denied them, so they can vote in the elections. The construction of bridges, roads and schools are also in full swing – with the help of UN money – obviously intended as a voter catcher for the deputy foreign minister who is standing for parliament in that area[59].

But all this is window dressing, and the deep-rooted resentment of the Burman and the Myanmar army will not be easily overcome. It will remain the key irritant to stable and peaceful country well after the elections unless there is genuine national reconciliation. The plight of Myanmar's ethnic minorities will not be resolved until there is a genuine political solution and their cultural and religious rights are recognised, according to analysts and ethnic specialists. "The first thing that needs to be done is to allow ethnic people to be educated in their own languages," Suboi Jum, a former Kachin Baptist Bishop[60].

---

[56] Interview with Chris Lewa, in Bangkok in April 2010

[57] Interview with Nural Islam in London June 2010.

[58] Interview with Dr Dipu Moni, at the ASEAN foeign ministers meeting in Hanoi, July 2010.

[59] Interview with WFP chief (Yangon), Chris Kaye in Bangkok August 2010.

[60] Interview with Suboi Jum in Bangkok Jan 2009.

The forthcoming elections are unlikely to help the process of assimilation or integration of Myanmar's ethnic minorities. "A Federal Constitution would be a start," said Ashley South, a historian of the Mon and an ethnic specialist. "Myanmar's ethnic nationalities will find it difficult to achieve lasting peace and security without a settlement that guarantees their social and political rights. But socio-political transition in Myanmar is likely to be a drawn-out process, rather than a one-off event[61].

The ethnic leaders understand that they are at a cross roads again – like they were in the early nineties after decades of fighting that got them no-where. The junta was also motivated by the military impasse and negotiated the series of truces as an interim measure that would be resolved when there was a new constitution[62]. Now that time has come and the end result is crucial to both sides.

The future for the ethnic groups now lies in the balance again. Just as it was important for their continued existence some two decades ago — to give up armed struggle and negotiate ceasefire agreements — they are faced with a bleak and unpleasant choice – to disarm or risk a return to civil war. The ethnic groups understand only too well what the prize is here. Do they join the legal fold as Khin Nyunt put it – and fight the elections – or return to the armed struggle. Neither choice seems appealing to the ethnic leaders.

Some ethnic groups like the Kachin plan to fight the elections, and have formed separate political parties to contest the polls, others have joined the NLD-inspired international boycott of the elections and a third group have remained silent so far.

Politically, the ethnic areas, especially in the north and Shan state will be key to the outcome of the elections: there are some 55 seats in the national parliament are in Shan State. And many of the regional parliaments are also in these areas. The ethnic groups are likely to decide the outcome of these elections. In many cases it is the ceasefire

---

[61] Email exchange with Ashley South, Dec 2009.

[62] Interview with Brig Gen Kyaw Thein, the most senior MI responsible for the ceasefire agreements in an interview in Rangoon in Feb 2004.K

groups who may be in a position – if they contest the elections to decide the Chief Minister in the states, and not the Myanmar army. There will be heightened tension between the ethnic groups and the regional parliaments on one hand and the central administration – especially over control of resources and the Myanmar army. Chief Ministers and the regional commanders will have to develop a new relationship.

So it is little wonder that the junta has postponed again the issue of the ethnic groups disarming and joining the BGFs. Now this will be tackled after the elections. The hope is that the new landscape will help them do what they have not been able to do for the last five years – finally remove the armed ethnic groups from Myanmar's political scene. The probable result is that this will give the ethnic groups renewed strength and vigour – seeing the constant dilly-dallying on the part of the junta as a sign of weakness. They certainly have their contingency plans in place. They are prepared to test the new military-backed civilianised government's resolve. In the end it may be the neighbours – China, India and Thailand — that decide whether this is resolved amicably and peacefully. In the meantime – and the incentive for the neighbours to act – there is certain to be a new increase in refugees seeking safety from uncertainty and possible conflict across the country's borders.

Since the junta seized power in September 1988, their attitude to the international community has been relatively cautious. They have been coaxed out of their shell on occasions over the last twenty years, but have quickly retreated into isolation whenever it proved more convenient and comfortable for them. But they have become the masters of splitting the international community when it suits them – and have generally turned to the region for support first. After all they have been patently aware of the divide between the West's isolationist approach towards them Asia's reluctant support.

This is no coincidence, for it was Asia which caused the first major schism within the international community by adopting a policy of "constructive engagement". [Chinese relations with Myanmar were cemented in the early years after the State Law and Order Restoration Council seized power in September 1988, and Beijing's temporary international isolation after the June 1989 crackdown on the pro-democracy movement may have also contributed to the burgeoning friendship]

But it was Myanmar's south-east Asian neighbours in the Association of Southeast Asian Nations that took the initiative. Having sorted out Cambodia, they now turned their attention to Myanmar. Malaysia was in the forefront of the move, as Dr Mahathir was keen to realise the ASEAN dream of the ten countries becoming members of the group by the time the organisation celebrated its 30th anniversary in Kuala Lumpur under the Malaysia's chairmanship.

There was significant resistance to joining ASEAN in Yangon. While Khin Nyunt was strongly in favour, other senior members of the junta, especially Maung Aye and Than Shwe himself, were reluctant. But the intelligence chief managed to convince his colleagues — and Myanmar became a member of ASEAN in 1997 and began participating in regional activities.

This was an important juncture for the junta for it began to expose the military to the region, and gave them a sense of what Myanmar was missing out on because of its isolationist policies. Singapore and Bangkok were beacons for the men in green.

Khin Nyunt's right-hand, Brigadier General Thein Swe often said Myanmar could and should emulate Thailand (he was also military attaché in Bangkok in the late 1990s). The deputy head of intelligence Major General Kyaw Win never hid his admiration for Singapore.[63] For the military intelligence crew it underlined the benefits that might accrue to Myanmar of accommodating the international community. Of course they also benefitted from that as they travelled in the region and were able to broker many commercial deals.

Myanmar's military leaders — from Ne Win onwards — have always sought limited but strategic partnerships that would protect them from international interference and pressure, help them develop the economy and provide financial assistance, and offer military hardware

---

[63] Several interviews with Maj-Gen Kyaw Win in Myanmar between 2002 and 2004.

and supplies. The current junta leaders, because of the internationally imposed isolation after the crushing of the pro-democracy movement in 1988, which left as many as 10,000 dead[64], have sought some respite from their predicament by forming strategic alliances – which often changed as circumstances necessitated. But China has remained the key to any notional security arrangement in the minds of Myanmar's military leaders.

US-led sanctions forced us into the hands of Beijing, according to the Myanmar military's spokesman, Col Hla Min[65]. The MIs under Khin Nyunt have consistently argued that Washington's position gave them no option but to seek China's assistance and support[66]. "We knew we could count on China, after thousands of troops massed on our northern border ready to help if the Americans invaded [in late 1988]", said Col Hla Min[67]. From that point onwards the relationship – despite the past tensions between the two countries – has developed and strengthened. But it has been a fraught partnership at times. Now the growing economic integration – especially with the building of the gas pipeline across the north of the country to Yunnan – will almost certainly make be the basis of any future government's foreign policy no matter what their outlook. Even the pro-democracy leader Aung San Suu Kyi is aware that good relations with Beijing are essential, even for a future democratic state.[68]

When in the early 1990s, India began to court the regime – for its national interest – the junta was a relatively willing suitor. Previously Delhi had been unswerving in its support for the pro-democracy leader and the students. But India soon realised that strategically that this was counter-productive: forcing the Myanmar military closer and closer to China. Since then a strong relationship has developed, though Delhi

---

[64] Conversations with many Myanmar military intelligence officers over the last 20 years. While academics tend to put the figure at 3,000, Khin Nyunt told his subordinates it was at least 6,000 and probably closer to 10,000.

[65] Interview with Col Hla Min in Yangon, March 2003.

[66] Senior MI officer, Brig-Gen Thein Swe.

[67] Interview with Col Hla Min in Yangon in February 2002.

[68] Interview with Aung San Suu Kyi, in Yangon on 10 March 2003.

understands it can only play second fiddle to Beijing[69]. In recent years India has tried to take a more nuanced position – supporting democracy in Myanmar in principle but not allowing that to stand in the way of improving pragmatic relations with the junta. "We cannot see our relations with our neighbours through a prism of democracy," said the then foreign minister, Jaswant Singh[70].

Russia has provided the necessary balance to these two neighbours – who are in reality rivals for influence in Myanmar. After some five years of being a member of ASEAN, the junta realised that their muted support was limited value, especially on the international stage. They were dismayed at the region's response to the international outcry that followed the brutal attack on Aung San Suu Kyi in May 2003 by pro-government thugs. The ASEAN foreign ministers at their annual meeting in the Cambodian capital Phnom Penh, effectively condemned the attack and called for Aung San Suu Kyi's immediate release. This certainly forced them to look towards Moscow as a more reliable ally.

The pecking order in Myanmar's external relations were further revealed at the ASEAN foreign ministers meeting in Hanoi in August 2010, when the Myanmar foreign minister Nyan Win left early and skipped the crucial security discussions at the ASEAN Regional Forum (ARF) attended by more than 17 dialogue partners – including China, Japan, India, Russia and the US. He had to accompanying the Myanmar head of state, Gen Than Shwe to India. China's premier Wen Jiabao was fully briefed on political developments during his trip to Myanmar in June 2010, and the Indian prime minister Manmohan Singh was also brought up to speed when Than Shwe visited Delhi at the end of July. "This is the state of things, China and India are being kept in the loop," said the Singapore foreign minister George Yeo. "That's why ASEAN must remain engaged with Myanmar – isolation and sanctions are not an option."[71]

---

[69] Numerous discussions and interviews wth Indian diplomats in Bangkok, Delhi and Yangon since 1992.

[70] Interview with Jaswant Singh in Yangon in April 2002.

[71] George Yeo's comments to journalists at the Hanoi A SEAN meetings in July 2010.

Since Burma's military leaders seized power more than 22 years ago, the international community has tried to restore democracy to the country through a combination of dialogue, engagement, goading and sanctions. Asia — largely China, India and ASEAN – the West (Europe and the US) and the UN have all taken key roles in this process over that time of either encouraging or putting pressure on Myanmar to reform. But the main problem has always been the major disagreement between those who favour sanctions and those who believe the only to encourage change, is to engage the regime rather than isolate them.

Part of the problem that stands in the way of the international community's efforts to convince the generals that change is both necessary and in their interests has been the general failure to understand the motivations of the Myanmar military. Myanmar's leaders are extremely insular, chauvinist and xenophobic. A few years ago Than Shwe told the Cabinet that all white people working for the UN and INGOs should be expelled from the country – four years later only two whites are now UN heads (WFP and the ILO) – even the deputy head of WHO (a white) was not been given a visa – and told to wait until after the elections to apply.

This was also highlighted during the aftermath of the devastating Cyclone Nargis which wreaked havoc in Yangon and the Irrawaddy Delta in May 2008. The regime resisted allowing a massive aid effort to swamp the country – and certainly initially rejected the help offered by the western countries – especially France, UK and the US. Two of whom sent ships into the area of the coast of Myanmar, which only served to alarm the regime and create renewed fears of a foreign invasion. However bilateral assistance from Asian countries – especially Bangladesh, China, India and Thailand was readily accepted. The major international effort only got underway a few weeks later, as a result of the ASEAN Secretary General Surin Pitsuwan's astute and diplomatic efforts to form a coalition – between ASEAN, the UN and the Myanmar Government – formalised as the Tripartite Core Group (TCG) — now defunct of course.

With the election looming there are signs that the international community may have greater opportunities to engage the new civilianised government. But the problem ill be the elections. "The election's will be a wonderful chance for Myanmar to prove that it has entered a new era and use the opportunity for national reconciliation," said Marty Natalegawa "We told Myanmar that the elections must be free and fair, and inclusive," he said[72].

ASEAN has adopted the public support and private pressure to nudge Myanmar towards democracy and greater transparency. "We can be quite strong behind closed doors," said Indonesia's foreign minister. "The junta cannot overlook the fact that ASEAN is on the record demanding Suu Kyi's immediate release," said Natalegawa. This was agreed by the ASEAN foreign ministers at their meeting in Phnom Penh in 2003 and put into the Chairman's Statement at the time. "If we don't specifically rescind it then the demand remains in force," Natalegawa said. "And the Myanmar leaders can be in no doubt that this is still the view of all of ASEAN," he added[73].

But the reality is that there is little room for ASEAN to manoeuvre and influence the junta. So in the end ASEAN will almost certainly accept the election results, even if they are flawed. "If they are not objectionable, then they will be acceptable," said the ASEAN Secretary General Surin Pitsuwan recently[74]. "Myanmar definitely wants us to rubber stamp the election results," a senior Indonesian diplomat on condition of anonymity. "And while we will use every opportunity to push the Myanmar authorities to greater democracy, in the end we will probably end up being a big rubber stamp."[75]

So the elections are going to be the crucial watershed – for the military, the ethnic groups and the international community. But the junta's military mindset will stay unchanged and determine much of what happens in the future. Fear of foreigners remains paramount, and will strongly influence any future engagement. But for the future, the biggest problem remains the ethnic minorities and this may yet subvert

---

[72] Interview with Indonesian Foreign Minister in Hanoi in July 2010

[73] Ibid.

[74] Interview with Surin in Bangkok in Nov. 2009

[75] Interview with Indonesian foreign ministry officials in Jakarta in Jan 2010.

the whole process of a civilianised government post polls. In some ways it is reminiscent of 1974 – when Ne Win realised naked military rule was a failure and experimented with a new constitution and elections[76]. This too was a failure in bringing peace, stability and development to Myanmar. The tragedy is that the new constitution adopted in the sham referendum in May 2008, will prove to be just as illusionary. After 22 years of naked power, the military are trying to formalise their control of Myanmar's political future, with little hope of success. Until the Myanmar military understands that there must be national reconciliation and the ethnic minorities given some autonomy and cultural rights the forces of instability will remain and a result continue to pose a the threat to the neighbours. The problem persists, the Myanmar military mindest.

---

[76] Ne Win established civilian rule under the one party state of the Burma Socialist Programme Party.

CONFLICT RESOLUTION IN MYANMAR: AN EVALUATION OF OPPORTUNITIES AND CHALLENGES FOR DIALOGUE AND RECONCILIATION

Ramu Manivannan

The political developments in Myanmar (Burma) are swiftly moving in a direction as per the itinerary designed and executed by the military junta. The developments such as the invalidation of the National League for Democracy (NLD), disqualification of its popular leader, Daw Aung San Kyi, to contest the future elections, and the decision to press ahead with the General Elections in November 2010 as per the guidelines of the military inspired constitution of 2008 are reasonable glimpses of the tragic future of democracy in Myanmar. Though we all desire to avoid contemplating the dreadful situations in politics, such developments may nevertheless happen. The role of military in politics for over sixty years and the political developments in Myanmar, in particular, for over two decades, are unequivocal indicators of the prevailing political circumstances in that country for long.

There were at least two major peoples' movements besides the several unrests in the last twenty-three years time beginning from the 8.8.88 Students' Movement for Democracy to the Saffron Uprising of the Buddhist Monks in September 2008. On the one hand, these two developments were both disconnected by several broken promises, betrayals of trust, lost roadmaps and the brutality of the military junta. The courage and determination of Daw Aung San Kyi and her commitment towards nonviolent transformation of the conflict as well as the role of National League for Democracy (NLD) towards restoration of democracy in Myanmar, on the other, are factors that bind these two major movements as part of the historical legacy of peoples' movements anywhere in the world.

Myanmar has been in simmer for too long but not too far from a genuine transition towards democracy. Until 1987, not many had imagined the course of politics and the unseen opportunity for democratic transition in South Africa within the next two years. The change had occurred in South Africa not because of the genius of political formula that was carved out but due to the genuineness of individuals committed towards peaceful and democratic transition. It took all the parties into confidence and encouraged them to trust the process of change through a simple but one of the most important tasks of addressing their fear and insecurity of transition.

We need to conquer this natural but crippling fear of transition. Once we overcome it and acquire the freedom to think about the unthinkable, we are better equipped to deal with the challenges. Myanmar has to address this fear and insecurity of transition. It has remained at the edge of political threshold for long and awaits transition without any doubt. The confinement of the popular leader Daw San Suu Kyi in a house arrest for over a decade, the derecognizing of the major opposition party, the National League for Democracy, the drafting of military inspired constitution through the National Convention, the holding of referendum when the entire country was reeling under the terrible impact of Nargis cyclone and finally the decision to conduct the General elections in November 2010 are acts borne out of fear and insecurity than political courage and determination of the military junta.

Role of Ethnic Minorities in Democratic Transition and Exploring the Opportunity for Multi-Ethnic Democracy

Any recourse to political process must recognize the element of fear and insecurity, about the impact of transition, prevailing in the minds of military rulers in Myanmar. More importantly, a more clear recognition of the parties to the conflict is required now than any general assumption that there are only two parties to the conflict. The NLD must consider that any wishful thinking about the future of democracy must encourage and cultivate ethnic representation as part of the dialogue process more than its existing component as part of the National League for Democracy. The recognition of role and influence of the ethnic minorities will help contain the manipulative potential of the military junta vis-à-vis the ethnic minorities and as well as check government's strategy of divide and rule. The decentralization of power, devolution of authority including more autonomy and representation for the ethnic minorities are issues that cannot be sidelined if democracy has to be achieved through a negotiated political settlement. This requires both the military junta and the National League for Democracy to recognize the role and existence of ethnic minorities as part of larger process of democratic transition. This also requires us to understand the fact that more than a large share of fear and uncertainty prevails in the minds of ethnic minorities, especially among the armed groups including those who had signed the ceasefire agreement with the Myanmar government, about the course and terms of transition. The National League for Democracy should address the role of ethnic minorities as part of its unconditional offer for reconciliation with the military junta which includes more autonomy and representation for the minorities in any future assessment of the transition than what was assured by the military inspired Constitution of 2008.

There is a need for shift in the way how the ethnic minorities are classified in the contemporary lexicon of politics in Myanmar. They are mostly classified as armed resistance separated into those who had signed ceasefire agreements with the military government and others continuing the armed struggle as non-ceasefire groups. There are at least twenty armed groups of varying composition from small to moderate units operating from remote, often mobile, camps along the border. There were originally seventeen rebel groups who had signed a ceasefire agreement with the military government in 1995. Among these only Shan State National Army (SSNA) broke its agreement with the military government and merged with the rebel Shan State Army-South (SSA) in 2005. Shan State Army(South), Karen National Union(KNU), Karen National Liberation Army(KNLA), Karenni National Progressive party(KNPP) are among, militarily speaking, the influential armed groups but without much operational base area any longer to contend with. The United Wa State Army(UWSA), Kachin Independence Organisation(KIO), New Mon State Party(NMSP) and New Democratic Army – Kachin (NDA-Kachin) are considerably large among other ceasefire groups which consist of more small and medium units. The protracted state of war-torn communities and desire for development addressing basic human development needs are conditions common to both the ceasefire and non-ceasefire groups/areas. The desire for dialogue with the government is a matter of political condition and military circumstances than factors, such as long term political objectives of self-determination and demand for equality, dividing them. A more common phenomenon is the overall trust deficit prevailing among the ethnic minorities in relation to any negotiation with the military government. This is an overall weak link in any possible projection of the democratic transition in Myanmar. The National League for Democracy should address this challenge in all its seriousness in order to keep its house in order before demanding the military junta to respond to its unconditional offer of negotiation. The military will continue to exploit the contradictions and play one against another until the process is completely dismantled in sheer frustration and disillusionment.

How do we transcend the impasse of trust building and negotiation with the ethnic minorities? First of all, the process of transition must be inclusive and necessarily remain as tripartite negotiation involving the military junta, the National League for Democracy and the representatives of the ethnic minorities than any bilateral arrangement between the military government and the National League for Democracy. Secondly, the recognition of political initiatives aimed at building common political platforms for the ethnic minorities must be encouraged. The revival of the United Nationalities League for Democracy (UNLD) in January 2001, an umbrella group of non-Burman political parties formed after the 1988 democracy movement; was another positive development in this direction. A draft constitution of this political forum was ratified and executive members were elected. It is difficult to ignore the fact that the political parties who constitute as part of this joint platform had won a combined 65 seats in the 1990 elections. Engagement of political forums with such a strong claim to political legitimacy will no doubt strengthen the basis for dialogue with the military government. It may also be observed here that the National Democratic Front (NDF), another coalition of ethnic groups, is also striving to promote common positions among ethnic minorities. It is crucial to recognize that without a just and amicable settlement of the country's ethnic conflicts it is not possible to achieve a genuine transition towards democracy in Myanmar.

A Brief Review of Opportunities for Dialogue and Reconciliation Process

The military government had released Daw Aung San Suu Kyi on 6th May 2002 after being placed under house arrest since July 1989. The military junta, at this stage, promised to initiate dialogue with her party about the course of democratic transition. The military regime, in a rare gesture, gave an assurance for open and unconditional dialogue with the National League for Dem,ocracy(NLD) and its leader Daw Aung San Suu Kyi. Though it appeared that the military was keen to seek reconciliation, yet its strategy of convincing the Western countries to withdraw sanctions against the regime could not be dismissed. But the rapid polarisation of political forces within the country created panic in the minds of military rulers. A sudden but sweeping wave of mobilisation against the military government was taking place. On the one hand, Daw Aung San Suu Kyi and other NLD members were keenly waiting for the announcement from the military government regarding the dialogue process that was announced as part of the open and unconditional offer at the time of her release in May 2002. On the other, the political leadership and the advocates of the democracy movement did not want to miss the opportunity for a peaceful and nonviolent transition in Myanmar as they closely witnessed the rapid transformation of the ground realities.

On 23rd April 2003 Daw Aung San Suu Kyi had announced during a press conference at the NLD Headquarters that the 'military junta does not want change but change is inevitable. She had even predicted that the country awaited democratic transition in October/November 2003. There were action plans for civil disobedience. Hence it was only a matter of time before the military junta acted and took Daw Aung San Suu Kyi into a protective custody after carefully organizing the Tabayin Massacre on 30th May 2003.

In reviewing the opportunities for reconciliation during period from 6th May 2002 to 30th May 2003 we can notice the absence of sound meditation despite the good intentions and best efforts of the United Nations. The UN mediation failed because there were very little political preparations for dialogue before the release of Daw Aung San Suu Kyi unlike the situation comparable to the release of Nelson Mandela in 1988 from the prison. He joined the process that was already under way with the tacit approval of the apartheid regime in power and the enormous hours of negotiation between the interlocutors of the apartheid regime and the African National Congress (ANC). The military government saw no need for such preparations because it was keen to mitigate the political and economic pressure that the country was increasingly coming under. Though Daw Aung San Suu Kyi acted with great poise and confidence yet her political dispensation acted in little dash and haste in making unilateral announcements concerning the political transformation. The military junta simply panicked at it watched the rapidly changing political environment in the country. It understood the fallacy of its own commitment and its failure to grapple with the situation. There was little or no common ground for dialogue at this stage. It must be recognized here that there was no clear understanding of the offer of reconciliation and dialogue by the military government at this stage. It was largely premeditated by the military junta to respond to the international pressure than any genuine consideration for dialogue with the political opposition inside Myanmar. The National League for Democracy(NLD) and its political leadership was unable to comprehend the rapid change of political environment in the country. It made certain unilateral announcements which created more risks for the party and leadership in terms of their ability to survive in the political arena. There was not much for the ethnic minorities as they remained vulnerable for political and military maneuvers by the military junta. Above all the offer for dialogue and reconciliation was yet to become genuinely inclusive of the ethnic nationalities.

The military government knew fully well in January 2003 that the time for change had come and the change had become inevitable. The NLD was too naïve in mobilizing the masses towards the imminent transition instead of offering engagement with the military regime. These two tasks could not have taken place simultaneously under the prevailing political circumstances then and the level of uncertainty about the transition itself. The military never stopped monitoring the movements of Daw Aung San Suu Kyi and the activities of the NLD. The military junta was more despondent in May 2003 than before in arresting Daw Aung San Suu Kyi under the ploy of protective custody on 30 May, 2003. The announcement of 'seven-step roadmap to democracy' was part of its strategy to contain the negative international opinion after the arrest of Daw Aung San Suu Kyi in May 2003 as well as convince the Western countries that the military junta was not only committed for transition but was also moving forward with a political solution to the stalemate. The enhanced pressure from the UN process and the Western governments during this period also made the military regime in Myanmar to seek the help of stakeholders in the region such as China, India and Thailand. The roadmap proposed by Thaksin Shinewatre, the then Prime Minister of Thailand, on 17th July 2003 helped to ease the international pressure on the Myanmar military government after the arrest of Daw Aung San Suu Kyi. This roadmap proposed by Thailand did not emphasis on any time frame. The seven-phase roadmap declared by Gen.Khin Nyunt on 30th August 2003 was a premeditated move of the SPDC to complement the roadmap proposed by Thanksin Shinewatre. Thailand hosted the first "Bangkok Forum for Burma"(then known as 'Bangkok Process') on15th December, 2003 which was attended by Australia, Austria, China, France, Germany, India, Italy, Japan, and Singapore besides the UN Envoy and the SPDC. The Bangkok Process backed the SPDC's seven-phase Roadmap declared by Gen.Khin Nyunt on 30th August, 2003. The roadmap proposed by Thailand in July 2003 and the SPDC's Seven-phase Roadmap of 30th August, 2003 virtually sealed the fate of UN process as well as any remaining hope for dialogue and reconciliation process to take root within the country in the next seven years.   The Seven-phase roadmap[1] became the beacon light of the military government and the military junta promised political

---

[1] Ramu Manivannan, *Burma: Freedom Behind Bar,* (New Delhi; Committee f or Non-Violent Action in Burma, 2004)

initiatives and justified its each move in the name of its seven-phase roadmap. A summary view of the seven-phase roadmap is given here as below:

1. Reconvening the National Convention that has been adjourned since 1996;

2. After the National Convention, step by step implementation of the the process necessary for the emergence of a genuine and disciplined democratic system;

3. Drafting of a new constitution in accordance with the basic principles laid down by the National Convention;

4. Adopt and enact the Constitution by the national referendum;

5. Holding of free and fair election for "Pyithu Hluttaw" (legislative body) under new Constitution;

6. Convening of "Hluttaw", attended by "Hluttaw" members in accordance with the new Constitution; and

7. Building a modern, developed and democratic nation by the state leaders elected by the "Hluttaw" and the government and other central organs formed by the "Hluttaw".

The summary outline of the seven-phase roadmap stated above reveals the fifth step as present engagement of the military junta with the holding of elections for "Pyithu Hluttaw"(legislative body) in November 2010. In the meanwhile the military government had become more bold and ruthless after employing the successful strategy of sabotage against any recourse to the politics of dialogue and reconciliation through the seven-phase roadmap. In May 2008 the military junta went ahead with the national referendum to adopt and enact the new Constitution amid the tragedy of one of the worst cyclones of recorded history. The military government did not yield to any international pressure and the world public opinion despite the magnitude of humanitarian crisis engulfing the country after the cyclone Nargis.

Myanmar had clearly drifted away from further explorations on holding dialogue and reconciliation process during the period from May 2003 to May 2010. This does not, however, mean that there were no political unrests within the country. UN processes and initiatives from the Western governments to restore democracy in Myanmar continued during this period. But the military government had clearly succeeded in creating a conflict of interests between the Western countries and the neighbours of Myanmar by cultivating the constituency of stakeholders committed to defending their interests vis-à-vis the military government of Myanmar. The Saffron Uprising of September 2008 was both preceded and followed by two unconditional offers for dialogue and reconciliation in 2006 and 2009 respectively by the National League for Democracy (NLD).

In 2005, the implications of the seven-phase roadmap and the oppressive control exercised by the military junta through this inconspicuous proposal became clear. National League for Democracy (NLD) had consistently maintained that the purpose of   the National Convention by the military was only to sustain the military dictatorship in Myanmar. It continued to advocate that the will of the people shall be the basis of the authority of the government. In February 2006, the National League for Democracy (NLD) came forward with an interesting peace offer to the military government which read as " that it is willing to extend *de jure* recognition to the State Peace and Development Council as a 'transitional government', the term of which is to be negotiated between the two sides, if the SPDC agrees to convene the Parliament in accordance with the results of the 1990 elections." The National League for Democracy (NLD) also requested the military government to respond to the offer before 17th April, 2006. The NLD also sought the release of Daw Aung San Suu Kyi, U Tin Oo, U Khun Tun Oo and all other political prisoners to create an appropriate for dialogue for national reconciliation. The SPDC had not responded to this peace offer made by the NLD on 17th February 2006. Though NLD had made this peace offer there was nothing in the peace offer that it could respond immediately. SPDC was unlikely to go back at once from the process of drafting of the new Constitution. The convening of the Parliament in accordance with the 1990 elections was unlikely under the circumstances. The extension of *de jure* recognition to SPDC as a transitional government was also dependent on negotiation of the term between the two sides. Hence this peace offer by NLD in February 2006 could be concluded as a tactical offer but not realistic in terms of the changing realities. Though the extension of *de jure* recognition to SPDC could be considered as a vital step forward in the direction of dialogue for reconciliation, yet the offer was underlined by the demand for convening the Parliament based on the 1990 elections which was more unlikely. The SPDC had little or no pressure either from within Myanmar or abroad. It was NLD that required to build the momentum that was not there yet. It may be observed here that the overall political environment was yet conducive for dialogue and reconciliation as both the SPDC and NLD found no common ground to appeal for peace and reconciliation. The role of ethnic nationalities in the proposed peace process and the inclusiveness of the ethnic minorities in the proposals announced by SPDC and NLD continued to remain as marginal until this period.

On 20th May, 2009 Daw Aung San Suu Kyi sent a message from the Officers Guest House, her place of confinement inside the Insein Prison that " it is still not too late to achieve national reconciliation." This announcement was followed by the release of a "Proposal for National Reconciliation : Towards Democracy and Development in Burma",(2009) by Sein Win, the Prime Minister (of the Exile Government) of the National Coalition Government of the Union of Burma (NCGUB). This was at large a more comprehensive policy statement of the NCGUB regarding the transition towards democracy than an exclusive presentation of the proposal for reconciliation. Another significant feature of this proposal was that it was far more open and accommodative of the representation of the ethnic nationalities in the future dialogue and reconciliation process. This is one of the most progressive developments as part of the preparations towards tripartite negotiations as part of the dialogue and reconciliation in Myanmar. This proposal was jointly presented by seven major alliances, which are broad-based,multi-ethnic political and civil society organizations working inside and outside Myanmar to achieve national reconciliation, peace and freedom in the country such as : National Coalition

Government of the Union of Burma, National Council of the Union of Burma, Democratic Alliance of Burma, Members of Parliament Union, National Democratic Front, National League for Democracy (Liberated Area), Ethnic Nationalities Council, Women's League of Burma, Forum for Democracy in Burma, Students and Youth Congress of Burma and Nationalities Youth Forum. Sein Win observes in his foreword for the document on "Proposal for National Reconciliation" writes that *"the people of all nationalities in Burma, who, for many reasons, remain divided since the Panglong Agreement, are again speaking with one voice. They want democracy, long-lasting peace, and development and to live in harmony in a single Union with enduring stability. Most importantly, they are willing to compromise to get there as elaborated in this Proposal for National Reconciliation towards Democracy and Development in Burma."* [2]

The Proposal for Reconciliation in Burma (2009) recognizes that Myanmar is entering into a constitutional crisis and also believes that the government emerging under the Constitution of 2008 will not be able to resolve the present crisis. On the other hand, this proposal encourages the military government to rethink about a set of basic constitutional principles proposed by the National League for Democracy (NLD) at the National Convention held in 1993 and also agreed upon federal principles with Ethnic Nationality political parties, including the Shan Nationalities League for Democracy and the United Nationalities League for Democracy, the confederation of ethnic nationality political parties. Another visible ground for reconciliation that needs to be acknowledged in the "Proposal for Reconciliation in Burma", (2009) was the preparedness on the part of Movement for Democracy and Rights of Ethnic Nationalities to commence discussions on constitutional reform on the basis of the 2008 Constitution. It also contained five basic principles which it believed should be included in a national constitution. They are: (1) National reconciliation, (2) Balance of power, (3) Safeguarding of human rights, (4) Recognition of the rights Governmentof Ethnic Nationalities, and (5) Full participation by all elements of civil society in the national political process. It also sought

---

[2] Cited in, *Proposal for National R econciliation: Towards Democr acy and Dev elopment in Burma,* (Washington: National Coalition of the Government of the Union of Burma, 2009).

the role of civil society in the political and socioeconomic matters that should unfailingly be carried out in the transition period, and in subject matters that should be reviewed and amended in the 2008 Constitution. Trust building was emphasized in this proposal as part of the principle on national reconciliation and this document also identified key areas where trust building is vitally needed. They include: 1. Transfer of power to people; 2. Fundamental Rights of the Citizenry; 3. Rights of Ethnic Nationalities; 4. Role of the military; 5. Acknowledgement that rights of people were violated and 6. Status of the 1990 elections. The Proposal for Reconliation in Burma (2009) also sought an unconditional and immediate release of political prisoners including Daw Aung San Suu Kyi; declaration of a nationwide ceasefire; cessation of all hostilities and mutual assurances of security as conditions for creating an environment for building trust.

In principle, the Proposal for Reconciliation in Burma (2009) was more inclusive, positive and confident. It also visualized a path forward as it advocated that there is a clear route embodied in this proposal. The proposal called upon the international community especially the United Nations and Myanmar's neighbours to lend an active and unwavering support. The military did not acknowledge the proposal with the seriousness it required to be addressed. The military junta was more keen on consolidating the developments following the referendum in May 2008 and the scheduled elections to be held in November on the basis of military inspired Constitution of 2008.

The major shortcoming of the 'Proposal for Reconciliation in Burma',(2009) is that it failed to address the fears of the military junta about the transition to democracy. It is also both premature and unlikely that a public document could absolve the military of its responsibility for the criminal acts committed against the political dissidents and the people of Myanmar. But without a sufficient scope for bail-out package that the military will also be reluctant to come to the negotiation table. It will be useful for the National League for Democracy and other federations of the ethnic nationalities to explore the constitution of truth and reconciliation commission in Myanmar on the lines of South Africa. The pain, bitter memory and the fear of change of both the oppressed and the oppressor must be addressed with the opening of the window of truth and reconciliation in Myanmar as was done in South Africa. In the case of South Africa, the reconciliation was supposed to bring the former enemies to talk and to build pacified links with each other in order to be able to co-exist. It did not necessarily mean forgiveness, even though there were several cases occurred of victims forgiving their enemies. It is almost essential that any reconciliation process should address the fears of both the oppressed and the oppressor. The lessons of peaceful change in South Africa should become the guiding spirit of this transition.

Military government in Myanmar has also been testing the limits of power. The country is virtually at the edge of constitutional crisis. It will be fully be blown and unmanageable if the   scheduled elections in November 2010 are held. The military government is neither legitimate nor can acquire legitimacy with the constitutional and electoral process devoid of popular will and peoples' support. The military inspired Constitution of 2008 and the electoral laws jeopardises the national reconciliation process. The military junta cannot misguide its neighbours and the ASEAN with another roadmap after being exposed of the process resulting in establishment of a government without popular support.   The seven-phase roadmap is a one-way process and the result is finally before us to see.

International Role in Reconciliation Process

In recognizing the role of Truth and Reconciliation Commission in the peaceful transition of South Africa, we need to recognize the role of political leadership in guiding the national reconciliation. The role of Nelson Mandela and Archbishop Desmond Tutu are more than significant in this process. Aung San Suu Kyi can be trusted to take a lead in guiding the peaceful transition. There is no better time than to act now. The best and brightest hope for future in Myanmar lies in the leadership of Aung San Suu Kyi and her unconditional openness for dialogue and national reconciliation. She is committed, as Nelson Mandela in case of South Africa, to guide and save her country from further bloodshed and violence.

This is the most inspiring component to the political transition that the international community must recognize and extend to the future as a thread of hope. We must recognize the global push for dialogue and reconciliation in South Africa with economic levers controlled by major powers including United States, United Kingdom and other economic powers that helped to sustain the apartheid regime despite the international boycott. The United States and the European Union have made it clear that the 2008 Constitution, under which the promised elections might be held, will not be conducive to democracy. The Chinese way of exploring reconciliation after the elections in November 2010 based on 2008 Constitution contravenes the notion of judicious process and popular legitimacy. It is also the most opportune moment for the United Nations to restore its engagement that served as a precious lifeline between the international community and the movements for democracy through its access to the military government in Myanmar. It will not hurt to combine a strategy of engagement with select sanctions as part of a tactical push.

There is a need for clear timeframe to the dialogue process and the time bound agenda for the democratic transition in Myanmar. Trust, Transparency and Transition (3Ts) are the keywords of this process towards democratic change in Myanmar. In summing up this discussion I am encouraged to record here the crucial developments that took place in South Africa well before the first democratic elections in 1994 in order to draw lessons as well as measure the realistic challenges involved in negotiation. In 1991 the Convention for a Democratic South Africa (CODESA) was held with the goal of establishing an interim government. In June 1992 Boipatong massacre took place and the entire negotiation came to standstill as the ANC chose to pull out. The, however, two representatives Cyril Ramaphosa of the African National Congress (ANC) Roelf Meyer of the National Party continued to meet and quietly took the negotiations forward. They discussed several important issues including the future of political system in South Africa, the fate of 40,000 government employees and other crucial concerns. The major outcome of this quite process was an interim Constitution not only provided constitutional continuity but also outlined the transition from apartheid to democracy. The rule of law and the state sovereignty was kept intact which was vital for maintaining political stability within the country. This process finally resulted in agreeing on the date for first democratic elections in South Africa on 26th April, 1994 and the rest is now history. The military must now shed its fear to come forward. The NLD and the federations of the ethnic nationalities should demonstrate more patience and endurance in addressing the reconciliation process without actually dislocating the opportunity for dialogue and negotiations. At the moment, Myanmar may stare into a barren and hopeless terrain of politics with the derecognition of the major opposition party, National League for Democracy (NLD) and its leader being virtually kept out of the electoral process scheduled for November 2010. There is an impending constitutional crisis awaiting the country and the legitimacy of the entire political system will be under test once again. This is, no doubt, an opportunity thrown with the dark realities of the military rule for over sixty years now. Political opportunities are not given in platter. The search dialogue and reconciliation remains the key to the political transformation in Myanmar. The situation demands the need for creating an appropriate environment for dialogue and developing constructive approaches to resolution of this long drawn conflict.

CONTRIBUTORS

Dr. Geeta Madhavan is an Attorney with specialisation in International Law. She is a consultant on International Law offering her expertise to the academic departments that feature International Relations programmes. She is Visiting Faculty handling International Law at the Tamil Nadu Dr. Ambedkar Law University. A PhD in International Law from the University of Madras, her doctoral thesis was on "Terrorism: Issues, Perspectives and Responses". She was awarded the Doctoral Fellowship of the Hague Academy of International Law, The Netherlands in 1997 for Advanced Research in International Terrorism - the only Asian to receive the award that year. She is a RCSS Alumnus (Colombo), Salzburg Alumnus (Austria) and has attended the Wilton Park Conference, UK. Her associated research interests are International Drug Trafficking and Control, Terrorism and International Extradition, International Law and Human Rights, International Law and Refugees and International Trade Law. Her most recent presentations have been in Terrorism and International Extradition, International Protection of Human Rights, International Law, Refugees and Human Rights, Trade and Terrorism, Terrorism and Human Rights, Counter Terrorism and National Security of India, South Asia's Encounter with Cross Border Terrorism, and Media and Terrorism. She has published several articles on issues of strategic security matters.

Dr. Tin Maung Maung Than is a Senior Fellow and coordinator of Regional Strategic and Political Studies at the Institute of Southeast Asian Studies Singapore. He is also editor of Contemporary Southeast Asia. He holds PhD degree in Politics from the school of Oriental and African Studies, University of London. He specializes in Myanmar issues. He has co authored with Kyaw Yin Hlaing the book *Myanmar: Beyond Politics to societal Imperatives.* Dr. Than has also written working papers, Journal

Articles and Book chapters on politics and development in Myanmar. He has presented a number of papers on Myanmar at various international conferences.

Kerstin Duell a PhD scholarship holder at National University of Singapore. She holds a Masters degree in South East Asian Studies from School of Oriental and African Studies (ASOS), University of London. She has done extensive research on political activists, refugees, migrants and ethnic rebel groups in Thailand, Northeast India, Burma and Malaysia. She has also worked with various think tanks including Friedrich-Ebert-Foundation (Malaysia and Singapore), Forum Asia Foundation (Bangkok), Friedrich-Ebert-Foundation, Division for International Development(Berlin), UNESCO, World Heritage Centre (Paris). Apart from contributing articles on Southeast Asian Issues at various International conferences, she has written for Himal South Asian Nepal, Buddhadharma: The Practitioner's Quarterly, US, UNESCAP bulletin, Bangkok. She has co authored/photographed *"Floating Lives on the Tonle Sap"* (forthcoming).

Dr Iftekhar Ahmed Chowdhury is a Senior Research Fellow, ISEAS, Singapore since 2009. He holds his PhD in International Relations from the Australian National University, Canberra. He joined the Civil Service of Pakistan in 1969 and was transferred to Bangladesh in 1971 upon its independence. He held many senior positions, including that of Foreign Minister (2007-2009); Ambassador and Permanent Representative to the United Nations (UN) in New York (2001-2007); Ambassador and Permanent Representative to the UN in Geneva (1996-2001); Ambassador to Qatar (1994-1996); and Special Advisor to Secretary General UNCTAD (2000).Dr Chowdhury has also been actively associated with the UN Reforms process as a Facilitator appointed by the President of the UN General Assembly. He was also awarded a Knighthood of the Order of St. Gregory the Great by the Pope. His area of interest and expertise include the South Asian Association of Regional Cooperation (SAARC), disarmament and UN issues such as peace keeping and social and economic development. His current research is on South Asian issues. He has contributed articles on international relations and economic development issues in a number of journals and newspapers including *"Hasina's Visit to India and Emerging Indo-Bangla Relations:*

Implications for the Future" (January 2010), *"The'Free Market' and 'Social Concerns': 'Asian Values' and 'Walking on Two Legs'"*(January 2010), *"India and Pakistan: Breaking the Ice"* (March 2010), *"The Roots of Bangladeshi National Identity - Their Impact on State Behaviour"* (June 2009)

Dr. LI Chenyang is a Senior Research Fellow and Director of the Institute of Southeast Asian Studies at Yunnan University. He holds PhD in History from Yunnan University. His main research interests are international relations in Southeast Asia, comparative politics among Southeast Asian countries and environmental issues in the Greater Mekong Sub-region and Myanmar. He has authored books on Myanmar in English and Chinese. His latest book is *Military regime and the Process of Modernization in Myanmar 1996- 2006.* He has also written many articles in peer reviewed journals.

Dr Bibhu Prasad Routray holds PhD in International Relations from Jawaharlal Nehru University, New Delhi. He has undertaken various assignments including research consultant at Centre for Development and Peace Studies, Guwahati, Deputy Director, National Security Council Secretariat, Government of India and as a research fellow at Institute for Conflict Management, New Delhi. He has done a number of field based projects and research, particularly in Northeast India and in areas of left wing extremism. His areas of interest are, non-military threats to state's sovereignty, radical islamist movements in South Asia, India's internal security challenges, insurgencies in India's Northeast, left-wing extremism in India and urban terrorism.

Pavin Chachavalpongpun is a Fellow in Regional Strategic and Political Studies Programme (RSPS) and Lead Researcher for Political and Strategic Affairs at the ASEAN Studies Centre, Institute of Southeast Asian Studies, Singapore. He received his PhD from the School of Oriental and African Studies, Department of Political Studies, University of London. He is the author of *A Plastic Nation: The Curse of Thainess in Thai-Burmese Relations* (2005), and the forthcoming *Reinventing Thailand: Thaksin and His Foreign Policy* (May 2010). He is also contributor to a number of book chapters including "A Fading Wave, Sinking Tide: A Southeast Asian Perspective on the Korean Wave", in

Korea's Changing Roles in Southeast Asia: Expanding Influence and Relations (2010), "Dealing with Burma's Gordian Knot: Thailand, China, ASEAN and the Burmese Conundrum", in *Myanmar: Prospect for Change* (2010), "Thailand", in *Southeast Asia in a New Era: Ten Countries, One Region in ASEAN* (2009) and "Confusing Democracies: Diagnosing Thailand's Democratic Crisis 2001-2008", in *Political Transition and Political Development in Southeast Asia* (2009). He is also editor of *The Road to Ratification and Implementation of the ASEAN Charter* (2009), and co-wrote with Moe Thuzar a book titled *Myanmar: Life After Nargis* (2009). He is a regular contributor to YaleGlobal, The Nation, Bangkok Post, Straits Times, South China Morning Post, OpinionAsia, Asia Sentinel and The Irrawaddy, writing mostly on topic related to Thai and Myanmar politics, nationalism and national identity, Thai foreign policy and international relations in general.

Dr. K Yhome is Associate Fellow with Observer Research Foundation (ORF), New Delhi. He holds his PhD from the Jawaharlal Nehru University, New Delhi. Before joining ORF, he worked for New Delhi-based South Asia Foundation as a content provider for the portal on South Asia and as an Editorial Assistant for Indian Foreign Affairs Journal. He also worked on projects covering energy, conflict, terrorism, etc. for various organizations in South Asia. He has contributed chapters in edited books and articles in national and international journals/ magazines. He has qualified National Education Test (NET) for eligibility for lectureship in Politics conducted by University Grant Commission. His area of interest is South and Southeast Asian Studies. He is currently working on Myanmar's relations with its neighbours.

Anna Louis Strachan holds a Masters Degree in Asian Politics from the School of Oriental and African Studies, University of London and a Bachelors Degree in Middle Eastern Studies with Arabic from the University of Exeter on Understanding of Contemporary Intrastate War. She has worked in a range of different environments including teaching, translating and research and recently completed a research internship, with a focus on Southeast Asia, at the Institute of Peace and Conflict Studies in New Delhi. She has travelled extensively in Asia, Africa and the Middle East and has also undertaken field research in Oman and Sri Lanka. Her research interests include intra-state conflicts, territorial disputes and the role of international organisations in Peace building and has published a number of papers on these subjects.

Mr. Larry Jagan is a free lance correspondent and analyst based in Bangkok where he covers the region — particularly Burma, Cambodia, Thailand and ASEAN affairs. He is the regional correspondent for The National (Abu Dhabi). He also contributes regularly to the Al Jazerra, Asia Times online, Bangkok Post, BBC World Service, Daily Star (Dhaka), Deutsche Presse Agenteur, Inter Press News Service, Radio Australia, Radio and TV Hong Kong and the Tribune (India). He is a renowned Burma expert, having covered the country for more than thirty years, and was the BBC's Burma correspondent between 1990 and 2003. He has written extensively on   Burmese affairs, including several scoops – the most noted Khin Nyunt's arrest. He also teaches media and international relations at Rangsit University (Bangkok) and is a media trainer and consultant. He graduated from Monash University (Melbourne, Australia) with a BA (Honours in History).

Dr Ramu Manivannan is a teacher, scholar and peace activist from India. He has been closely associated with the Alternatives Movement in India and other parts of Asia, and is the founder of the Spirit in Life Movement. He is an Executive Member of the Nonviolent Peaceforce, USA/Belgium, an associate member of JUST, Malaysia, and was co-convenor of the Nonviolence Commission of the International Peace Research Association (IPRA). His many voluntary roles in India include serving as co-ordinator of Friends of Tibet-India in Delhi, and of the Burmese pro-democracy movement. A Reader in Political Science at the University of Chennai, he is the author of several books, including Shadows of a Long War: Indian Intervention in Sri Lanka (1988), and (editor) Social Justice, Democracy and Alternative Politics: An Asian-European Dialogue (2001).

www.ingramcontent.com/pod-product-compliance
Lightning Source LLC
Chambersburg PA
CBHW060838100426
42814CB00016B/420/J